Universities and the Europe of Knowledge

Universities and the Europe of Knowledge

Ideas, Institutions and Policy
Entrepreneurship in European Union
Higher Education Policy, 1955–2005

Anne Corbett
Visiting Fellow
Interdisciplinary Institute of Management
London School of Economics and Political Science

First published 2005 by
PALGRAVE MACMILLAN
Houndmills, Basingstoke, Hampshire RG21 6XS and
175 Fifth Avenue, New York, N. Y. 10010
Companies and representatives throughout the world

PALGRAVE MACMILLAN is the global academic imprint of the Palgrave Macmillan division of St. Martin's Press, LLC and of Palgrave Macmillan Ltd. Macmillan® is a registered trademark in the United States, United Kingdom and other countries. Palgrave is a registered trademark in the European Union and other countries.

ISBN-13: 978–1–4039–3245–7 hardback
ISBN-10: 1–4039–3245–X   hardback

This book is printed on paper suitable for recycling and made from fully managed and sustained forest sources.

A catalogue record for this book is available from the British Library.

Library of Congress Cataloging-in-Publication Data
Corbett, Anne.
    Universities and the Europe of knowledge : ideas, institutions, and policy entrepreneurship in European Union higher education policy, 1955–2005 / Anne Corbett.
       p. cm.
    Includes bibliographical references (p.) and index.
    ISBN 1–4039–3245–X (alk. paper)
    1. Higher education and state–European Union countries. 2. Political entrepreneurship–European Union countries. 3. European Union. II. Title.
LC93.A2C67 2005
378.4′09045–dc22   2005047735

10   9   8   7   6   5   4   3   2   1
14   13   12   11   10   09   08   07   06   05

Printed and bound in Great Britain by
Antony Rowe Ltd, Chippenham and Eastbourne

For Graham

Contents

List of Abbreviations

CAME	Conference of Allied Ministers of Education
CCC	Council for Cultural Cooperation
CERN	Centre Européen de la Recherche Nucléaire
COMETT	Programme for cooperation between universities and enterprises regarding training in the field of technology
COREPER	Committee of Permanent Representatives
CRE	Conférence des Recteurs Européens
DG	Directorate General/Director General
EAEC	European Atomic Energy Committee
EUA	European Universities Association
EURASHE	European Association of Institutions in Higher Education
EC	European Community
ECJ	European Court of Justice
ECTS	European Credit Transfer Scheme
EEC	European Economic Community
ECF	European Cultural Foundation
ECSC	European Coal and Steel Community
EHEA	European Higher Education Area
EMU	European and Monetary Union
EP	European Parliament
ERA	European Research Area
ERASMUS	European Community action scheme for the mobility of university students
ESIB	The National Unions of Students in Europe
ESPRIT	European Strategic Programme for Research and Development in Information Technology
EU	European Union
Euratom	European Atomic Energy Community
GATS	General Agreement on Trade in Services
GDP	Gross Domestic Product
ICED	International Council for Educational Development
JSP	Joint Study Programmes
IGC	Intergovernmental Conference
LINGUA	Programme to promote foreign language competence in the European Community
MEP	Member of the European Parliament

NGO	Non-governmental organisation
OECD	Organisation for Economic Cooperation and Development
OJ	Official Journal of the European Communities
SSV	Short Study Visit
TEU	Treaty on European Union
UK	United Kingdom
UKREP	United Kingdom Permanent Representation to the European Communities
WEU	Western European Union

Preface

I have long been puzzled that the leaders of the European Union, and before that the European Community, have not built more on the public appeal of a Europe of Learning, or a Europe of Education. I grant that there is an established argument that Europe needs more and better research – a product of higher education. And that there is a successful programme, Erasmus, which provides grants for students to undertake part of their studies in other parts of the EU and, increasingly, other parts of the world. It helps around three in a hundred European students to do so. And that there are now some lively exchanges between schools, thanks to a spin-off programme called Comenius, and that there are parallel efforts in vocational education. But is educational Europe on par with technocratic or economic Europe – the single market, the common agricultural policy, competition policy – or the 'secure' EU of asylum and immigration? As some might say, 'get real'. But why isn't the Europe of education as familiar as the Europe of the euro? And wouldn't Europeans as a whole be better off if it were. As anyone who works in this area knows, Jean Monnet is alleged to have said 'If I were to start again, I would start with education.' It was so out of character that he probably never did. But it is an aphorism which makes sense, where ever it comes from.

Suddenly some sort of Europe of Learning *is* emerging, and it is on a continent-wide scale. Thanks to the 'Bologna process', backed by more than 40 European governments, and the EU's own recent strategy to exploit the knowledge economy more effectively, we are seeing governments almost everywhere in Europe accepting the need for congruence between their systems, if not for convergence. They positively want a European Higher Education Area by 2010 in which governments have agreed they will put in hand measures in their own systems so that students and academics can move freely around European systems of higher education, and, so they hope, European higher education in general will become a beacon to the rest of the world. What we cannot know as this book goes to press, is whether the public disillusion with the EU, expressed in votes against the Constitutional Treaty on European Union, will sabotage much of the coordination and shared sovereignty established over 50 years.

But there are good reasons for thinking that the policy change represented at least in higher education is now institutionally embedded.

This book is intended to be both a detective story of the early attempts to Europeanise higher education and an academic study of policy change. It follows the idea of a Europe of higher education from the moment the issue came before governments, and through many of the twists and turns which have led to the Bologna process. The EC's Erasmus programme did constitute a breakthrough, just as the experts and the scholars believe. And the Bologna process is novel in that governments and university and student bodies have a better basis on which to be fully engaged than in the past. But what this account shows is that the ambition has always been present in some sort of form even where the policy capacity has been lacking.

The challenge has been to understand why. This account encourages us to understand those policy outcomes in terms of the opportunities and constraints of politics and process, including the part played by actors tenaciously committed to the idea of an EC or EU role in higher education. Despite the EU not being a classic form of government, there is much that is familiar about the politics, which in a particular context, in particular institutional configurations, using identifiable policy-making processes, enable an issue to be moved forward – or shelved. This account aims to bring to the fore the politics of policy-making in the EU as it affected the process, hidden from the general view, of agenda setting and policy modification before decisions get taken.

My own interest in the topic started in the early 1990s when writing a column for the *Times Educational Supplement* on the Europe of education. The chance to do the research and to write the book came from the London School of Economics and Political Science. My first thanks are to the Interdisciplinary Institute of Management and its director, Professor Diane Reyniers, for generously making me a Visiting Fellow. That allowed me to continue to work with Michael Barzelay, who, as my PhD supervisor, had put me on the track of the political science ideas which underpin this book. I thank Michael Barzelay, again, and the international and effervescent group of academics and research students who have been associated with the continued research. I am especially grateful to Roger Morgan, doyen of European studies, and currently external professor of the European University Institute in Florence, who was a Visiting Fellow at LSE's European Institute of Education when I first met him. He has given me much wise advice on European history and politics. He has read the whole of the manuscript. And he has been merciless in the pursuit of clear writing. Others at LSE who helped the course of this book with interventions of different kinds, each at key moments, are Kevin Featherstone, Francisco Gaetani, Howard Glennerster, Geoffrey Owen, Francis Terry and William Wallace. I associate with them the late Richard Neustadt, co-examiner with Featherstone of my PhD.

In and around the institutions of the EU, key individuals willingly provided private papers and gave me their time. There have also been many academics who, in the best collegial spirit, invited me to make presentations and/or offered useful critiques or contacts. I thank most sincerely Dave Allen, Ian Bache, Ivar Bleiklie, John Brennan, Michelle Cini, Howard Davies of London Metropolitan University, Helen Drake, Roger Dillemans, Nicoline Frøhlich, Raymond Georis, Andy Green, Elsa Hackl, Guy Haug, Hywel Ceri Jones, Maurice Kogan, Christine Musselin, Jean-Marie Palayret, Pauline Ravinet, Michel Richonnier, Clive Saville, Kathleen Saville, Jo Shaw, Alan Smith, Peter Sutherland, and Lesley Wilson. Helen Perry made helpful comments on an early draft of the manuscript. I also acknowledge the grant in 2001 from the EU scheme for shared library resources, EUSSIRF, to visit the European Community Historical Archives and the European Documentation Centre of the European University Institute in Florence.

Needless to say, I assume responsibility for the mistakes which remain. One last point is that, as I neared the end, I found myself in friendly rivalry with Luce Pépin, author of the official Commission history of EU education policy. I think we both believe our books, which have significant differences in their treatment of some common ground, are mutually reinforcing.

For that other precious support without which few books get written, Graham, my husband, heads the list for reasons he will know – down to bearing with excuses so feeble for not getting the book finished that they matched 'the dog has eaten my homework'. My Anglo-French family provided other much valued support of the sort needed from children and grandchildren.

Part I

Universities and the Europe of Knowledge

1
Ideas Do Not Arrive Out of the Blue

This is a book about European Union (EU) policy-making in one policy sector, and over a specified period of time. The 'plot' of the book centres on the idea that there should be a higher education dimension to EU policy. Why do we know so little about a policy area which has interested European leaders for all of the 50 years of the Community and Union's existence? More generally, why might the particular case of higher education have something to say about Community policy-making in general?[1]

This 'plot' is topical. There is a new and Europeanising process of change sweeping through the universities of Europe at the beginning of the 21st century. European universities, especially those on the continent, are frequently represented as being in crisis. Many of the best known cast envious eyes across the Atlantic. Their dream is to be Harvard or Yale, with their research incomes and endowments larger than the Gross Domestic Product (GDP) of small nations. But there is another and largely ignored story: this is the story of the efforts of European governments, and universities themselves, and the EU to bring about the changes which will put the regionally integrated universities of Europe in a leading position on a world stage.

Some commentators suggest that over the next ten years, the change that will drive up quality – or make it more evident – will be that increased competition and more cooperation will make the universities of Europe more focussed in what they individually do best. If this is so, the European university scene will shift dramatically. The significant differences in Europe will not be, as traditionally, *between* the culturally different national systems. The most marked diversity will be *within* national systems. This even raises the question of whether all institutions will keep the linkage, which is fundamental to the European conception of the university, of teaching and research.[2] There is a general forecast of shakeout which puts the elite research institutions in one camp, and the local universities which have absorbed the bulk of student expansion in another. Officials in Britain, if not elsewhere, use analogies with the commercial world of World Cup football. We'll see a university world which has its 'Manchester United' and 'Arsenal' and 'Real Madrid'. But whether or not the future is that dramatic, and that commercial, there is surely a conflict foreshadowed for resources and respect.[3] There are other scenarios, which reflect national higher education-government structures designed to limit competition. But underlying them all is some shared conception of a problem which might be mitigated by turning to European solutions – in terms of a European labour market, European-wide research, and why not, more co-operation between the increasingly familiar university systems of Europe.

The new factor is that we are seeing an astonishing consensus among the governments of a greater Europe, which stretches from the Iberian peninsula to Russia, from Scotland and Northern Scandinavia to the Mediterranean. All believe, albeit more or less strongly that greater unity, in some form, will provide greater strength. Since 1999, over 40 governments have opted for an unprecedented form of *regional* integration of universities. They are anxious to make these universities – over 4,000 of them,[4] more than half of them founded since the end of the second world war, and with over 16 million students – part of a *European* academic area. By signing up to the terms of the so-called 'Bologna process',[5] launched in 1999, governments are committed to building bridges between systems to create a 'European higher education space' by 2010. This potential 'space' is variously interpreted as a barrier-free market and/or a zone of cooperation. It will be characterised by the 'compatibility and comparability' which comes from a common commitment to recognised frameworks for crediting studies, assuring quality and recognising qualifications. The aims are external to Europe, and internal. The goal is not only to make the European higher education area (EHEA) attractive enough to the rest of the world to draw in more of the best foreign students and scholars, but also to boost quality within Europe itself, as a way of making universities more effective within the knowledge-based economy which the world's richest nations regard as the *sine qua non* of economic growth.

The political decision to create the EHEA, covering EU and non-EU institutions alike, coincides with moves by EU leaders, similarly targeted on 2010, to boost the Europe Union's competitiveness and growth. One strategy for this is the Lisbon process, agreed in 2000, and dedicated to creating 'a Europe of knowledge'.[6] The – possibly unattainable – goal is for the EU to have 'the most competitive and dynamic knowledge-based economy in the world, capable of sustainable economic growth, with more and better jobs, and greater social cohesion.' At the same time the EU, having created its single market in goods, is now engaged in creating a single market in services, as part of the 'growth and jobs' strategy.[7]

While both of these EU strategies would introduce new practices into national systems, the Lisbon process does not operate under the classic Community method of directive and regulation, but under an 'open method of coordination', by which governments themselves agree to peer review and benchmarking of relevant policy areas. However, the single market legislation on services, if it is applied to higher education, would be regulatory. It would suppress the right to provide public funding for some university activities. Though the legislation has its supporters, there is widespread resistance to treating higher education as a trade.[8] In any event it will increase volatility and uncertainty. On a minor scale this is already apparent with the competition between universities throughout the continent for the lucrative, or potentially lucrative, market for masters' courses given in the English language and demanding high fees.

The 'plot' also focuses on the European higher education as an exemplary policy area for study. There is a gap in our knowledge. That is to say, much has been written on the impact of *globalisation* and *internationalisation* on universities. Many of the leading exponents foresee 'radical and disruptive' change for essentially national institutions, 'forged in the successful scientific, industrial and democratic revolutions of the past two centuries'.[9] But we know relatively little about the processes of *'europeanising'* policy for higher education, and how EU initiatives interact with institutions which are a byword for their claim to intellectual autonomy and national governments which regard education as an element of national sovereignty.

Yet Europe offers a distinctive frame for action. There is a strong case for saying that aspects of educational policy are now an established part of 'europeanisation' of national policy-making[10] – at the least in the sense of 'europeanisation' as the progressive emergence of common norms of action, the evolution of which may escape the control of any particular member state and yet decisively influences the behaviour of public policy actor.[11] But history, too, weighs heavily. It was in Europe that universities grew their cultural and intellectual roots back in the

12th and 13th centuries. The European tradition of teaching, scholarship and research as it developed in the 19th century, has given rise to different models which have been taken up and translated world-wide. At the risk of over-simplifying, we can say that there is the German or Humboldt tradition, primarily concerned with preparing students to do research; the French model which has set out to provide elite training, and which treats the *grandes écoles* – which grew out of an engineering tradition, and until recently did no research – as superior to the universities; and the British model, exemplified by Oxford and Cambridge, seen as providing an 'all-round' education for a future political and administrative elite.[12]

As of today, the European Union's interest in having universities on its side appears to be in the largely instrumental terms of the Lisbon process. For in advocating this Europe of Knowledge, policy-makers want to see not just an economy which is better geared to strategies of wealth creation derived from world-beating research and innovation, but the wealth itself making it possible to maintain the famous European social model or welfare state in some form. This task is complicated not just by markets shifting to low-cost economies but also by the demographic shift within Europe to older age groups.[13]

A political strategy which supports a knowledge society clearly has to meet a number of conditions – the appropriate economic and institutional regimes, the innovation systems, the informational and communication practices, the human resource policies – but universities are seen by the EU institutions as a key to an expanding knowledge economy.[14] They are characterised by their mass of intellectual resource and their functional involvement in all the processes on which a knowledge economy depends. Through research and teaching and various types of partnership to exploit research, they participate in the production of new knowledge. They provide highly skilled manpower through teaching students, and training them in techniques of learning and research. They are usually a stimulus to local and regional economies. Even today, despite the development of private research institutes, universities pursue 80% of the fundamental research within the EU. They employ a third of the researchers in Europe; and over a third of Europeans now work in the knowledge-intensive industries which themselves are major sites of job creation and wealth production.[15]

Such an analysis leads the EU Commission, at any rate its research arm, to plunge into the politically contentious area of a future pattern for university research. It advocates 30–50 centres of excellence Europe-wide, much better cooperation with business and industry, more efficient spending – but also a recognition that universities need adequate and sustainable income. Behind the EU concern is that the EU – on the basis of its membership before the 2004 enlargement – lags behind the US and Japan in resources allocated to universities and research, and in added value – and has the chagrin of seeing many of the best students going to the US.[16] It has few mobile students – 2.3% studying in another country, although there are big national disparities. It has fewer engineering students. Yet the overall higher education effort of the EU matches the US. The EU of 15 member states already had around the same number of graduates annually as the US and the same number of institutions – 12 million and 3,300 respectively.

The university Europe of the Bologna process may be running in parallel with the Lisbon process, at any rate for the governments of the EU member states. But the Bologna process, in working for means of convergence which will allow the creation of a common academic 'space', gives universities a political voice. Governmental decisions have been significantly shaped by an academic input. Governments are committed to respecting the fundamental characteristics of universities q*ua* universities and not simply seeing them as economic engines. The Bologna process is explicitly underpinned by a university 'Magna Carta', *the Magna Charta Universitatum*, which combines both aspirations and a process to challenge governments taking action to infringe their autonomy.[17]

The Bologna process also relies on mechanisms which have been pioneered within the EU to support and sponsor different forms of direct inter-university cooperation. The instruments are neither the full EU method of directives and binding legislation nor the gentlemen's agreements of intergovernmental cooperation, but more supportive regimes, which range from incentive funding to voluntary forms of organised cooperation, and voluntary agreement on common practices, such as the use of a credit system and of quality assurance on criteria which can be understood Europe-wide.

There is thus a situation of significant, if ambiguous, political momentum in favour of a stronger European dimension to university systems. This book sets out to explore that momentum with two aims in mind. One is to provide a better understanding of the historical development of the policy of cooperation in higher education as it developed in the days of the Community, as a contribution to understanding contemporary developments and particularly the Bologna process. The second is to provide a new explanation of how policy has been made, focussing on the processes of policy-making.

In embarking on this course, I have made three assumptions which are current in political science. The first is that no idea arrives out of the blue.[18] If the basic question is 'how and why the Community has developed a higher education policy?' a sub-question we ought to be able to answer is 'what made the idea of a Community involvement acceptable?' The second assumption is that policy develops as much by the operation of day-today processes as by the 'history-making' decisions of treaties and high-level political events.[19] The third assumption is that the story can be told in ways which make it not just a *sui generis* case for specialists, but something of interest to a wider political science community. That requires setting the policy scene.

The changing Community context, 1955–2005

The study which follows takes place in a precise context – that of the Community's evolution in the last 50 years, and in particular in the years 1955–87. One measure of the general evolution of the European Community (EC) lies in the statistics. In the years 1955–2005, the Community has grown from six members to 25, and its population from 185 million to 456 million, and its land area has more than doubled from the original Community of 1.2 mn kms^2.

If we regard the treaties as the major landmarks, we can talk about three periods.[20] The years from 1952 to 1957 marked the creation of three European Communities – the European Coal and Steel Community (ECSC) in 1952, the European Economic Community (EEC) and the European Atomic Energy Community (Euratom) in 1957. The second produced the common market with implications for higher education, due to freedom of movement commitments, and especially freedom of establishment. The third demonstrated that signatories were ready to create a university institution under Community rules.

A long second stage from 1958 to 1991 transformed the EC – effectively the EEC – into the EU. Key moments within this period were the 1965 Treaty establishing a single council and a single commission of the European Communities, generally known as the Merger Treaty. Next came the Community's acquisition of its own resources with the 1970 Treaty amending certain budgetary provisions of the treaties, and the 1975 Treaty amending certain financial provisions of the Treaties, which laid down a budgetary procedure and allocated budgetary powers between the EC institutions. The Act concerning the election of the representatives of the European Assembly by direct universal suffrage 1977, effective 1978, made the European Parliament (EP) an important player. The final decisive agreement of this period was the Single European Act, setting a target for the completion of the single market by 1992. It made research a partial Community competence. The Act was signed in 1986 and ratified by the last of the member states in 1987.

The Treaty on European Union (TEU), more commonly known as the Maastricht Treaty, signed in 1991 and effective in 1993, should, in this account, be seen as the beginning of a third stage. It furthered the integration process by agreeing the timetable and criteria for moving to Economic and Monetary Union (EMU) and creating the conditions for intensified or new EU political cooperation in two of the most fundamental areas of national sovereignty: foreign and security policy on the one hand, and justice and home affairs on the other. It also laid out the conditions for the first time on which the Community, in becoming the Union, could intervene to support education. The Treaty of Amsterdam, 1997, and the Treaty of Nice, 2000, shaped by the prospect of EU enlargement to 25 or even 30 member states, were designed to deal with both left-over issues from Maastricht, including institutional reform, decision-making procedures, and the social dimension of the single market, and concern with new issues, notably immigration and asylum and the shape of a common foreign and security policy, in the expectation of EU enlargement to 25 or even 30 member states. The Treaty of Amsterdam, at least, also reflected the changing goals of the EU in an increasingly globalised economy, making it an explicit goal of the EU member states 'to promote the development of the highest possible level of knowledge for their peoples through a wide access to education and through its continuous updating.' It also, to the despair of scholars, re-numbered the treaty articles.[21] The draft constitutional treaty signed in Rome in 2004 was a further development in this process.

Another way of looking at these years is to observe the major events and changing political climate.[22] The 1950s in Europe were marked by strategies of reconstruction and reconciliation, following the Second World war, and then the onset of the Cold War. For western Europe, this was the beginning of European integration, as envisaged by Jean Monnet and Robert Schuman in 1950, leading to the three 'Community' treaties by which six continental governments agreed to pool some of their sovereign powers in relation to coal and steel and atomic energy and agreed to create a common market. From 1958 for a decade, this model of European unity was challenged by the French president, General de Gaulle, whose alternative model was based on the idea of the Community as cooperating nation states – *L'Europe des patries*. The years from 1969 to 1979 are seen by some as a Community in flux, due *inter alia* to the impact of the first Enlargement bringing in the United Kingdom (UK) (1973) and the economic slump which followed the 1973 rise in oil prices. But it was also a period initially of reconstruction and re-launch, symbolised by the call at the Hague summit of 1969 for a Community which was to be widened, deepened and enlarged. The years 1979 to 1984 marked the resolution of some festering problems. This period extended the principle of enlargement to three newly democratic Mediterranean states, which also happened to be poor. Greece joined in 1980. The period also saw the institution of direct elections to the EP, the resolution of the British budget problem, the Community commitment to high technology and the single market, and the European Parliament's draft Treaty establishing the European Union. The years 1985 to 1988 saw the Community at a high point, universally recognised as being transformed. These were the years in which Delors headed the Commission and was strongly backed at European Council level by François Mitterrand and Helmut Kohl. Spain and Portugal joined the Community, the single market strategy was devised and the Single European Act ratified. The years 1989 to 1993 saw the EC transformed into the EU. These were the years of the collapse of the USSR and the commitment of the twelve Member States to the inter-governmental conferences and the TEU, signed at Maastricht in 1991. The years since Maastricht's crisis-ridden ratification have marked the emergence of a potentially pan-EC. In May 2004, the Community completed its biggest enlargement, taking in eight countries of central and eastern Europe, formerly part of the Soviet Empire, the islands of Malta and Greek Cyprus, and committing itself to a constitutional treaty.

EC higher education in the literature

On the higher education front, the received view is that the Community had nothing to do with universities, or education in general, before the 1970s. The policy sector was 'taboo', according to Guy Neave, author of the earliest account of EC education policy, because national governments had not given the Community competence for education when they signed the Treaties of Rome.[23] Though this was not strictly true – there was the basis for building up a law of education, if not an education policy, as Bruno de Witte and colleagues powerfully demonstrated in 1989.[24] But the literature has generally accepted the assumption of the post-enlargement Commission, which took office in 1973, that the first Community education activity was opportunistically rooted in vocational training and the education of migrant workers' children, both issues which did fall within the EEC Treaty, and which attracted political interest during the 1960s.[25] Between 1971 and 1984 Commission and the Council of Ministers worked to agree to an education dimension. A combination of actions by the Commission and the EP, and some favourable interpretations by the European Court of Justice (ECJ), enabled the Commission to propose funded pilot programmes, notably the Action Programme on education of 1976, where initiatives included action for the education of migrant workers' children, school leavers and the young unemployed and for higher education and the promotion of languages. The foundations of cooperation had been laid.

In the literature generally, the period from 1985 to 1993 is seen as the period of transformation which put education policy on the road to Maastricht. This began with a new wave of integration in the mid-1980s, stimulated by the appointment of a new activist Commission in 1985, and by success in agreeing the Single European Act for completing the single market. This led to the formal adoption of a number of EC programmes in the late 1980s and early 1990s, including Comett (Community Programme for Education and Training in Technology), Erasmus (European Community Action Scheme for the Mobility of University Students), Lingua (to fund and promote training and skills in foreign languages), Tempus (Trans-Mobility Programme for University Students) in the late 1980s. Erasmus itself stimulated much activity within the university policy domain. The Commission also initiated the Jean Monnet system of chairs to promote teaching and research on European integration. The Community's subsidiary competence in education was defined for the first time by the Treaty of Maastricht in 1991 after which new and reorganised programmes could be developed by the EU institutions. The Leonardo da Vinci programme was designed to stimulate innovative training policies, and the Socrates programme, which incorporated both Erasmus and Lingua, and extended the EU's educational action to schools, through the Comenius programme. By the 1990s, and in Shaw's much-cited phrase, education had moved from the margins to the centre of Community policy-making concern.[26]

Yet a focus on higher education itself, rather than on education policy as a whole, immediately reveals a potentially different version of history. The other Treaty of Rome – the Treaty of Rome (European

Atomic Energy Community) of 1957 – made provision for the Community to create an institution of university level. In 1971 when ministers of education from the EC met for the first time, they had come to agreement in principle to set up the European University Institute in Florence, as a postgraduate humanities and socials sciences institute, under intergovernmental rules, and to cooperate on EC educational issues. In other words, much had happened before the 1976 action programme although that programme launched a pilot scheme for networking among volunteer universities, and set some of the scene for Erasmus (1987). A direct focus on higher education also reveals the extraordinary role played by the European university community. It has been a major agenda setter and a shaper of policy for the Bologna process.

Furthermore, some of the founding figures of the EC were determined advocates for a university dimension to the Community right from the start. People often think of Jean Monnet as saying 'If I were to start again, I would start with education'[27] – a proposition which those closest to him say would have been entirely out of character.[28] Rather more to the point are the recorded declarations from those who ran the Community in the early days: Walter Hallstein, first president of the EEC Commission, Etienne Hirsch, president of the Euratom Commission, and Altiero Spinelli, a life-long European federalist and the moving spirit behind the draft treaty on European Union, adopted by the European parliament in 1983.

They were expressing ideas which would make perfect sense to proponents of the Bologna and Lisbon processes, Hallstein – as we shall see in this account – was arguing in the 1950s to the 1970s for a 'common market of the intelligence' to exploit the electronics-based industries of the future, to close the technology gap with the US, to educate a more European-minded young. But he in a way which seems to have been forgotten today glorified the university as an institution. Was it not 'the most magnificent form of cultural institution created by the European mind?'[29]

It was in coming across these ideas, and discovering that higher education had a longer policy history and almost certainly a more political one than generally assumed, I thought it relevant to re-ask the question of how and why the Community developed an education policy of cooperation with a focus on higher education. The familiarity of ideas expressed a generation ago piqued my curiosity. How do those individuals who emerge in the policy process as the promoters of ideas affect policy change?

Policy change: the conceptual and theoretical choice

The Community's policy activities in higher education have attracted relatively little attention from a political science perspective.[30] But those who come from an EU specialist perspective have almost all been attracted by issues of Community competence and indeed, in Mark Pollack's phrase, the Community 'creeping competence'.[31] This has produced explanations which are variants on neo-functionalism, i.e. the belief that integration would follow the performance of a functional policy role. That had been the argument of Jean Monnet in pressing for European integration via the creation of sector-oriented bodies, such as the ECSC and the Euratom. Scholars tended to see the functional field of education in the same light, servicing the training and human resource needs of the Community. Hence explanations which present the development of education policy activity as spillover from the Community's general policy, such as the development of the single market, and the linkage between education and vocational training.[32]

The dominant explanation of the 1980s and 1990s derives from the evidence of the important role of the ECJ in widening the interpretations of the EEC Treaty's stipulations on vocational training, and the trend in the 1980s to broadening interpretations of non-discrimination between Community citizens.[33] This finds a theoretical form in historical institutionalism and path dependency as in Jo Shaw's well known article on how and why education and training have moved from the margins to the centre of Community concerns since the 1970s with, as she sees it, the gradual establishment of an education common market. Path dependency is evident in a situation in which

> [T]he Commission has been adept at opening up spaces opened up by the European Court of Justice. This is not to discount the importance of political judgments nor to decry to the discretion and autonomy of policy-makers in 'applying' opportunities opened up by interpretations of the legal framework of the EU. At the same time the policy-makers continue to be constrained by formal decision rules and constitutional principles governing EU law in general and the field of education and training in particular.[34]

But as of 2005, there is a situation in which competence issues for education and training are no longer in need of explanation. They have been defined, giving the EU a supporting role only, competence resting with the member states. This clarification of the EU's 'subsidiarity' role was an achievement of the Treaty of Maastricht, 1991. It is confirmed in the draft constitutional treaty, signed by the EU governments in 2004 and since submitted to Parliamentary scrutiny or referendum.[35]

Another strand in the literature, and which emerges from higher education specialists, is distinctive in being refracted through conceptual debates which do not interact with EU policy-making – internationalisation, globalisation, marketisation, massification. Guy Neave, Ulrich Teichler and Peter Scott have all been active chroniclers of trends since the late 1970s and an influence of much contemporary comment.[36] Many of those who have worked from a comparative politics perspective – names that come to mind are Maurice Kogan, Mary Henkel, Ivar Bleiklie – have been more interested in the national level than the EU. That has also applied to such internationally known centres as CHEPS in the Netherlands. The Bologna process however looks like changing this as Marjit van der Wende's work testified.[37]

In sum, the pointers to an unexploited and rich political history around the idea of a European dimension to higher education are sparse. The major exception is Palayret's study of the pre-history of the European University Institute in Florence, drawing on EC and state archives.[38] Actors such as Ladislav Cerych,[39] and the actor and historian, Walter Rüegg,[40] have given us glimpses of the conflicts of the early days on the one hand, related to university hostility to the EC as a supranational organisation, and the innovative range of non-governmental higher education activity, epitomised by the College of Europe.

But if we want to understand the policy significance of this history for contemporary developments such as Bologna and Lisbon processes, we might – I suggest here – try another tack. I have chosen to look at the development of an EC policy of higher education cooperation in terms of the general literature of policy change, that is to say I anchor the case in one of the major theoretical preoccupations of political science. This opens the door to a research frame which gets us closer to the political process than in previous studies of EC/EU interest in higher education. In particular, there is a range of relevant scholarship under the umbrella of 'new institutionalism'. This 'new institutionalism' has historical, sociological and rational choice variants which in different ways make institutions part of a causal chain.[41]

Of the two variants most relevant here, historical institutionalism seeks to explain change by the interaction of institutional and idea-related variables, and contingent events. In this school of thought, institutions interpreted to include formal and informal rules and procedures – structure political situations. It is institutions which shape not just actors' strategies but their goals by mediating their relations of cooperation and conflict.[42] There tends to be in consequence a 'path dependent' flow of policy, punctuated by 'critical junctures' or moments when substantial change takes place.[43] There is much that is helpful in historical institutionalist interpretations for this study. But it is a conceptualisation which, through notions of path dependency, resurrects the a-political neo-functionalism, and naturally provides room for dispute as to what the critical junctures are, and the relevance of different time-frames.[44]

Sociological institutionalism has the attraction of defining institutions much more broadly. Its advocates wish to explain the 'frames of meaning' which help to account for actors' acceptance of institutional rules as due to the rules' legitimate authority, rather than to the objective costs or benefits which rational choice conceptions emphasise. Thus actors orient their thinking to certain ideas not because they are directly persuaded to value them, but because they are placed before a *fait accompli* that they come to accept as an unalterable part of the institutional context. Instead of becoming 'infused with value' through persuasion, certain strategies become 'taken for granted' because certain actors are outmanoeuvred or ignored by those who are successful in advancing their ideas. Over time, arguments for alternative strategies are forgotten.[45] This is a theoretical approach which derives from the observation of culturally specific factors in organisations, akin to the myths and ceremonies of particular societies, and is a new generation's attack on the assumptions of rationality made by the founding fathers of social science, notably Max Weber.[46]

From my perspective, sociological institutionalism offers the advantage for this study of a linkage to models of policy *processes*.[47] These models are based on assumptions which reject any expectation of rational behaviour. A strong theme derived from the sociology of organisations is to explain decision-making in terms of what their proponents back in the 1970s called 'garbage can' or 'organized anarchy' models. James March and Johan Olsen, two of the scholars most associated with these terms, specify a model of decision-making which assumes a match between the situation, the identity of the actor and his/her action.[48]

In this conceptual family, though claiming 'more organization, less anarchy', John Kingdon has also challenged the idea of rational policy processes proceeding in clear stages between agenda setting, decision making and implementation. His own most famous work, *Agendas, alternatives and public policy* (1984), presents a model of policy-making in the agenda-setting phase, in which ideas advance because of the linkages between three processes with different dynamics: problem definition, policy formulation and the evolution of political mood.

Given my interest in the trajectory of an idea, Kingdon's immediate attraction is that he provides a way of structuring a narrative account as a preliminary to analysis. His analytic separation of agenda-setting events, which determine the issues or problems to be dealt with by decision-makers, and of 'alternative specification' or policy modification events which determine which solutions decision-makers consider when a decision is made, is a helpful – and distinctive – contribution to policy analysis. It enables us to distinguish analytically the type of scenario in which a government wants a policy solution rapidly because there is an urgent political problem to resolve – a new administration has a new programme to put into effect, a catastrophe requires an urgent policy response – from a 'processually' different scenario in which officials, or office holders, who are attached to a particular policy idea, detect a favourable political climate in which to advance it. Kingdon identifies the individuals promoting the idea as 'policy entrepreneurs'. He models the linkage, which explains the advance of ideas, in terms of the opportunity mechanisms which arise out of the interaction of predictable and unpredictable events, and the action of individuals.[49]

However, for a study based on the EC in which institutions are unstable, Kingdon is less helpful. Possibly because of the relative stability of American institutions, his model pays little attention to institutional resources. The present account draws for that on another model, conceptualised by Frank Baumgartner and Bryan Jones. Though their aim is not processual – they set out to explain the moment of policy change in terms of equilibrium, or not, between institutions[50] – they emphasise the salience of what they call policy domain, as linked to 'issue' and 'venue', and as such draw our attention to the issue of policy capacity or resources.

The concept of entrepreneurship

The reason for lingering, nevertheless, over the Kingdon model, is that the particular analytic twist I have wanted to give to this account of the creation and development of higher education policy in the EC is to explain the action of individuals in the policy-making institutions considered here. For the historical narrative reveals a number of individuals who played an important part in advancing policy, either as agenda setters or as advocates for a policy solution, or for significantly expanding policy capacity. I detected around 30 – officials from national ministries, ministers of education, commissioners and desk officers, and two dynamic presidents of the EEC Commission, Walter Hallstein and Jacques Delors.

Their presence produced research questions within a general conceptual framework of new institutionalism with a processual bias. How and why do individuals in Community institutions affect policy change? How do position and procedures create resources for them? To what extent are issue careers related to individual careers?

In this account I shall be focussing on seven individuals who can be classified as policy entrepreneurs, all of whom were active at European level, in the Commission or the Council of Ministers. They are, firstly, Walter Hallstein, in his role of head of the foreign ministry of the German Federal Republic in 1955, Etienne Hirsch, President of the Euratom Commission in 1958–61, Olivier Guichard, the French minister of education in 1969–71, and Altiero Spinelli, who was commissioner for industry and technology in 1970–72. Next, Hywel Ceri Jones, who holds the record for longevity as an entrepreneurial individual in European higher education and education, was the Commission's most active policy official on education from 1973, and the top official from 1979–93. (In 1987 when the Erasmus decision was taken he was director for education and youth within DGV Social Affairs). Peter Sutherland, who was commissioner for education, training and youth, and for social affairs in the year 1985, and Michel Richonnier, the Cabinet official working to Peter Sutherland, on education and training questions in the same year make up the seven.

My claim is that if we wish better to understand policy change within the EC we need to take careful account of these individuals. The concept of entrepreneurship derives from economics. Joseph Schumpeter, writing in 1934, gave it currency in defining the heroic identity of entrepreneurs: 'What drives the entrepreneur are primarily three things (i) the dream and the will to found a private kingdom (ii) the will to conquer (iii) the joy of creating.'[51] It was Kingdon who tailored the concept to the political process and stressed the function. The function of the policy entrepreneur is to advance an agenda issue – an idea – towards decision, his or her goal to manipulate the *dominant* understandings of issues and influence the institutions which exert jurisdiction over them.[52]

The political science literature takes the policy entrepreneur to be both a type and a role, with a place in the policy process.[53] The skills of the policy entrepreneur are most evidently those of the advocate. They need creativity, guile and judgement, expertise and tenacity. They have to 'soften up' the policy communities and larger publics, exploit political connections, and use negotiating skills, and above all to be ready to seize opportunities. Like the business entrepreneur, policy entrepreneurs are ready to invest their time, their energy, their reputation and sometimes their money in the hope of future returns. These can come in the form of policies of which they approve, satisfaction from participation or personal aggrandisement in the form of job security or career promotion.[54]

Much of the European-oriented literature of policy entrepreneurship has attempted to explain identity, aspirations and interests – agency – in terms of EC institutions. This literature includes studies of the decisions of the ECJ,[55] the agenda-setting powers of the Commission,[56] the Single European Act,[57] EMU,[58] structural policy,[59] technology policy[60] and telecommunications.[61] In this institutional perspective, the view of the Commission as an entrepreneurial or purposive actor, intent on enhancing its role and powers, is entrenched. Some have noted its educational activities in this connection. Cram's 1994 characterisation of the Commission as a 'purposive opportunist' has been widely used. She cites the Erasmus programme as an example of Commission agency, explained by the Commission wishing to extend its influence by mobilising citizen support at minimal expense.[62] A doctoral thesis by Gertrud Schink 1993 which covers much the same period as I do and which even had policy entrepreneurship in its title, though its focus was competence – *Kompetenzerweiterung im-Handlungssystem de Europäischen Gemeinschaft: Eigendynamik und 'Policy Entrepreneurs'* – drew attention to institutional policy entrepreneurship as driving 'an inner dynamic' of policy-making.[63] A more recent doctoral thesis by Gaetane Nihoul, taking 30 years of educational policy-making beginning in the 1970s as a case study for improving the theory of historical institutionalism, detected policy entrepreneurship at the directorate and unit level of the Commission, at three critical junctures of policy-making: 1986–87, 1992–93 and 1998–99.[64]

However if the interest is in individual policy entrepreneurs, as suggested in the Kingdon analysis, I suggest here that we should look to an emerging and, to me, enlightening EU literature, which is both historically specific, and which considers the impact of *individual* agency and contingency upon structure. For instance, Dudley and

Richardson, in a study of the transference of policy ideas across national boundaries, and into the supranational arena of the ECSC, identified six individuals, during a 50 year period, who intervened as policy entrepreneurs to change policy 'frames'.[65]

Dyson and Featherstone in *The Road to Maastricht, Negotiating Economic and Monetary Union*, provide a convincing analysis of the policy significance of 'flesh and blood people, whose motives were very complex and preferences by no means fixed, whose likes, aversions, ambitions and manners played an important part in the dynamics of the process.'[66] They note that in playing a part in events which have their 'own process of development, their own particular rhythm and shape, specific to the subject matter and the precise historical context', the beliefs and knowledge of these policy entrepreneurs functioned as 'road maps' and were vital in informing how their interests were defined.

This literature persuaded me that that we need to show how the beliefs of policy entrepreneurs, and the opportunities open to them, helped to structure the policy process in EC higher education, within an institutional framework, broadly defined in sociological institutionalism terms.

EC higher education as a case study

What follows is a case study of policy change.[67] The particular research episode covers the years 1955–87. This period is chosen because it covers four distinct policy decisions or outcomes which mark the creation and development of a policy-making function by the EC institutions. The first which needs to be explained is the Treaty of Rome (European Atomic Energy Community) of 1957, which permitted the nuclear energy Community to establish a university institution. The second is the decision in principle in 1971 to agree to establish the European University Institute in Florence – ratified by treaty in 1972. This was historically linked as part of a deal for ministers of education to pursue educational cooperation within the Community under intergovernmental rules and marked the creation of an educational policy domain. The third is the Action Programme in Education of 1976, and the fourth is the Erasmus Decision of 1987, the first EC decision in education made under full Community rules.

The two main questions which have structured the account as an analysis of EC policy change are – as suggested earlier – first, how and why did the EC developed policy making activities in higher education, and second how do the actions of individuals working in, or otherwise related to the Commission, affect policy change? This second, and theoretical question, gave rise to such second level questions as how position and procedures create resources for individuals who want to influence the 'career' of an issue and policy choice, and also how the trajectory of an issue is related to the career of an individual. In other words these were questions intended to bring into focus the identities and motivations of individuals as well as the repertoire of procedures by which organisations function.

In order to answer these questions I have drawn on both political science and historiography, treating the sequence of policy outcomes as a historical narrative,[68] theoretically underpinned by an agenda-setting framework. The primary explanatory framework used is that of Kingdon (1984) whose agenda-setting framework structured the historical narrative. The Kingdon framework is supplemented by Baumgartner and Jones (1993) on issue-definition and venue. The analysis of policy entrepreneurship relies heavily on the concepts in compatible frameworks from the family of sociological institutionalism, and notably those developed by March (1994) on decision processes.

As will be obvious from the text, I have made heavy use of interviews.[69] The case for and against interviews is well known. There is a real problem that actors often rewrite the script. Their stories are ones in which they are the heroes. However I found interviewing participants or observers of the EC higher education policy process of irreplaceable value in a study which looks for part of the explanation in the beliefs or motivations of actors, and felt myself fortunate to have talked to some whose memories went back to the earliest days of the Community.

The three types of primary documentary sources for this study are the documents of the EC institutions, the historical archives of the EC and the private papers of some actors. The choice of a historical approach made the splendid archives and library of the EC Historical Archive in Florence an obvious goal.[70] The unexpected prize, thanks to the director, Jean-Marie Palayret, author of the study of the history of the European University Institute, was being able to use material relevant to the higher education issue from the personal files of Emile Nöel, the Secretary-General of the EEC Commission 1958–87. Coming across his marking up and personal commentary on official documents, and his exchanges of correspondence with EC actors was to have confirmation of the need to get behind the official documents with actors' own accounts if we want a better understanding of how the EU works.

The structure of the book

The case study is in three parts: the theoretically underpinned historical narrative of the creation and development of EC higher education between 1955 and 1987, the analysis of policy entrepreneurship based on the outcomes in those years, and what I have termed an epilogue, though it can be considered part of the 'case'. It is a study of the creation and early development of the Bologna process.

Part I consists of the historical narrative, its 'plot' being how the idea or vision of EC higher education has progressed, and at times was blocked, under the pressure of events, institutional rules, the mechanisms of the policy process and the tenacity of particular individuals.

Chapter 2 – 1955–57 – recounts the emergence of the idea for a European University to be set up by the Community and its incorporation in a rather vaguer form into the EC's forgotten Atomic Energy Treaty – the Treaty of Rome 1957, EAEC.

Chapter 3 – 1958–61 – recounts the attempt to implement the Treaty article concerning a university institution and the failure of the first policy design for Europeanising all higher education in 1960.

Chapter 4 – 1961–69 – recounts the failure of the alternative model: intergovernmental cooperation through the Council of Europe.

Chapter 5 – 1969–72 – recounts how the idea of some kind of Community-driven cooperation was taken up by EC ministers of education, solving en route the problem of the European University, and how the Commission responded in creating a rudimentary bureaucracy for education.

Chapter 6 – 1973–76 – recounts the effective way in which a policy design was agreed and the inventive solutions to policy development and decision-making which made pilot action possible.

Chapter 7 – 1977–84 – recounts the new clash over competences between and within the Commission, the Council and the Parliament and how the European Council revived activity in EC higher education policy.

Chapter 8 – 1985–87 – recounts how the Erasmus programme was devised and eventually decided, surviving breakdown to become an exemplary (if small scale) achievement in europeanising higher education and thus contributing to the Europe of Knowledge or the Europe of Learning, about which so many had dreamed for so long.

Part II takes up the theoretical question of policy entrepreneurship and draws general conclusions in the light of what we have learned about policy-making processes and policy entrepreneurship from the historical narrative. It presents the argument as to why, if we accept that the beliefs of well placed individuals matter, we should understand their life experience, as well as the institutional rules under which they function.

Chapter 9, analyses the efforts made by policy entrepreneurs and the opportunities open to them as a partial explanation of the creation and development of EC higher education policy.

Chapter 10 discusses the general conclusions we can draw.

Part III, the Epilogue looks at the Bologna process in the same analytic terms as have been applied to the issue of the European University and of Erasmus. It concludes with a discussion of the opportunities and constraints of 'europeanising' higher education.

Part II

The Creation and Development of an EC Higher Education Policy

2
Origins: The Proposal for a European Community University, 1955–57

Messina, for anyone interested in the history of European integration, is a name to conjure with. The Sicilian hillside town beside Mount Etna is the place at which between June 1 and the dawn of June 3, 1955, the crucial first step took place to create the European Economic Community (EEC) and the European Atomic Energy Community (Euratom). The governments of Belgium, France, the Federal Republic of Germany, Italy, Luxembourg and the Netherlands, who from 1952 had pooled resources within the European Coal and Steel Community (ECSC), had embarked on a still bolder experiment to unite Europe.

It was also at Messina, at this same meeting, that a proposal was made that the Community should create a European University – the starting point of the European Community (EC)'s higher education policy history. This chapter explains how and why this unexpected idea came about and survived into the Treaty of Rome.[1]

Presenting a novel idea

The fact that the representatives of the six ECSC governments were gathered in Sicily was a goodwill gesture towards the Italian foreign minister, Gaetano Martino, who was in the midst of an election campaign.[2] Belgium, France, Luxembourg, and the Netherlands had sent delegations headed by their foreign ministers. The British, though invited, responded with a mere observer, a middle-ranking civil servant from the Board of Trade.[3] In the case of the Federal Republic of Germany, Chancellor Konrad Adenauer, who had held the foreign office job himself until only a few days previously, also sent a civil servant. His emissary, Walter Hallstein, the permanent secretary in the foreign ministry, had full negotiating powers. Furthermore, he was well known to the ministers present as the respected veteran negotiator for the ECSC.[4]

When it was Hallstein's turn to present his country's case, he drew attention to a German paper, submitted late, on European integration. One phrase in particular attracted other delegates' attention:

> [T]he Federal Government hopes to show that tangible testimony to young people of the desire for European union through the foundation of a European University to be created by the six ECSC states.[5]

The Belgian foreign minister, Paul-Henri Spaak, who initiated the meeting, and Willem Beyen, his Dutch colleague, initiator of the idea of an EEC, both reacted immediately:

> These aren't issues for our present work![6]

But as the same witnesses record, Hallstein persisted. He explained the Bonn government's position as being that integration ought not to be limited to the economic domain but should also include some form of cultural integration. Spaak neither argued nor encouraged further discussion on the issue. According to a disappointed Alfred Müller-Armack, also in the German delegation, and the man behind the European University idea, Spaak paid only 'lip service to the idea'.[7] But nor did Spaak or others talk it down.

The West German government had powerful reasons for going against the grain of university opinion in proposing a supranational university. A post-Nazi government had had cause to worry about its universities. By 1955 this concern was perhaps less pronounced than it had been. (One English commentator recalled the Hitler era as 'thousands of students forsak[ing] the books of Kant for the loudspeakers of Goebbels and the jackboots of the elite guard, the professors... forsaking their standards of critical thinking.'[8]) Indeed, a British member of the post-war educational reconstruction team in Germany was explicit in his view that the 'first Rektor and Kurator' he worked with were certainly not Nazis.[9]

The importance of the German view was indirectly confirmed by other British evidence. The more influential British personalities involved in the post-war reconstruction of Germany's educational system included Sir Robert Birley, first educational adviser in the British Zone and a man steeped in German scholarship. Birley believed there was a political failure to be remedied within German universities, and that its resolution required taking on the self-promoting caste of professors who, he said, 'display the worst failings of a subservient civil service. The universities are entirely cut off from a large part of German society by which they are despised and hated.'[10] However by 1955, when the Germans were once again in charge of their universities, the rectors and their senates had defeated proposals to make their academic structure more open to talent.[11]

However there was a lobby within the German government in favour of ending the universities' wartime scientific isolation, thereby hoping to stimulate reform of university leadership and improve academic capacity. This group advocated the creation of a European University as a model for innovation – a line heard at the Congress of Europe in 1948, and in the debate in the early years within the European Movement.[12] The foremost reformer was Alfred Müller-Armack, a former economics professor and, in 1955, adviser to Ludwig Erhard. Müller-Armack wrote well-received books on the social market economy but, more relevant here, he is also credited with the idea for the European University[13] and writing the best account of its genesis, according to Max Kohnstamm, Monnet's right-hand man, and future first president of the European University Institute.[14]

Müller-Armack's view was that the German universities 'were too conservative, too separated from big political issues of day. Disciplines were too specialised, too linked to national culture.[15] He describes leaving a meeting to prepare for Messina with Carl Ophüls,[16] a colleague of Hallstein's in the Ministry of Foreign Affairs.

> We began to talk about our 'favourite thought'. ... The European Community should be completed by 'a Community of the Intelligence'. We were convinced that German universities would be immediate beneficiaries of a European community with a strong European cultural dimension.' A European University would also provide a base for European research that would help overcome the gap with the US, and would act 'as a model for innovation.[17]

It would seem that Chancellor Adenauer, like his advisers Hallstein and Ophüls – themselves a law professor and a former rector – saw the political advantages to presenting a proposal for a model of innovation at Messina. The German government was split between the Adenauer view that European integration was an essentially political project – 'it was in W Germany's interest to find a European answer to the German problem' – and those who agreed with the economics minister, Ludwig Erhard, that the value of Europe was essentially as a larger free trade area.[18] A proposal for a European University chimed well with Adenauer's view.

The second factor that helped to keep the European University issue alive was the process required for dealing with an overcrowded and high risk agenda in which the question for ministers was whether they should recommend their governments to negotiate on the proposals for a EEC, and a Euratom for sharing nuclear energy for peaceful purposes. There was, as Spaak said with almost British understatement, 'a certain degree of confusion'.[19] Each country had its own agenda. The French, whose greatest anxieties were what they would lose by staying out, pressed for agricultural cooperation, supported by the Italians and the Dutch. The Belgians were keen on the atomic cooperation and greater integration in transport.

Neither of the ideas for European communities got universal support, but neither encountered unanimous opposition. The idea of the EEC or common market was strongly promoted by Spaak in Belgium, Willem Beyen in the Netherlands and Joseph Bech in Luxembourg – three countries that had already formed the Benelux customs union. But a common market was not acceptable to the political class of a largely protectionist France, nor, for the opposite reasons, to the liberal wing of the German government. However, the proposal for a Euratom – generally known by its French acronym, Euratom – was of great interest to France, the continent's one nuclear power, but opposed by Germany. The idea that the European integration achieved for the 'old' source of energy in coal and steel should be followed by integration in the 'new energy' of atomic fuel for peaceful purposes, had originated with Spaak and Monnet. Indeed Monnet – mistakenly, as it turned out – believed the issue to be much more important than a customs union.

Though all governments concerned found it hard to agree on a model to follow on from the ECSC, none wanted to repeat recent failures. In 1954, the French Parliament had crushed a joint proposal of the Six for a European Defence Community. This was a second failure within two years. In 1953, ECSC governments, represented by their foreign ministers, could not reach agreement on a proposed European Political Community.

Nonetheless, for much of the two-day Messina meeting it appeared that Spaak and Beyen were unlikely to get agreement from all foreign ministers to the two main proposals. As accounts of Messina emphasise, success came very late indeed: it was only after the closing dinner that negotiations began in earnest, back at the delegates' hotel. Talks concluded in the early hours of the morning when Pinay was finally brought round to the position of the other representatives. With Spaak singing a triumphant *O Sole Mio* from his balcony – above Pinay's bedroom – officials were left to clear up.[20] Hallstein, while attempting to represent the ambiguous official position that was the result of domestic divisions within the German government, was observed by those keenest on integration to spend much of his time at Messina with the hesitant French foreign minister, Antoine Pinay.[21] The attention may have been a crucial input and, paradoxically, the saving of the European University idea.

Although the European University was not specifically mentioned in the final communiqué signed by ministers, the proposal had survived its first hurdle and was somewhere in the *melée*. The final communiqué stated:

> The governments... believe that the time has come to make a fresh advance towards the building of Europe. They are of the opinion that this must be achieved first of all in the economic field.

> They consider that it is necessary to work for the establishment of a united Europe by the development of common institutions, the progressive fusion of national economies, the creation of a common market and the progressive harmonisation of their social policies.

> Such a policy seems to them indispensable if Europe is to maintain her position in the world, regain her influence and prestige, and achieve a continuing increase in the standard of living.[22]

Negotiating a policy commitment

The successful transplant of the European University issue from the German domestic agenda into negotiations for a treaty came with one unpredicted twist. Hallstein had expected that the European University proposal would be fitted into the EEC Treaty.[23] But by the time the Treaties of Rome came to be signed in March 1957, the one reference to the creation of a university institution was as an offshoot to the commitment to create a nuclear energy community.

It was Spaak's impatience with the negotiating process after Messina which precipitated the events which ensured that the European University proposal became a Euratom issue. Spaak, frustrated by lack of progress, took it upon himself to get a small group of experts, representing each member government, to write a draft treaty in the comfort – and isolation – of the south of France.[24] The French official, Pierre Uri, who records that the first day he wrote only 15 pages, but the whole of the Euratom chapter on the last evening between 1930 to 0200,[25] would have seen a logic for linking the European University to a French proposal for a nuclear sciences research and training institute for the atomic energy community. The model of the French research and training institutes supporting the technical require-ments of an industrial sector had already been applied in the ECSC Treaty.[26]

By the time the drafts were ready for submission to ministers, officials had approved the idea that 'the joint atomic research centre and schools to train European specialists ... might constitute the base for a European University where scientists from various countries would teach together; like any university it would have to have recognised autonomy.'[27]

It would have been surprising if the minor issue of the European University had attracted the attention of the foreign ministers meeting in Venice in May 1956 to give the go-ahead to negotiations. Once again the larger political scene was fraught, and again on account of the French. Up to the last minute those most closely associated with the meeting thought the foreign ministers were at an impasse. But according to the French foreign minister Christian Pineau, Spaak's comprehension and his own interpretation of the ambiguities was able to produce what they both termed 'the miracle of Venice'.[28]

It was only when formal negotiations for the EEC and Euratom Treaties began in the Val Duchesse chateau, just outside Brussels, that was there any serious attempt to discuss what the European University might be. In July 1956 the German team of diplomats argued at some length for the European University as a full university, albeit within the terms of the Euratom Treaty. According to a junior member of the French delegation, Félix-Paul Mercereau, the French tried to argue the German delegate down, saying a proposal to establish a full university was inappropriate in a nuclear treaty. There was also the fact that, as the only continental nuclear power, Mercereau recalls, 'we thought we "owned" the Euratom Treaty. We thought of the Euratom Treaty as "our property". No other Member State rivalled France in this domain. The UK would have been the only competitor but of course was outside the EC.' However there was no decision. The French backed off. As Mercereau recounts:

> We were always embarrassed by this German official. He was physi-cally handicapped. We assumed he had been wounded in the war. We did not like to persist in our opposition.[29]

At the same time, the Belgian, Dutch and Italian delegations began to find the idea of a European University interesting. The Belgian remembered it was in the Spaak 'Bible' agreed at Venice and therefore had to be decided.[30] On the other hand, the issue was complex and the Treaty on atomic energy not obviously appropriate. They agreed to defer discussion.

Once again it took Hallstein's and Ophüls' determination to ensure that the proposal was not lost to the treaty process. In a tidying-up session addressing unfinished business, Hallstein ensured that the European University proposal was in place, albeit ambiguously, in the Euratom Treaty.[31]

> *Article 9 (2):* An institution of university status shall be established: the way in which it will function shall be determined by the Council acting by qualified majority on a proposal from the Commission.

> *Article 216:* The Commission proposals on the way in which the institution of university status referred to in Art 9 is to function shall be submitted to the Council within one year of the entry into force of the Treaty.

The two Treaties of Rome, signed in their final form on March 27, 1957 by the foreign ministers of the six ECSC states, appeared with a number of politically integrative elements made explicit. The Treaty establishing a EEC had a preamble that:

- Determined to lay the foundations of ever closer union among the peoples of Europe
- Resolved to ensure the economic and social progress of their countries by common action to eliminate the barriers that divided Europe
- Intended to confirm the solidarity that binds Europe and the overseas countries and desired to ensure the development of their prosperity in accordance with the principles of the Charter of the United Nations.
- Resolved by thus pooling their resources to preserve and strengthen peace and liberty, and called upon other peoples of Europe who shared their ideal to join them
- Stated a commitment to creating a EEC

Furthermore, the Common Market Treaty, as it was called, included articles that foreshadowed future activity in higher education and vocational training.

In order to make it easier for persons to take up and pursue activities as self-employed persons, the Council shall issue directives for the mutual recognition of diplomas, certificates and other evidence of formal qualifications. In the case of medical and allied and pharmaceutical professions, the progressive abolition of restrictions shall be dependent upon co-ordination of the condition for their exercise in the various member states.

Though it could not have been foretold at the time, two other articles concerning vocational training, one of which addressed non-discrimination, were to be relevant to higher education:

Article 7 (1): A worker who is a national of a Member State may not, in the territory of another Member State, be treated any differently from national workers by reason of his nationality... (3) He shall also, by virtue of the same right and under the same conditions as national workers, have access to training in vocational schools and re-training centres.

Article 128: The Council shall, acting on a proposal from the Commission and after consulting the Economic and Social Council, lay down general principles for implementing a common vocational training policy, capable of contributing to the harmonious development, both of the national economies and of the common market.

The Euratom Treaty, signed as the Treaty of Rome, which created a Euratom, contained in Article 9(2) and 216 the provisions already cited for a University Institution, as a subsection to the Joint Research Centre.

So there it was: the proposal for a European University had become embedded in a treaty unambiguously oriented towards nuclear energy. As the preamble of the treaty states:

- Recognising that nuclear energy represents an essential resource for the development and invigoration of industry and will permit the advancement of the cause of peace
- Convinced that only a joint effort undertaken without delay can offer the prospect of achievements commensurate with the creative capacities of their countries
- Resolved to create the conditions necessary for the development of a powerful nuclear industry which will provide extensive energy

resources, lead to the modernisation of technical processes and contribute through its many other applications to the prosperity of their peoples

- Anxious to create the conditions of safety necessary to eliminate hazards to the life and health of the public
- Desiring to associate other countries with their work and to cooperate with international organisations concerned with the peaceful development of atomic energy
- Have decided to create a European Atomic Energy Community (Euratom)

A first phase had closed with an outcome that the newspapers of the time and Chancellor Adenauer thought was not very impressive. But the 'founding fathers' themselves looked back on as a success. If the creation of the EEC and the European atomic energy community were the great achievements, for at least, Hallstein and Christian Calmès, later Secretary General of the Euratom Commission, the European University was also a noteworthy achievement of Messina.[32]

We can see that contrary to the *idées reçues*, higher education in the Community was an issue from the European Community's earliest days. But we also see that right from the start the prospects for a European University were uncertain and potentially controversial. The initial vision to attract the young to Europe, to incite the universities to think innovatively and to stimulate Community-wide research, was clear and ambitious. But the 'fixing' that was needed to achieve its incorporation in a Treaty of Rome rendered the project ambiguous. It was left to subsequent decision-makers to make the definitive choice – as we shall see in the next chapter.

So how do we explain the survival of the European University proposal? My argument is that a key element in its survival was the interlinking of several factors linked to the policy process of agenda setting – seen as the list of subjects or problems to which government officials and those closely associated with them pay serious attention.[33] The most important factor was the congestion of the Messina agenda, which resulted in a rationing of time rather than logic. Issues that had not been ruled out at Messina or Venice were left in the process. There was the recognised option of leaving issues pending during the negotiations, or for settlement by the Council of Ministers once the treaty was operative – the European University benefited from both. As is characteristic of major political occasions, a minor issue had got carried along on the tide.[34]

It would be consistent with the literature that a second factor accounting for the survival of the European University idea was the fact that the proposal had been put forward by an individual with authority – what has been called a 'certified' actor.[35] Hallstein had sprung a surprise on foreign ministers.[36] The risk of non-discussion was acceptable, given the source of the idea. With the assumption that the issue could be discussed at a later stage, the fact that no time was allocated for Hallstein to develop the multiple reasons for supporting a supranational university – was thus not an immediate disadvantage.

We should not discount the French account which is revealing of the particular atmosphere of the immediate post-war period. Arguing against a war-wounded German – as in the negotiations at Val Duchesse – made the French uncomfortable. The easy option at this stage was to obtain an ambiguous formulation which satisfied both Germans and French and to postpone substantive discussion. Nor can we ignore the personal factor. Walter Hallstein was persistent. He had pursued the idea through all the stages of the process from agenda setting to the final formulation of the draft Treaty. In this Walter Hallstein was a typical policy entrepreneur – a concept to be discussed in greater detail later.

3
Conflicting Visions of Europeanised Higher Education, 1958–61

May 1958 marked the start of a new sequence of events in the history of the European University. This was the date at which the institutions of the new European Communities first discussed Articles 9(2) and 216 of the European Atomic Energy Community Treaty – the duty of the atomic energy community to create a university institution. The two Treaties of Rome had come into operation in January 1958, the one to establish the European Economic Community (EEC), the other the European Atomic Energy Community (Euratom). While the establishment of the Communities is seen with hindsight as marking the most ambitious act of peaceful integration ever seen on the European continent, the higher education issue has been a forgotten footnote – Jean-Marie Palayret's archive-based account of the pre-history of the European University Institute is the major exception.[1] The Euratom treaty provision for a supranational university institution was never implemented. This chapter tells us why.

Establishing a venue for policy-making

Once the Communities were established, the survival of the European University idea depended on new institutions and a larger group of actors. The new institutions most immediately concerned were the Commissions of the EEC and of Euratom, as the initiators of policy and guardians of the Treaties of Rome, and a Council of Ministers as the principal decision-making body. Each Community had its own Council, usually led by foreign ministers. They usually met jointly in the early stages. The other institution with a role to play at this stage was the future European Parliament (EP), at this stage an appointed Assembly with a basically advisory role, composed of delegates from national parliaments.

However although the institutional settings were different, at Community level many of the individual actors were the same. Among the veterans of Messina, Walter Hallstein had become President of the EEC Commission. Louis Armand, who had led the French delegation in the Euratom negotiations, was President of the Euratom Commission, respecting the tradition that it was indeed French 'property'.[2] Müller-Armack, the instigator of the European University idea, headed the diplomatic delegation of the German Federal Republic when economic ministers took the lead. Another German, Hans von der Groeben, one of the three draughtsmen of the Spaak report, was a German-nominated EEC Commissioner. Christian Calmès, another supporter of the European University, was Secretary-General of the Euratom Commission.

The wider policy community also became involved once the process of implementing the treaties began. The EEC treaty provisions for the recognition of degrees and other qualifications, and – far more immediately – the Euratom treaty proposal for the creation of a university institution brought to the fore university rectors from throughout the Community. By 1958, rectors of universities in western Europe had been meeting collectively for three years. They were about to take the step of creating a corporate body, the Conférence des Recteurs Européens.[3]

The rectors, with the rectors of the West German conference of rectors in the lead, opposed the European University. Having suffered – or resisted – the extremist nationalism of Nazis and fascists in the years leading up to and during the second world war, university leaders were deeply suspicious of a European supranationalism.[4] The rectors' concern to have university autonomy guaranteed had been made clear at the Congress of the Hague in 1948, a glittering meeting of politicians and intellectuals, chaired by Winston Churchill. The congress is most usually remembered for a host of economic, political and cultural initiatives, including the creation of what would become the Council of Europe and the EEC itself. But the congress also has a place in university history. The rectors wholeheartedly supported the resolution of its cultural committee calling for 'efforts tending towards a federation of European universities and towards a guarantee of their freedom from state or political pressure'.[5] Hallstein, who was then rector of Frankfurt University, had himself been present as part of the West German rectors' delegation, though he is not recorded as speaking.[6]

The initial prompting for rectors to meet collectively had come in 1955, when the Western European Union (WEU) set up a meeting in

Cambridge for rectors of universities from much of Western Europe. On their agenda was their common interest in strengthening their autonomy in the largest framework possible, and distancing themselves from supranational institutions. The fact that it was the WEU that prompted this development – an issue unexplored in the WEU literature – is linked to two factors. One is the background to the 1948 Brussels Treaty, a treaty of mutual defence between the 'victors' – the United Kingdom (UK), Belgium, the Netherlands, Luxembourg and France – which included cooperation in education and culture, sectors consistently seen as tools of diplomacy[7] and of new relevance with the onset of the Cold War. The other factor was the presence of the British. The British had been active in educational reconstruction in Germany immediately after the war and were sympathetic to the rectors' concern for a flexible European structure.[8]

Hallstein's proposal was unwelcome news to those in the higher-education linked foundations and voluntary movements which had emerged in the post-war period. The European Cultural Centre was one of several foundations established at the time, based on the idea that they were the natural sites of experiment, and by the same token hostile to state initiatives in education and culture. The College of Europe at Bruges founded as a voluntary initiative in 1949 to train future European cadres, and the European Cultural Foundation, which was established in Amsterdam, with the support of a Dutch public funding – including a percentage of the Dutch lottery – were also products of this context.

An emblematic figure in this context was the Swiss philosopher, Denis de Rougemont. De Rougement was a leading figure in the pro-federal European Movement. He had come to prominence in post-war congresses for European unity as the most powerful exponent of the view that it was the drive of individuals, rather than that of states and supranational institutions, that would change post-war Europe.[9] Arguing that organisation was a property of states, but culture was a property of spontaneous groups or individuals, he fought unrelentingly, where he could, against state takeovers or nationalisation of cultures. Cultural networks were the Rougemont 'method'.[10]

De Rougemont had been the driving force behind the European Movement's creation in 1950 of the European Cultural Centre in Geneva – which, as he was wont to remark, was not the Centre of European Culture.[11] Installed as director, he intended the centre to be the nucleus of a future European Centre for Research and Education.[12] One of de Rougement's achievements in this setting was to bring

together the group of physicists who went on to create Centre Européen de la Recherche Nucléaire (CERN), the collaborative nuclear
particle laboratory.[13]

Many in the European Movement worked for the kind of spontaneous grouping envisaged by de Rougemont, setting up summer
schools and organising periodic meetings of professors and students
from across Europe to provide teaching in a European context. They
regarded such activity as providing the nucleus of a European
University or universities, or even an itinerant European University.[14]
Others were keen to organise networks for postgraduate or advanced
studies and training. Prominent among them were institutes in Nancy,
Saarbrucken, Rome, and Bologna – the Bologna Center of the John
Hopkins Washington-based School of Advanced International Studies.
Only a minority of the federalists of the European Movement wanted a
single European University from the start.

Once the treaties creating the new European Community (EC)
treaties began to be implemented, the universities started to mobilise
and Denis de Rougemont – although not a university figure himself –
provided the initial impetus. In January 1958, he wrote to the Secretary
General of the Council, Christian Calmès, to say he would be organising a major conference on the proposed European University. It was a
warning of what was to come.

Devising a design

Within the Community institutions, Hallstein, though not a member
of the Euratom Commission, and the German delegation, headed by
Müller-Armack, moved swiftly to try and impose their view at the joint
Councils at which the first discussion of the European University took
place. They re-iterated their view that the European Communities
needed an institution that both embodied the idea of a common
European 'intellectual homeland', training an elite, and which would
be capable of closing the technological gap with the Americans,
That meant a university with the full disciplinary range, not merely an
institution to train atomic scientists and technicians.[15]

Furthermore, Hallstein and Müller-Armack maintained that such had
been the intention of the Messina delegates. Had there been time to
discuss the cultural implications of integration – which Hallstein said
participants had intended to discuss – they would, in his view, surely
have avoided the 'fortuitous' solution of recourse to the Euratom
Treaty. Moreover Hallstein had a proposal to make to advance imple-

mentation. He could tell them that the Ford Foundation was willing to make a significant grant to such an institution, as would his government. Müller-Armack proposed that a preparatory committee be established composed of representatives of the Six to decide on next steps.

The French delegation immediately declared their opposition to such an institution. In their view, Article 9(2) was intended to allow for the creation of an atomic studies centre to supply the scientists and technicians the Community needed, and should be proceeded with in accordance with Treaty. This, the French maintained, did not mean that the idea of a European University needed to be dropped, but the university was a different, intergovernmental issue, which should be studied in those terms.

However, none of those present at the May 1958 Council meeting appeared willing to sabotage – or be seen to sabotage – the European University project. At the end of these first discussions, the joint Councils agreed on a resolution stating:

> It is planned to found a European University as an autonomous permanent institution for teaching and research, bringing together professors and students coming chiefly from the Community countries.[16]

They also agreed on a method for proceeding with the project. Consistent with the treaty, the Councils deputed the Commission to draft proposals. In response to French arguments, the Council requested that a working group be established consisting of representatives of the Six and of the three Commissions, to report by October 1958.

With the Euratom vice-president, the Italian physicist, Enrico Medi, in the chair, the working group's design for the European University – presented as 'the university of Europe for Europe' – ended in stalemate. This was despite the fact that a broader coalition in favour of the university had emerged, within the Commission working group consisting of the Italians, Germans, Luxembourgers and the Commission itself. The group essentially backed the line pursued by Hallstein and Müller-Armack that the European University was a necessary motor for European integration.[17]

The Medi report, in December 1958, favoured the German idea that the Europoean University should be used to promote integration. 'It would be a very grave error not to supplement it by general European studies', including a traditional range of faculties such as literature and philosophy. The group also suggested that the university could run courses for diplomats and European officials. This, in the group's view, was possible under the terms of the Euratom Treaty. The one concession to the French, who maintained their opposition to the European university was that it should start from small beginnings.

But Medi stirred up a common front of opposition including from the universities. His working party ignored the proposal that the French delegation had presented for an intergovernmental institution. The French proposed that policy should be made by a European Higher Education Council of Ministers. Medi's proposed instead that the European University should have an administrative council that would report to the Commission. This crystallised concerns. No member state would support the idea of Commission control. The issue was shelved at the joint Council's meeting in December 1958.

A new attempt by the joint Councils to resolve the European University issue began officially in October 1959, with the appointment of an Interim Committee on the European University, under the chairmanship of the new President of the Euratom Commission, Etienne Hirsch. A number of factors had altered the political dynamics since December 1958. First, a change in the executive leadership of the Commission in April 1959 brought new energy to the body. The ailing Louis Armand, who, according to Mercereau, never had the strength to drive forward the European University issue,[18] was replaced by Etienne Hirsch, a forceful Frenchman who was a former budget minister under de Gaulle and successor to Monnet at the French Plan. Hirsch made it clear from the start that he wanted a successful outcome on the European University issue.[19]

In the meantime, it was apparent that the opposition of West German rectors to the idea of a supranational European university had already had an effect on the German government position. As soon as the Euratom Treaty was operational, the universities started to mobilise. Calmès, Secretary General of the Council, received a letter from the philosopher, Denis de Rougemont, as early as January 1958, warning that he would be organising a major conference to ensure the universities' (hostile) views were known to Euratom.[20] Hallstein believed the opposition to the European University came from one person who had made it his life work to oppose the project[21] – he meant the president of the West German rectors' organisation, Hermann Jahhreis. Hirsch shared his view.[22] The rectors had chalked up a major success in December 1958 in persuading the Federal Government Ministry of Foreign Affairs that the European University was an error. Once the West German ministry of foreign affairs started to investigate the issue, they realised also that the European University was difficult to support under the Federal republic constitution. Higher education was a matter for the *lände*. As a result, the delighted French were able to report back to Paris that the German government had beaten a tactical retreat on the issue.[23]

But as against this opposition, as Palayret recounts, the French foreign ministry started to support Hirsch. In early 1959, the head of cultural affairs at the French Ministry of Foreign Affairs, Roger Seydoux, convinced his minister, Maurice Couve de Murville, to change strategy. He argued that it was in French interests to use the European University proposal as the basis for a wider scheme that could generate benefits for France.[24] Seydoux proposed that Article 9 of the Euratom Treaty should be used to create a nuclear studies centre. Since students would need access to a fully equipped laboratory, the French should campaign for such a centre to be established at the French National Institute of Nuclear Science and Technology at Saclay, south of Paris. Second, European institutes should be established at the best equipped universities, with staff and research students from other parts of the EC. Seydoux even proposed that a postgraduate European University should be set up in France, judging that such a body would be internationally subsidised and would help promote the French language. This French European University was envisaged as a federating institution for the specialised teaching and research institutes already in existence at national universities. Third, a system of European university cooperation should be established by bringing existing universities under a European Higher Education Council, with a mandate to supervise and coordinate university courses and degrees.

Seydoux's opportunity arose because the French had been reconsidering their strategy from December 1958. They wanted to escape the isolation of their position. The person who had the original idea – and who would convince Seydoux to act as advocate – was Gaston Berger, director of higher education in the French Ministry of Education. His starting point was that 'Europe' should be used to benefit French higher education. His greatest concern was that French research institutes were not meeting high enough standards. He argued that France should take the initiative and provide the Councils with new thinking on higher education, using EC interest in higher education to boost the quality of national research institutes throughout the Community and to import a European element into university life in general. Hirsch was receptive to the ideas of fellow Frenchmen, Berger and

Seydoux, and was encouraged in this by his *chef de cabinet*, Mercereau, who knew Berger well.

By July 1959, however, it became evident that the French position was shifting again. The European University issue had attracted the attention of the French president, Charles de Gaulle and he was opposed. His foreign minister, Couve de Murville, arrived early for a joint Councils meeting to warn Hirsch that the French government could not now approve Hirsch's recommendation that the European University be established under Community law. As Couve put it, there was opposition to the European University 'from the highest level'. Mercereau recalls: 'We knew that meant General de Gaulle.'[25] Hirsch was perplexed. Couve had been kept in constant touch when Hirsch, while Mercereau had worked with Seydoux and Berger on the research institutes idea and he had not demurred.[26] But for Couve, the issue was apparently of little significance: the European University receives no mention in his memoirs.

After the rectors' organisations began meeting collectively in 1955, the Belgian, Italian and Dutch governments started to express concern about the European University as a costly diversion of resources that could otherwise be spent on their own systems. They noted that the German government had already reduced its support for the European University, while still preferring an institution under Community rules to one under the intergovernmental structures that would have made the *lände* the responsible bodies.[27]

At that point, the Dutch unexpectedly came to the fore with a view that put them in tactical alliance with the French, and strengthened opposition to a Treaty-based European University. Until 1959 the Dutch had opposed the European University merely on the grounds of cost. Their new, young Minister of Foreign Affairs, Joseph Luns – who later made an international reputation for himself as the head of NATO – had developed a strategic case that a European University should be expanded beyond the six member states and should certainly include the UK. He suggested that the Council of Europe's Cultural Committee or the WEU, where the university rectors of the Conférence des Recteurs Européens (CRE) were already ensconced, were more appropriate venues.

By this stage the strongest national supporters of the European University were the Italians. Gaetano Martino, foreign minister from the days of Messina, had been saying since May 1958 that a European University was needed in order to advance the cause of European integration. From December 1958 onwards, Attilio Cattani, the Italian's able secretary-general of the foreign ministry, made the case that they would like to see the university based in Italy, preferably Florence.

However a significant new actor was the EP in which Italians and Germans were active. The German Member of European Parliament (MEP), Hugo Geiger, the rapporteur on the European University[28] was particularly active, steering MEPs towards two important jurisdictional ideas. One was that the European University should be linked to the EEC Treaty's provision for the mutual recognition of qualifications, the other that non-signatories of the Treaties of Rome might be associated, an idea the Dutch had strongly supported. MEPs backed the idea of a full university furthering science and technological progress, social and economic sciences, philosophy, historical research and the elaboration of Community law.

Walking into conflict

Faced with this diversity of views, and despite the known opposition of General de Gaulle, Hirsch's strategy was to develop a package of proposals and engage in wide ranging consultations, in order that as great an array of actors as possible had some stake in the outcome – including the French Atomic Energy Authority and the rectors.[29] One explanation for Hirsch's action lay in the events of June 1959. Hallstein had obtained from US President Eisenhower an invitation for the heads of the three European Commissions to make an official visit to the US. A session at the Institute of Advanced Studies at Princeton University was included in the itinerary. There Hirsch and his colleagues met Robert Oppenheimer, famous as the father of the nuclear bomb, and Robert Lilienthal of the Tennessee Water Authority, an organisation that had inspired Monnet in the development of the European Coal and Steel Community (ECSC).

The visit to the Americans established the policy priority of the European University in Hirsch's mind – and, despite the Cold War, it was not scientific. It was 'the Americans [who] convinced us to abandon the idea that the European University idea needed to be linked to the nuclear sciences'.[30] Hirsch found this remarkable given Oppenheimer's background, and his knowledge of the comparatively low levels of science education and research.[31] As he interpreted the situation, for the Americans the idea of an innovative university to teach future EC leaders was the most important strand of the project. This elite would be best educated for European leadership by working and living together. Such a structure would also mitigate the likelihood of professors creating 'islands of knowledge' – which they regarded as a disaster of the modern university world. Possibly reflecting the Commission leaders' elation at clarifying a contentious issue, Mercereau, the delegation's *rapporteur*, entitled his account *A Weekend at Princeton*.[32]

The American advice suited Hirsch and Hallstein, given their view that the European University was an instrument of European integration. As Hirsch later put it: 'the sciences already had a common language. But such a language needed to be created among the lawyers, economists, historians and social scientists'.[33] Following the 'weekend in Princeton', Hirsch was ready to sort out the legislative implications. He and Hallstein and Medi agreed that the EEC Treaty provided a more appropriate instrument than the Euratom Treaty, and that the political unanimity formula of Article 235. This respected the idea that the European University needed specific political legitimacy, as well as escaping the awkward relationship with the nuclear science-based Treaty.

By October 1959, the idea of the humanities-based European University was sufficiently solid for Hirsch to propose it to the joint council of ministers. Embedded in what was essentially the French plan, the European University was placed in the context of the existing higher education structures in EC member states. Hirsch asked that the Councils resuscitate the Interim Committee on the European University on the basis of five subcommittees – three working parties on the European University to reflect on its academic, legal and financial status; a fourth on the European institutes of higher education and research, chaired by their protagonist, the Frenchman Berger; and the fifth on the issues of mobility and exchange, including the EEC Treaty issues of the recognition of qualifications and curricular harmonisation, under Commissioner Sattler.

The committees would be asked to deliver recommendations on how the European Community could structure co-operation in higher education. The Interim Committee should include Hallstein, Müller-Armack and Ophüls – the established supporters of the European University – alongside other representatives of national ministries and the universities. Later commentators thought the Hirsch strategy – and his authority and negotiating skills – worked wonders.[34]

Presenting a strategic plan

The climax of this work came n 27 April 1960 when the rationale and a design for EC involvement in the higher education of the Member

States was presented in Florence, in the splendour of the Palazzo Vecchio, to the Councils and an invited public, in the form of the Interim Committee's report. According to Hirsch and Muller-Armack,[35] it was a glittering occasion – it also provided the Italians with a chance to restate their wish to host the European University in Florence. Palayret calls the *Report of the Interim Committee on the European University* 'a founding charter for any real European university policy'.[36]

The committee was agreed that the aim should be to strengthen 'the common heritage of European cultures and civilisations, of high-level institutions which the Community needs, and of universities extending their brilliance and influence (*'rayonnement'*) beyond national frontiers'. In adding to the existing and varied national structures, the 'original and essential characteristic of the European University would be its role in reinforcing Europe's cultural and scientific potential'.[37]

The strategy behind the Interim Committee's proposals was to weld together the diverse higher education elements in the public sector within the EC: the European University, the European institutes for higher education and research, and university exchanges between existing universities. The European University would cater for an eventual total of 500 students – no more than a third of whom would be of any one nationality – registered for a two-year postgraduate course leading to the award of Doctor of the European University. In a reflection of lessons learned during the Princeton weekend, it was recommended that the University be residential, covering disciplines with particular relevance to European integration (*'la construction européenne'*). The European University would also have a crucial networking role in Europe-wide co-operation through exchanges, seminars and research.

The second element to the plan was that national research institutes could have access to EC funding by applying for a 'European' label on the basis of their scientific standing, and a commitment to recruiting at least one-third of their academic staff and students from other countries. The idea, so strongly and consistently advocated by Berger, was the first instance of possible EC incentive funding for higher education.

A third idea – also foreshadowing the 1970s and 1980s – was that there should be 'structured co-operation' and exchanges among existing universities. Alongside this, the Interim Committee made suggestions for the development of some common features among the different university systems of the six member states. There should be university twinning, common languages and common publications.

Various administrative measures were also recommended, including a student passport and a database to facilitate the mobility of academics. The report suggested that the equivalence of degrees should be associated with a minimum harmonisation of curricula, in the light of EEC Treaty Article 57. A working group should be set up to suggest how harmonisation might be achieved.

The Interim Committee's recommendations for the planning and the management of the 'University of Europe' followed the best practice of the time explicitly.[38] A Council of Ministers, composed of representatives from member governments, would have ultimate control. Its responsibilities would include naming a rector. But this would be on the advice of a professorial senate – seen as the innovatory practice at the time. These proposals were a major change from the Medi proposal to give the Commission ultimate control. There would, as the French had wanted, be a European Higher Education and Research Council, consisting of Community as well as national representatives, which would be the executive agency charged with implementing directives from the Council and drawing up a budget.

The European University's internal regulations would be in the hands of an administrative board that would include the rector and an administrator, as well as at least one representative from each Member State. The report proposed adopting the best current practice on university autonomy by putting academic management in the hands of an academic body, and financial management in the hands of a board of trustees.

But the strategic plan for higher education in Europe was incomplete in two important respects. First, there was no agreement in committee to the legal basis in Community law. Nor did the Interim Committee know how to fund this plan. Hirsch, Hallstein and Albert Coppé of the ECSC had each given their opinion that the European University legally fell within the rules of one or other Treaty: either the Euratom Treaty, Articles 9(2) and 203, or EEC Treaty Article 235, which gives Member States powers to extend Community competence to attain objectives consistent with the Treaty. ('If action by the Community should prove necessary to attain one of the objectives of the Community and the Treaty has provided the necessary powers, the Council shall, acting unanimously on a proposal from the Commission and after consulting the Assembly, take the appropriate measures'). But Couve de Murville's announcement in July 1959 that the French could not support a Treaty-linked university had deterred other diplomats from trying to agree the jurisdictional issues at that time.

Removing Community competence

Within six months the proposals of the *Interim Report on the European University* were rejected and within 18 months a new intergovernmental structure was in place for higher education at the European level. On 19 July 1960, the Euratom Commission lost the power of initiative on the European University issue. After two months of fruitless discussion on resources and the legislative basis for a European University, the Councils agreed 'to continue study of the proposals in the framework of the Committee of Representatives, in close liaison with Mr. Hirsch, and to resume discussion at the next meeting'.[39]

All the dismantling of the European University project took place under French pressure. On 22 October 1960, when the Councils next met with the European University on the agenda, the French representative made an alternative proposal for 'tackling the question of the University in the framework of a European cultural co-operation agency, if it were set up'.[40]

One explanation is that although technically the issue of the European University was one for majority decision, none of the other representatives objected to moving the European University into an intergovernmental arena. The European University had low status on the agendas of those Kingdon describes as 'visible' participants – i. e. the decision-makers.[41] The Belgian foreign minister, Paul-Henri Spaak, told Hirsch that Belgium could not take on the defence of the report on its own.[42] The German representatives, having been told to keep a low profile by their government, could not challenge the French. The Dutch representatives agreed with the French. Furthermore France's partners were unwilling to risk a row over this low status issue, knowing there were likely to be high status issues about which they would quarrel in the future.

Hence once General de Gaulle's attention had focussed on EC issues – the nuclear deterrent and the Algerian war had been major previous preoccupations – he did not have to manoeuvre for support to bury the European University. Fellow heads of government were to hear of de Gaulle's alternative strategy of intergovernmental cooperation in foreign affairs, defence, cultural and scientific cooperation and education for the first time in Paris in February 1961 – a story pursued in the next chapter.

Alternative specification and the building of shared beliefs

There are processes – as well as political – explanations for the failure of the Hirsch 'grand design'. A condition of a viable proposal is that it requires widespread support. The process Hirsch was engaged in was essentially that of modifying a proposal in the process of building shared beliefs. What emerges from this account is that the Euratom Commission never had the necessary support of a key group of major actors – the national rectors. They were able to convince their ministers that a supranational university would be a dangerous precedent. Hirsch's packaging of several issues, a typical strategy to garner support, was insufficient.

Another crucial weakness was the failure to get agreement on the financial and legislative base for setting up a supranational university. The residual sympathy of the representatives of the member states drained away and their attention turned to de Gaulle's criticisms of creeping EC powers. Their support for de Gaulle ensured that the European University could not be created under the terms of the Euratom treaty. In summary, factors in the immediate as well as the wider context combined to make agreement of a European University unlikely. In sum, there was no agreed issue, no accepted policy domain and no appropriate venue.[43] Thus we should not be surprised at the EC leaders' policy choice, confirmed at the Bonn Summit of 1961, for the alternative of removing competence for the European University from the Community, hand the dossier to the Italians and make education an intergovernmental matter. It was only on paper that the Hirsch plan would have given higher education institutions serious incentives to 'europeanise'. Its biggest impact at the time was on the 1960s generation of players in the EP and in and around the Council of Ministers who wished to keep the project alive. The next chapter turns to how they did so.

4
Experimenting with Intergovernmentalism, 1961–69

The 1960s were a turbulent period for higher education in Europe – both within European Community (EC) institutions and within the universities. At the start of the decade, the issue of higher education moved from its position as a potential policy area for Community structured cooperation, with the European University at its centre – an idea proposed in 1960 – to an issue in which the European executives were instructed not to intervene. Yet in 1969, the issue of education, including higher education, was back on the agenda of EC heads of state and government. When their predecessors had set the conditions for higher education intergovernmental cooperation at the Bonn Summit of July 1961, there were few grounds to predict that the issue would become an established policy domain within ten years. This chapter recounts how and why that reversal took place.

Finding a venue for cooperation

Heads of government heard the details of de Gaulle's alternative strategy for the European University and higher education at a summit in Paris in February 1961, in the context of his broader plan for intergovernmental cooperation in foreign affairs, defence, cultural and scientific cooperation and education. Arguing that such cooperation would make the Community more politically effective, de Gaulle proposed the appointment of the French diplomat and politician, Christian Fouchet, to chair an intergovernmental committee to work out a plan.[1]

The de Gaulle plan did not mean that substantive thinking on higher education contained in the report of the Interim Committee on the European University was put to one side. Fouchet set up a sub-committee to reformulate proposals in intergovernmental terms, covering the three issues of the European University, higher education cooperation and the research institutes, and giving priority to exchanges.[2] This sub-committee was chaired by Pierre Pescatore, a Luxembourgois, and later a judge in the European Court of Justice (ECJ). Having been a member of the Interim Committee, when he was faced with the new situation, Pescatore took on Etienne Hirsch – Euratom Commission president and designer of the Interim Committee report on the European University – as an informal and energetic adviser.[3]

The Pescatore 'solution' hastened the end of any involvement in policy-making on higher education topics. The French authorities, having engineered the ending Community competence for a European University, were enraged to see Hirsch actively involved in the new process and systematically opposed what Hirsch and the Commission supporters of the project advocated, for example that the University should award a full doctorate.[4] Neither of Pescatore's two drafts for a legal framework achieved consensus. His defenders insist he was the source of many good ideas, including a plan to establish a committee of ministers of education, able to influence the education systems of member states. Anthony Haigh, who became interested in the subject as a Council of Europe official, blames external events for Pescatore's failure to realise these plans. This was indeed the time at which de Gaulle vetoed the British application to join the European Economic Community (EEC) (in 1963) and the Fouchet committee itself collapsed the same year under the determined opposition of the Dutch, and the absence of Fouchet himself, whom de Gaulle had sent to be the French ambassador to Denmark. The outcome of Pescatore's mission was to be filed away in the archives.[5]

With the Euratom Commission ruled out of action, there was only one EC actor with the freedom to be consistently interested in higher education and the European University. This was the European Parliament. It continued to keep higher education on its agenda. Parliament's interest in the issue was largely due to the efforts of the president of the Committee for Research and Development, the German Member of the European Parliament (MEP), Hugo Geiger, and Enrico Medi, who had become an MEP for Italy after his time as deputy chairman of the Euratom Commission and his chairmanship of the first working group on the European University in 1958. Having failed to get any agreement from the Council from a base in the Commission, Medi used his new forum to signal continuing Italian interest in the project. At the same time he worked as a member of the organising committee working to secure the European University a base for Florence.[6]

The evident interest in the European University, and the unstable situation of higher education issues within the EC, shifted heads of government towards a decision which changed the course of higher education policy-making. On 18 July 1961, heads of state and government, meeting in Bonn, made two decisions. They changed the venue in which the issue of higher education would in future be discussed, and ensured that future developments surrounding the European University would need to be intergovernmental.

The first decision was that the European University should be made the responsibility of the Italians. The story is told that the conclusion was reached in the course of a meeting, at which de Gaulle discussed the issue with Adenauer, literally over the head of the Italian head of state, Amintore Fanfani. De Gaulle argued that the European University project should be downgraded to the creation of a university institute, and that the process should be intergovernmental. Despite his links with Hallstein, Adenauer had become as much a hard-line opponent of the original European University idea as de Gaulle, and had already turned down Hirsch's request to intervene with the West German rectors organisation. Taking the view that only states could set up a university, Adenauer agreed that establishing an institute was the right way to go.[7]

Bonn was not a 'bonne decision', was the wry summary of the Italian head of the foreign service, Attilio Cattani. He believed the Italians had been outmanoeuvred, if they had to take total responsibility for establishing a blueprint for a European University and securing its funding. Yet the Italians had been lobbying for it. And the second higher education decision of the Bonn council gave the Italians their reward. Not only was Italy's claim to the European University formalised, the choice of Florence was secured. Hirsch was satisfied too. In 1959, Walter Hallstein, as president of the EEC Commission, wanted to do a deal with the Grand Duchy of Luxembourg. It should have the university in exchange for allowing Luxembourg-based Community institutions to move to Brussels. It was Hirsch who had prevented the deal and secured agreement to the Florence site, should the university be established.[8]

Leaders had agreed that the ministers responsible for education and/or international cultural relations – rather than foreign ministers – should meet periodically in order to negotiate conventions on issues pertaining to higher education. And proving the persistence of ideas, the Bonn Summit communiqué also advocated several of the recommendations of the Interim Committee report. Among these were the possible creation of other European institutes devoted to university

teaching or scientific research – the Berger-Seydoux proposals of 1959 –
co-operation and exchanges among member state universities, and a
definition of the 'European mission' that could be assigned to national
university institutions. The communiqué also established that the
Florence-based European University should be largely funded by the
six member states.

Thus in proposing a new framework of cooperation, the Bonn
summit communiqué opened a new agenda. But this was to benefit
the Council of Europe. The Bonn Summit did little to advance co-
operation in the short term. EC ministers of education made no effort
to follow up with EC ministerial meetings. The main reason was that
ministers had found an alternative venue in the Council of Europe.
In 1961 membership of the intergovernmental Council of Europe
embraced a wide western European membership, including the UK
and Scandinavia. Its charter specified the commitment of signatories
to democracy and human rights. Founded in 1949, largely thanks to
British determination to establish an intergovernmental forum on
educational and cultural issues, the Council had been the first international institution to introduce measures to facilitate co-operation
in higher education. In 1959, the status of the Council of Europe in
higher education received a boost when the national rectors' organisations broke their established relationship with the Western European
Union (WEU) and agreed to meet under its auspices as the Conférence
des Recteurs Européens (CRE).

The fact that the WEU – whose membership consisted of the EC
Six and Britain – had initiated the first contacts between the national
rectors' bodies was characteristic of the Cold War climate of the mid-
1950s, in which higher education was seen to have a 'cultural propaganda' mission. Every country was doing it. Moscow and the
West divided up much of the world between them.[9] The WEU's particularity was that it had inherited something of the spirit of the British-
inspired wartime conference of allied ministers of education (CAME)
dedicated to the reconstruction of educational systems in the defeated
countries.[10] That organisation had then been associated with the
Brussels Treaty agreed by the 'victors' of the second world war – i.e. excluding the German Federal Republic and Italy. Under that treaty the
contracting parties had agreed

> to lead their peoples to a better understanding of principles which
> form the basis of the common civilisation and to promote cultural
> conventions themselves and other means.[11]

By all accounts the WEU efforts in the realm of higher education were innovative and sometimes unexpected. This was possibly due to the WEU's cultural officer doubling as literary critic for the leftist British magazine, the *New Statesman*, while its higher education officer would almost certainly have been the well known French novelist and Resistance hero Romain Gary, if he had not unnerved his interviewers by turning up with a gun.[12] The job went instead to Raymond Georis, a young graduate from the College of Europe in Bruges.

The fact that the WEU recruited Georis brought into a member of the newer, younger integrationist elite. A Francophone Belgian, he was born just before World War II, and was to become later, secretary-general of the European Cultural Foundation (ECF). Georis had become politically conscious in typing a book on world governance for his father, a senior civil servant who had refused to work for Belgium's Nazi occupiers. After the experience of the College of Europe, his early career was spent on development projects in India.

In the mid-1950s, Georis was a proud defender of the WEU's role in higher education. He believed in the link to the rectors, and wrote a strongly critical memo of their proposal to move under the umbrella of the Council of Europe's Council for Cultural Cooperation (CCC). But Georis was swimming against the tide. Today Georis recognises he was wrong, and that his judgement was politically motivated: 'I have to say it was partly to do with keeping culture and education away from the French who were strong in the Council of Europe.'[13]

Ministers of education of Council of Europe signatories followed the rectors in 1959. The CCC provided a secretariat. Though ministers collectively had no juridical existence, they met seven times over ten years and passed a number of resolutions. Anthony Haigh, a British official who was secretary to the CCC, captured the policy style that differentiated the Council of Europe from the WEU.

> Two streams of education and cultural co-operation were flowing in Europe. The WEU stream ran fast and deviously, giving irrigation to some interesting educational ideas in its circum-ambient path. The Council of Europe stream moved slowly. Members of the Council for Cultural Co-operation were versed in the old fashioned techniques of cultural propaganda ... and bilateral cultural co-operation. In the field of collective cultural co-operation, the Conference of European Ministers were pioneers.[14]

In 1959, the year of the rectors' and the ministers' arrival, the Council for Cultural Cooperation had agreed an important strategic change. Haigh recalls:

> To Dr Reinink, director-general of the Netherlands ministry of education, belongs the credit of discovering that the new machinery could be turned to good account to ... pick the brains of their partners for specific educational aims of their own.[15]

This was the first evidence of a fundamental shift in ideas towards cooperation deriving from shared educational – as opposed to diplomatic – ideas. According to Haigh, the Dutch initiative owed much to their holding to their conviction that it was inappropriate for the Council of Europe to be an instrument of the Cold War. The Dutch minister of education, Joseph Cals, shared his official's distaste at foreign ministers and diplomats attempting to use education to serve state purposes. He was instrumental in persuading his fellow ministers to agree to the Council of Europe device of a standing conference.[16]

Returning to EC institutions

Its supporters pronounced the standing conference to be the nucleus of a European 'ministry' of education. But by the late 1960s several ministers of education had begun to criticise the Council of Europe's intergovernmentalism. The most audible voice was that of Edgar Faure, the French minister of education, who had had the job of kick starting the country's universities after the shock of the 1968 student revolts.

Once again the issue was not so much the vision as the venue. In 1969 Faure, as chairman of the standing conference of ministers of education, made an impassioned call for 'Europe' as a vehicle for national university reform.

> The European university, or if you like a European university community, and, through it, Europe itself, will help us to overcome our troubles and to solve the crisis undergone by the universities ...
> We must not permit Europe to be no more than a 'geographical expression' ...
> I believe the time has come to seek to define together through the European university community, through educational Europe, a cultural pattern, a pattern of European civilisation ...
> Why not set up a European information centre, why not envisage a European institute of technology ... to co-ordinate effort in

the field of educational reform ... a European Education Office to intensify exchanges of information ... to induce each country by means of proposals to harmonise the content of education and of the structures of the education system.[17]

With its scant secretarial and financial resources, however, the Council of Europe could not deliver what Faure was demanding. Among papers kept by Hirsch, who continued to follow university affairs after leaving the Euratom Commission, was Faure's complaint that his ideas had got 'nowhere' in the Council of Europe.[18]

Then, in December 1969, came the EC's Hague Summit. Faure's criticisms of the Council of Europe coincided with moves by Community leaders to schedule a summit to discuss re-launching European integration. The other heads of government accepted the Dutch EC presidency's invitation to debate ambitious proposals for 'completing, deepening and widening' the Community. A meeting was scheduled for 1 and 2 December 1969 at The Hague. General de Gaulle's sudden retirement from the French presidency on 27 April 1969 provided an opportunity for the new leadership of France and Germany – Georges Pompidou and Willy Brandt – to settle with the other four member states the issues that de Gaulle had refused to entertain. High on the leaders' agenda was offering the UK the chance to join, a compensation for de Gaulle's two vetoes. At the same time, Brandt's Ostpolitik – the policy of ending hostile relations between the German Federal Republic and its eastern neighbours, including the Communist German Democratic Republic – was a new subject of controversy, prompting member states to think of ways to more firmly anchor the Federal Republic to the West including economic and monetary union.[19]

The European Parliament (EP) also seized the opportunity of the new atmosphere in 1969 to move beyond the bitter legacy of de Gaulle's disputes with Commission presidents, Hallstein and Hirsch on the extent of Community competence. It took the lead in pressing for the crucial budgetary issue of Community resources to be resolved.[20] It also brought higher education back on to its agenda. This was in the form of resolutions resurrecting the Bonn declaration on co-operation.[21] One resolution of its session of 6–9 October urged the Commission to submit a proposal for the creation of a Council of Ministers of National Education, to work, like other EC Councils of Ministers, in close collaboration with the Commission. Another resolution urged the preparation of draft conventions, as provided for at Bonn, on exchanges between Community area universities.[22]

The French, having been the key players, in 1960–61, in getting higher education and education moved to an intergovernmental venue, now jumped in with a proposal for action within EC institutions. Olivier Guichard, one of de Gaulle's key administrators, and a minister of whom the new French president, Pompidou, thought highly, had replaced Faure. Guichard, like Faure, believed the events of 1968 had shown that every education system was in the grip of 'an intellectual and institutional crisis'.[23] This was not merely a reflection of the student revolts of May 1968. A 1968 best seller on America's technological advance over the rest of the world – *Le défi américain* by Jean-Jacques Servan-Schreiber – had shaken the French political class.[24] This book implied that educational reform was urgent.

Guichard, who was to be the French minister of education from 1969 to 1972, seized the opportunity to re-launch the idea of an European Education Centre as an aid to national problem-solving. A guide to Guichard's thinking lies is an article published in *Le Monde* two years after the Hague Summit, when he still hoped his proposal would be carried through. His disillusion with the Council of Europe was, he said – like Faure's – that no political or policy initiative emerged:

> The Council undertook a heavy programme of research and development ... no precise or concrete notion has been engendered ...[25]

Guichard proposed that an EC Council of Ministers of Education be set up to act as an instrument of political co-operation, with support from a permanent team of EC officials to negotiate on educational matters of common interest, strengthening cooperation and diffusing ideas. In Guichard's view, it was essential that such a council move beyond the one direct concern of the European Economic Community (EEC) Treaty, Article 57 on the recognition of qualifications:

> Indispensable as such negotiations are it is even more important that we go deeper and create a new tool with clearly defined aims. [That tool should be] a strong and flexible European Centre for the Development of Education, reporting to the Council of EC Ministers of Education. Its task would be to 'inform, co-ordinate and promote change.

Like others before him, Guichard linked national concerns to the promotion of European integration. In his view, the Community's future would be determined by how member states prepared in terms of 'educating and training those people who would tomorrow run Europe.... The Community provided the best framework.... The harmonisation of conditions of entry to different levels of university education and to university laboratories[26] was a task [that] demands more than intermittent meetings of various committees. It needs a permanent team with contacts between different administrations and with the power and the means to make recommendations to responsible ministers.'[27]

But Guichard was not alone in seizing the opportunity to advance an education-based idea for the Community. For the Italians, the summit provided an opportunity to put the European University back on the decision agenda. Indeed, by February 1969 the ambassador Cattani had established that all foreign ministers, bar the French, were in favour of reaching a solution. He believed that a deal could be done with a new French leadership.[28] Cattani – who was widely respected and liked[29] – was sent on a mission the same month to the other member states to ascertain support for the principle of the European University.

As the final communiqué of the Hague Summit reveals, EC leaders responded to pressures for new activity on higher education and education by commenting favourably on numerous issues raised. They proclaimed that 'creative Community action' could only be a success if the young were associated with those actions. They re-affirmed their interest in establishing a European University. They approved that EC ministers of education should meet. And they affirmed 'the need to safeguard in Europe an exceptional source of development, progress and culture'.[30] Furthermore, they agreed that the Guichard proposal should be studied.

Hence the way was open to the permanent representatives in Brussels to work with the Commission to try to turn the new co-operation 'vision' into a blueprint for policy and organisation. As all the participants knew – whether they were implementing summit commitments to Enlargement, or dealing with co-operation on higher education and education – they were operating within a tight timeframe. Enlargement, scheduled for 1973, would bring in new players and new ideas.

In short, this return to Community institutions offered the promise of dynamism and competition in ideas and instruments. However, some watchful observers in the new member states were already on guard. Fred Jarvis, a senior official in the biggest teachers' union in the UK, in bringing to his members' attention the educational implications of membership of the EEC, wondered whether *European Community*, an official publication of the EEC, was purveying 'the view of some editorial zealot ... or official EEC thinking' in its February 1972 issue, which ran thus:

> ..Member states are already committed to some degree of integration in education, as a by-product of economic and monetary union, This process involves budgetary harmonisation, and national education budgets in all member countries form one of the major constituents of the total sums spent; as a result greater coordination of educational spending and therefore planning seems inevitable.
>
> Why should the Community need a common educational policy of its own? The logic of economic union demands it, and in the longer term, it must be one of the factors turning the concept of a separate European identity into something more than a distant dream.

On the other hand, as Jarvis was able to point out, the British minister of education, one Margaret Thatcher, had assured the UK Parliament on 8 July 1971:

> No changes in the British educational system will be required as a condition of entry into the Common Market.[31]

This political climate suggested change coming from several directions.

Matching ideas and venues

This account challenges the view that education was a taboo issue for the Community up till the 1970s.[32] If we focus our attention on the progress of the idea of higher education at European level, the 1960s were already a second stage. They marked the development of an alternative agenda to the Messina idea of creating a Community university. Policy makers developed instead a definition of a European role in education which achieved consensus and led to the recognition that an effective policy sub-system was also needed if ministers of education were to take action. In process terms the shift can be explained by the shift in the policy-making venue from the foreign ministers to ministers of education. What from the point of view of foreign ministers was a solution to the issue, was to ministers of education a new opportunity to define what was useful to them collectively – i.e. the chance to exchange experience. Failure in one venue can lead to the shelving of an idea, but as Baumgartner and Jones have demonstrated, it is just as likely to lead to a search for a new venue in a bid to make the process dynamic.[33]

The fact that opposition to the Community venue built up slowly is probably best explained by issues of trust between the different missions that gathered weight until a tipping point when most governments concluded that there was no viable solution under Community rules. It is notable that French opposition to using a nuclear sciences treaty to run a university did not gain widespread and immediate support – despite the apparent common sense of the position. Perhaps their self-interest was too visible. The French, after all, wanted the Community finance implicit in Article 9(2) to be invested in a training institute attached to their national nuclear sciences centre.

However the member states did not want to kill off the idea of higher education cooperation altogether. The dilemma was how to match idea and appropriate policy-making venue. The experience of the Fouchet Committee and the Bonn Summit illustrates the unpacking of ideas, separating out the European University from other aspects of cooperation such as academic exchange and the 'europeanising' of the research institutes. But having dispatched the European University to the Italians, the ministers of education, the new key players, were to discover that the alternative venues of the WEU and the Council of Europe could not provide the dynamism they had come to expect. The dissatisfaction with the new venue can also be explained by the fact that ministers of education did not share a key belief of the diplomats. In ministers' view the purpose of educational cooperation was to improve education, not to create cultural propaganda, as implicit in the Brussels Treaty of 1948 and in the WEU.

But a better match of ideas and players could not guarantee dynamic policy-making. The Committee on Cultural Cooperation and the Council of Europe failed ministers despite some concrete achievements – as in the conventions on mutual recognition of qualifications. Where ministers or their staffs attended meetings, agreed resolutions, and went home to their respective capitals where they took the action – or not – which officials recommended to their ministers, there was plenty of scope for inertia. Guichard's remark is highly significant in this respect. 'No precise notion has been engendered'. In contrast the Community secretariats were seen as having the mission and the machinery to develop activity.

There was thus a presumption of dynamism, which in the late 1960s attracted ministers of education. The Hague Summit was the kind of focussing event that directed attention to a problem already at the back of people's minds.[34] It provided the opportunity to bring forward alternative policy proposals, in which policy ideas and policy capacity might be better matched. But Enlargement, by definition, also brought in new players and, with them, new uncertainties.

5
Creating a Policy Domain for Education, 1970–72

The years 1970–72 marked an intensely creative period for the development of European Community (EC) policy-making on education. This chapter reveals how and why educational cooperation became recognised as a policy sector for which the Community could promote action.

Doing a deal on cooperation

In 1969, the French minister of education, Olivier Guichard, proposed to fellow ministers of the six European Economic Community (EEC) member states that the EC Council of Ministers of Education be established as an instrument of political co-operation, with backing from a permanent team of EC officials. He used the traditional argument of pro-European politicians that the Community's survival depended on some shared European identity. Its future would be determined by how member states took on the role of 'educating and training those people who would tomorrow run Europe'. But Guichard, in fact, was a politician primarily motivated by a national crisis. As minister of education, he was charged with implementing French university reforms in the wake of student revolts in 1968. He expected to rally his fellow ministers because every minister of education was faced with systems in the grip of 'an intellectual and institutional crisis'.[1]

Guichard's solution was to add extra tasks to the EEC Treaty commitment to the recognition of professional qualifications in an EEC-wide labour market, as defined in Article 57. One would be some 'harmonising' of conditions of entry to institutions of higher education, in order to encourage academic mobility. That task, in his view, was beyond the capabilities of the Council of Europe. In terms which later policy initiators can recognise, he maintained that such a function 'demands more than intermittent meetings of various committees. It needs a permanent team with contacts between different administrations and with the power and the means to make recommendations to responsible ministers'.[2] The EEC had technical services which could do the job he prescribed. But even better, in his view, would be a new tool with clearly defined aims, a strong and flexible European Centre for the Development of Education, reporting to the Council of EC Ministers of Education. Its task would be 'inform, co-ordinate and promote change'.

To Guichard's disappointment, the permanent representatives in Brussels of member state governments could not even agree on a date for the meeting of education ministers. It was twice postponed.[3] In contrast, in July 1971, the social affairs ministers provided an example of how to promote education indirectly, approving a resolution for a Community programme 'to provide the population as a whole with the opportunities for general and vocational education, further education and life long education which will adequately allow individuals to develop their personality and to follow a skilled occupation in an economy in which the needs are constantly changing'.[4]

The Council set up a working party drawn of senior officials to recommend how such a centre might be structured.[5] In a foretaste of the difficulties that were to plague future efforts, this working party could not get over immediate procedural hurdles. There was no clear agenda. A call for agenda items issued by the Belgian presidency and the Commission in October 1970 showed that the West German government, for example, wanted a variant on ideas debated in 1960, focusing on an overall framework in which mutual recognition of professional qualifications would be tied to the establishment of postgraduate teaching in the European University and Europe-wide collaboration between universities. Belgium wanted trans-national universities.[6]

A decision – or rather two decisions – became more likely in the second half of 1971 when the Italians took on the presidency of the Council. They had been preceded by the Luxembourgeois, who were highly supportive of Community action on education, culture and social progress.[7] With the respected Italian ambassador, Attilio Cattani, still in his post, and sure of other governments' support, the Italian government prepared for their presidency by proposing an intergovernmental conference on the European University. The two conferences held in the course of 1971, agreed a modest proposal for an institute rather than a university, and as foreshadowed that it would be postgraduate and based in the humanities. With the French still holding out, the Italians brokered a deal. They would support the Guichard centre if the French would support the European University Institute.[8]

On 16 November 1971, the long-awaited meeting of EC ministers of education took place, chaired by the Italian minister of education, Ricardo Misasi. Secure in the knowledge that a deal had been reached with Guichard, the ministers first met intergovernmentally to agree the project of a European University Institute in Florence, to be established by international convention. Their officials were to be set to work on the legal document – which was eventually signed on 19 April 1972, enabling the EUI to be established in 1976.[9]

Then, sitting as ministers for education meeting 'within the Council' – the phrase signifying the group was working under Community non-binding rules – the ministers made the first decision to affect higher education since the European Atomic Energy Committee (EAEC) treaty, and the first as EEC ministers of education. The decision – in the non-binding form of a resolution – is considered by many as the first step towards an EC educational policy.[10] They committed themselves to a broad and cultural view of education by their resolution on co-operation in the field of education, and agreed that it was logical to co-operate on education if they were already co-operating on training,

> considering that the Treaty of Rome already provided for and organ-
> ised activities concerning, *inter alia*, the right of establishment
> and vocational training, but that they should be supplemented by
> greater co-operation in the field of education as such.

Second, the ministers described European integration as a cultural project. As they put it, the 'ultimate aim being to define ... a European model of culture correlating with European integration, it is first necessary to establish a framework enabling that aim to be achieved'.

The ministers of education also took account of an issue of great importance to the university community, in declaring their determination that co-operation should take in wider Europe, outside as well as inside the Community. Educational cooperation needed, as they put it, 'to take account of historical affinities of civilisation and culture ... [S]uch action must not be limited to Member States of the Community alone.'

The fourth – and most concrete – aspect of the accord was the ministers' agreement to establish a working party to consider the tasks and organisation of a European Centre for the Development of Education and to define its relationship with the European Communities and the legal base for co-operation. The working party, said the ministers, would also be able to make suggestions on other ways of establishing active co-operation in the field of national education.[11]

The terms in which the ministers described cooperation faithfully reflected the Hague Summit concern with the cultural dimension of the Community – the Cold War continued to cast a heavy shadow. But the ministers also seem to have been trying to achieve the broadest possible consensus between the different educational actors. They responded to Guichard's plea for common action by asking for ideas for cooperation. They agreed with the Conference of European Rectors and other university lobbies that the cooperation should not be limited by the frontiers of the EEC.[12] They responded to evidence that 'education as such', was emerging in other EEC policy areas. These included the 1963 Council decision on vocational training policy which provided for general education,[13] the Social Affairs Council of July 1971, a regulation of 1968 that included education as one of the policy sectors that needed to make provision for migrant workers' children – an issue which provided an unexpected opportunity for policy-making in education, and the increasingly contentious issue of the mutual recognition of qualifications required by the EEC Treaty commitment to freedom of establishment. A sign of its importance was that the Conférence des Recteurs Européens (CRE) had reversed its long-standing policy of arms-length dealing with EEC institutions and set up an EEC experts' office.[14]

An English commentator thought that the ministers' resolution of 1971 was proof that nothing much would happen quickly in education, although the instruments, when used might be unpalatably powerful. But from within the Community institutions, the novelty of 1969–72 was that EC leaders had shown they wanted the Community to expand into new areas – industry, technology, scientific research, environment and culture, and ministers of education had used the opportunity to settle an outstanding issue and to look forward to something new on cooperation.

Establishing a rudimentary bureaucracy

The Commission had also been deeply involved in creating the conditions for a decision on cooperation. From 1969, the senior officials of the Commission were well aware that the EC was going to be dramatically changed by their agreement to expand from six members to a possible ten – to include the eternal candidate, the UK, as well as Ireland, Denmark and Norway.[15] They also knew that they had little time – a three-year term of office as opposed to the usual four, to enable a new Commission to be appointed with enlargement.

Five people within the Commission took a particular interest in the change in the political landscape as it affected education: Commission secretary-general, Emile Noël; Jean-René Rabier of the information division, who maintained links with university associations teaching about EC politics and policies, and gave them grants; Félix-Paul Mercereau, the official who had been responsible for the European University dossier at the Euratom Commission under Etienne Hirsch; and Commissioners, Altiero Spinelli, who had been in charge of industry and technology, and Albert Borschette, in charge of youth and information.

Spinelli and Noël were both ready to secure effective Commission input for the promised meeting of ministers of education in what they judged to be a promising context for action. The rectors, collectively in the CRE, had toned down the hostility to the EC they had demonstrated in the early 1960s. Though they were still wary of involvement with the EC, they did not pose the threat they had in 1959–60 when they so strongly opposed the European University. Moreover they themselves were divided over their leadership's priority to bridging the Cold War gap with academics in Eastern Europe.[16]

But a determining factor in getting the rectors to work with Community institutions was that the Commission was getting ready to prepare directives for the recognition of professional qualifications in application of Article 57. The Commission appeared to favour basing equivalence on length of studies – anathema to rectors who believed that was simplistic in view of national variation in qualifications.[17] But by 1970; there were also signs of positive support for working with the Community institutions. Various university associations were attracted to the EC as an object of study, and in general supportive of European integration. These had been nurtured by the Commission.

A conference to consider cooperation between universities in Europe held at Grenoble on 29–31 October 1970, and in which several of these associations were active, was particularly encouraging for the Commission. The event was hosted by Jean-Louis Quermonne, president of Grenoble's innovative social sciences university, with working groups presided over by major figures on higher education in Europe, including Professor Henri Janne, an eminent sociologist, whom Mercereau and Spinelli were to select for an expert appointment, Alexander King of the OECD, and Max Kohnstamm, future president of the EUI, and at the time president of the Institute of the European Community for University Studies.[18]

The tone of the meeting was summed up by the mathematician and conference *rapporteur* André Lichnérowicz, Professor at the Collège de France, who declared that if a EC of universities could be constructed of institutions that were both 'compatible and diverse', each institution would better fulfil its role. Universities were committed to cooperation in a new and intense way in order to meet their varied obligations. They were anchored in their regions, where they had a public role, while the boundaries of knowledge were global and their students not limited to nationals. Initiatives needed to come from the universities, with students among the artisans of reform.

The conference made seven recommendations to support its argument that cooperation in higher education was essential, opening up the universities, stimulating research, and benefiting the standard of living and cultural life of the population as a whole – in short, cooperation was indispensable to the vitality of every university. These recommendations also required that states suppress nationality clauses for the recruitment of teachers and researchers where such clauses existed, and that each university periodically make explicit its strategy for teaching and research. This latter requirement would include a statement of the cooperation a given university wished to undertake and the services it could render to the community. University resources should be used throughout the year, with cooperation activities organised during the summer in initial teaching, *formation permanente* and research. National awards should be transferable from one university to another within Europe, with compensation where appropriate and low interest rate loans made available to encourage the mobility of students – and there should be research into why there was so little mobility, producing recommendations for reform. Finally, no teacher should get tenure without having spent at least one term at a foreign university.[19]

The universities' diagnosis was received with enthusiasm in the Commission. The Commissioner, Altiero Spinelli, took the view that the conference ideas 'perfectly fitted the ideas of co-operation being developed at Council level'.[20] Emile Noël, the Commission's Secretary-General urged Commissioners to take note of the Lichnérowicz report[21] and sent a message to assure the conference organiser, Henri Lesguillons, of his personal sympathy.[22]

Spinelli began to put pressure on his fellow Commissioners to act on the education issue, suggesting, via his *chef de cabinet,* that the Commission should fully support the Grenoble statement of the universities' position and aims. On 16 March, Spinelli met Lesguillons and Lichnérowicz,[23] while Noël circulated Spinelli's suggestions to the Commissioners to clarify 'the problem of education policy' in the light of the forthcoming meeting of Ministers of Education.[24] On 1 February1971, Emile Noël sent a memo to Commissioners to take note of it.[25]

By March 1971, Spinelli – at the time Commissioner for Industry and Research and a well-known advocate of European federalism – had officially secured the position of Commissioner in charge of education as a possible new policy area. He had had to beat off a challenger, the Commissioner for youth and information, Albert Borschette, who thought the domain of higher education and education was naturally his. But Spinelli was a man Borschette could not begin to match. Although Spinelli had surprised many when he was appointed a Commissioner in 1970, after a period spent working as an adviser to the Italian prime minister, he immediately exploited the new opportunities for creating an institutional base within the Commission for new policies. Following the Hague Summit, he had thrown himself into initiating and developing Community policies on industrial policy, research, environment and culture, none of which existed when he joined.[26]

Spinelli believed higher education to be a strategic and interesting domain for the EC. The 'crisis' in EC higher education – not just the shock of the French student revolts of 1968 and the challenge posed by the Americans' technological advances – made it so. As he was to write in a Commission document in June, whereas education at school level was a national responsibility,[27] 'higher education and [other] education were bound to become more important within the EC (*'porteur de l'avenir'*) in the wake of the Hague summit decision to work for economic and monetary union'.[28]

Spinelli had an ally in Emile Noël. Not only did Noël have a long-standing interest in the Community assuming a role in education,[29] he had been Secretary-General of the Commission since the EEC's beginnings in 1958. As such, he was the 'memory' of the Community, and a powerful person to have on-side.[30] Though bound by his office to be discreet – a trait that went with a personality once described as soft-slippered and Levantine[31] – Noël could make things happen. He was widely admired as a supremely good administrator, working as both a strategist and a broker, and one who was always well informed from across the organisation. A graduate of the elite French Ecole Normale Supérieure during World War II, and a member of the French Resistance, Noël was of the generation that viewed European integration as the best defence against further war. His conviction that the Commission should work actively with universities to provide resources for teaching and research about the EC was part of his integrationist strategy. Indeed, according to those who had worked with him, Noël was the power behind the initial subsidising of university studies on European affairs, the conferences and liaison work targeted at making teachers and academics the 'multipliers' of Community knowledge, and the interaction with students focussed on those interested in pursuing a career in 'Europe', especially those who would become judges, politicians or senior government officials.[32]

Spinelli, who saw the promised meeting of Ministers of Education as 'preparing the embryo of an institutional mechanism that would open the way for future progress',[33] began to put pressure on his fellow Commissioners to act on the education issue at the same time as Noël was urging Commissioners to 'take note' of the outcome in the shape of Lichnérowicz report.[34] On 22 February 1971, following his support for the Lichnérowicz report, Noël circulated Spinelli's suggestions to the Commissioners to clarify 'the problem of education policy' in the light of the forthcoming meeting of Ministers of Education.[35]

Spinelli said he wanted a precise statement of the activities the Commission was currently managing. This may have been a Mercereau initiative: Mercereau insisted in an interview that Spinelli had told him that as far as education was concerned, 'get on with it'. This statement is not entirely unconvincing. Spinelli, for all his interest in devising a strategy for Commission involvement in education, never talked to his collaborators about it in terms they remember. Nor in his 1972 account of the challenges the Community faced did Spinelli mention education.[36] Mercereau recalled that when asked to assume responsibility for education he had one question only. Would he be allowed to deal with the European University? 'Spinelli said, 'I don't suppose you will succeed. It was easier than I thought.'[37]

On 11 May 1971, the Commissioners agreed that Mercereau should map the Commission's existing educational activities and make recommendations on a future structure and the resources required in its support.[38] Mercereau was already heading an *ad hoc* group on the Commission's educational activities, which had been stimulated by a number of different EC decisions: a Council decision of 1963 that vocational training needed a general educational component; a regulation of 1968 on the education of the children of migrant workers; and by concern to make progress on the mutual recognition of qualifications.

Mercereau also knew the history of the issue, based on his experience as Etienne Hirsch's *chef de cabinet*, during the period in which Hirsch was deciding how to tackle the issue of the European University, and a continuing interest in education as an advocate of Community-backed European Schools for the children of EC officials among others.[39] Furthermore, Mercereau had a link to fellow Frenchman Olivier Guichard, whose project for EC educational cooperation was being discussed in Committee of Permanent Representatives (COREPER).[40] They had worked together on the press and information for the French Commission for Atomic Energy in the 1950s.[41]

On 4 June 1971, Mercereau completed his mission, reporting that there were already eight Directorates-General (DGs) undertaking education-related activities, as well as the Commission's legal service and the statistical office, all under different rules and in a policy area in which the Commission officially had almost no role.[42] The eight DGs involved were DG 1 (External Affairs), DG II (Economic and Financial Affairs), DG III (Trade and Industry), DG V (Social Affairs), DG VI (Agriculture), DG VIII (Development), DG X (Press and Information) and DG XIV (Internal market and approximation of legislation) – each organisationally diverse and working to different legal frameworks.

Given the fragmented nature of education in Community institutions, Mercereau recommended co-ordination rather than major structural change. He argued that the best way forward was for different EC sectors to address higher education/education questions 'in the same spirit of consciousness of their long-term importance'.[43] The existing *ad hoc* group, for which he had been working, should be transformed into a Group (unit) for Education and Teaching, while Commission activities in education across the DGs would be co-ordinated by an inter-services Group. According to Mercereau's proposal, the Group (Education and Teaching) would be supported by four A grade staff.[44] The task of the first group should be to organise co-operation, the exchange of information and co-ordination of activities undertaken in the Directorates-General dealing with teaching, and the education of young people and adults. The task of the second group should be to conduct studies, encourage reflection and compile proposals for the Commission, drawing on the various technical services concerned in order to obtain a 'global' view of problems, and some 'coherence' between short-term action and long-term vision.[45]

Spinelli, as the Commissioner who wished to address the 'crisis' in education, presented the Commission with a view that stressed the need for some EC policy-making capacity, and a clear mission.[46] Despite claiming to have no wish to enlarge his responsibilities, Spinelli wanted to take over fundamental research activities from DGIII, and higher education mobility from DGX. He did not, however, want to impinge on DGX's informational role.[47] Spinelli apparently thought it would be dangerous to attempt to incorporate the university liaison activities that Noël supported so strongly.[48] Spinelli won this round too. He was supported by Noël's old friend, the future creator of Eurostat, Jean-René Rabier.[49] The distinction between policy making and information endured until 1999.

If the Commission were to propose something different than Guichard's idea of an intergovernmental centre, it needed resources and a strategy. On 16 June 1971, Spinelli presented the Commission with recommendations for policy-related education, in a paper written jointly with Albert Coppé, the Commissioner responsible for personnel.[50] Mercereau anticipated this operating through two groups: Mercereau's *ad hoc* group, transformed into an established Group (Education and Teaching) within Spinelli's Commission, and an inter-service co-ordination unit, chaired by Mercereau. The Education and Teaching Group would report directly to him on such strategy issues as the preparation of the Council of Ministers meeting and the European University. The unit would be charged with policy development, starting with an analysis of the current education crises and the possibility for education systems to develop along a 'European route' (*'voie européenne'*), 'as a way of resolving problems which bear such striking similarities among existing and new Member States'.[51]

Even this modest proposal raised concerns among the other Commissioners. When the *chefs de cabinet* met to discuss forthcoming business – as they did each week before the Commissioners' meetings – they challenged the premise of Spinelli and Coppé that Community activities should extend to education.[52] Was the Commission not encroaching on Member State prerogatives? Nöel combined reassurance with some revision of the text to make it clear that the role in education envisaged for the Community was quite different from the development of teaching and the management of education systems within member states.[53] On 19 July, a complementary note to the SEC document explicitly assured Commissioners that 'the role would not be confused with that of Member States for the curriculum and for [the management of] their education systems'. On 27 July, 1971, the Commissioners approved the decision on what they called 'l' affaire

Mercereau'.[54] Within the Commission, Mercereau and Spinelli were to register with satisfaction that the Ministers of Education agreed to 'active cooperation' when they met in November 1971.

A policy domain had thus been created by the time Spinelli relinquished his education-related responsibilities in December 1972. He believed that the coordination group, under Mercereau's chairmanship, had provided 'conclusive evidence' of the benefits of getting the DGs to think globally about the problem of higher education and education. Foreshadowing an issue that was to be controversial in the 1980s and 1990s, he said:

> There was always the risk that the issue would be confined to a sector rather than taking on a real Community dimension.[55]

Spinelli himself was satisfied. As he put it to his Commissioner colleagues just before the handover of office with Enlargement, he regarded the Ministers' meeting as 'preparing the embryo of an institutional mechanism which would open the way for future progress'.[56]

Staking out a Community agenda

This was in many ways an anxious time for the larger Community project. As the proposed new member states proceeded with ratification of their membership – successfully, except for Norway – the issue preoccupying the EC institutions was how much of the reform activity since the Hague summit would be acceptable to the new members who would be attending a summit in Paris planned for October 1972. One reason for anxiety was that the Commissioners, presided over by their Italian president, the politician, Franco Maria Malfatti, were marching forward to Enlargement divided in their aims.

Spinelli was on the side of expanding Community powers before enlargement. On 13 October 1971, at a special meeting of the Commission at the chateau of Val Duchesse, Spinelli argued for a revision of the Treaty to take in 'new common policies' on industry, scientific and technological research, environment and the regions.[57] Willy Haferkamp, a German commissioner throughout the 1970s, argued for a strategy of subsidiarity – long before the idea became commonplace. He hoped, he said, 'that the period would be used to destroy prejudices, and to create a sober, realistic but welcoming image of the Community framework and particularly of the Commission.'[58]

Borschette, Spinelli's rival for building an education base, contented himself with arguing that 'Europe's strength was not being a military union and demonstrating that it was not obliged to behave like one'.[59]

Nöel expressed his anxiety by making great personal efforts to smooth the path of UK entry at the official level. He dined with the head of the UK civil service, urging that able civil servants be sent to Brussels, and he took immense care with a speech delivered at the Civil Service College.[60] As he said in a private letter to a good friend and future Commissioner – Karl-Heinz Narjes, former *chef de cabinet* of Walter Hallstein – the scene was one of 'great political animation'.[61]

Although the Commission communication of last Friday was welcomed, the British ministers and the ministers of the other three adherents indicated extremely clearly that they were not ready to envisage significant institutional modifications, especially any Treaty modification of institutions, until their countries had acquired an effective experience of the functioning of institutions as they are ....

I think there is lot of uncertainty as to how much the summit might do to build European construction. I think the success of the summit is far from guaranteed at this precise moment.[62]

The febrile atmosphere and weak Commission leadership[63] gave Spinelli a chance to advance on the content and method of educational cooperation. Mercereau, on hand with ideas, suggested that the best way forward in devising a Community policy – as opposed to an intergovernmental process – was to call in an education expert to conduct enquiries among well known names in the policy field, and report back on a possible Community policy on education. This was not an unreasonable proposal. According to Hywel Ceri Jones, the top official on education after 1973: 'The Commission could *never* have accepted the Guichard inter-governmental structure.'[64]

On 19 July 1972, the strategy of getting an expert contribution to policy making came to fruition. Following Spinelli's proposal – on Mercereau's advice – to that effect, the Commission appointed Professor Henri Janne, one of the key figures at the Grenoble conference.[65] Janne was a prestigious figure with a Resistance past, a respected Belgian sociologist at the Université Libre de Bruxelles, and former Minister of Education. In 1972, he was presiding over the education aspects of the European Cultural Foundation (ECF)'s prospective on the year 2000, *Plan Europe 2000*. He was known for his enthusiasm for

Europeanising higher education. And he was liked. Interviewees stress Janne's charm and capability for the job – 'somebody who drew people to him';[66] 'a genial Mr Fixit for the Commission – he obviously knew his way around Brussels';[67] 'our master;[68] 'impressive and charming'.[69]

The starting point for this new initiative, for both Janne and the Commission, was that in the EC, educational and cultural issues were national and diversity was to be preserved.[70] Within that frame of reference, Janne was to discuss with the agreed experts the issues and instruments for effective higher education and education co-operation, in areas such as language, teaching and mobility, and the relationship of the EC to other interested international organisations, notably the Organisation for Economic Cooperation and Development (OECD). Should the Community make 'regulations' for the compulsory teaching of a second language in the interests of understanding culture?[71] Should the Community not make a semester of study abroad within Europe 'obligatory', and given 'official sanction'? Was not the Community in the 'best' position to act and to produce results on mobility? ('It is above all a question of conceiving and creating institutional and financial machinery', went one line of argument. 'The Community should play the role of promoters of university consortia with well-defined goals ... the best method for exchanges and the best framework for mobility ... by creating the necessary means encouraging the preparatory contacts and suggesting objectives.'[72])

Contemporary sociological preoccupations shaped the thinking of Mercereau and Janne. They saw the objective as being 'to define and draw up ... an education policy to be implemented at Community level ... so that the educational process (transmission of learning and diffusion of culture, teaching and adaptation to the cultural environment) will satisfy the aspirations of the individual and at the same time respond to the present and future needs of society.'[73] The background – reflecting the shocks of 1968 – was one of 'profound' change in education systems, and a 'veritable [cultural] revolution rocking social classes in all European countries.' The Commission envisaged EC institutions playing a part with national and other elected authorities 'in adapting education as a whole.'

There was an auspicious beginning to Janne's work. In October 1972, the summit about which Emile Noël and many of the Commissioners had been so anxious, had been held in Paris, attended by the representatives from the new member states.[74] Contrary to their fears that the brakes would be applied to integration, the final communiqué confirmed the vision of Spinelli, Mercereau, Noël and their contemporaries, that the EC had a cultural and educational dimension. Partici-pants understood that higher education, along with education in general and culture, would have a place in the re-launched EEC. The communiqué stated that: 'Economic expansion ... is not an end in itself.... In the European spirit, special attention will be given to non-material values and to protecting the environment, so progress shall serve mankind.'[75]

Christopher Audland, a Foreign Office 'high flyer' with exactly the profile Noël had asked for – and Noël's deputy for nearly ten years, says this communiqué marked the beginning of an EC education policy.[76] It clearly marked a Commission commitment to the sector. Bearing out the view that widening of the Community has also produced deepen-ing,[77] the Commission reorganisation for the enlarged community included a commissioner was to be appointed with a portfolio that explicitly included education, linked to science and research.

But Enlargement to include the UK, Ireland and Denmark, proved a watershed. When Janne delivered his report on 27 February 1973, Spinelli had moved to another post in a new and enlarged Com-mission. Mercereau had retired.[78] The new Commissioner, as we shall see, had very different ideas from Spinelli.

Deciding on a Community policy domain

The years 1970–72 were highly significant in the history of higher edu-cation in the Community. It was not in fact the beginning of Com-munity policy-making in education as many sources maintain.[79] It was already the completion of one policy cycle with the decision of the European University Institute and the start of another one with the res-olution on cooperation. The two decisions of November 1971 enabled ministers of education of the Six to put behind them one old problem and to start on something new. The problem of the European Univer-sity, on and off government agendas for 16 years, was at last resolved by a much more modest reformulation of the original idea, and the agreement that this new institution – the European University Institute in Florence – should be subject to intergovernmental rules defined by a treaty.

Part of the explanation of these outcomes lies in the spillover between Community level events and the sector. The Hague Summit, which had agreed on an expansionist agenda for the Community, created the climate in which both the European University and educa-tional cooperation would have a place. But also these decisions were being taken in the knowledge that the climate could worsen in the near future, once Enlargement brought in the suspicious British and Danes. In short, there was a policy window that the Commission, the Italians and Guichard all recognised.

However the decision to cooperate on educational issues within an EC framework must also be explained in part as consistent with the interlocking mechanisms of a stable image of education, and the formation of shared beliefs.[80] The idea of educational cooperation on a European scale had been acceptable – and practised – since the Council of Europe's foundation. The unresolved problem had been finding the policy capacity to establish higher education – or education – as a European policy domain. For all its weak status – the resolution of the ministers of education never appeared in the *Official Journal* – it was a significant decision for ministers of education to agree that the Community institutions provided the best venue. It was also a break with the Cold War framing of higher education cooperation as primarily a foreign policy issue.[81] Ministers believed they had common problems and had accepted the need to promote a European dimension to higher education (and education). As Mercereau's survey had shown, within various Commission directorates-general there was already much education-related activity taking place. Individuals within universities were active in pro-Europe associations.

Another essential element in advancing the solution for a dynamic form of cooperation was the capacity-building to control activity and resources within the territory over which the Community institutions were claiming jurisdiction.[82] Until 1969–71 the question of policy capacity had not been an issue for education. In the Euratom years, the resource most needed was Commission initiative to frame the issue acceptably, with the understanding that had there been agreement on the European University, ministers could have drawn on Community funding. In the years of intergovernmental activity within the Council of Europe, in contrast, it was known that there were almost no resources available. It was not surprising that it was veterans of the resource-poor Council of Europe – Guichard, like his predecessor Faure, – who campaigned so vigorously for a more robust alternative. They were attentive to the problem of capacity, specifically stating that there needed to be more than 'intermittent meetings of various committees' to solve such complex problems as the harmonisation of qualifications, and an administration needed to be given the power to make recommendations. Not that Guichard's admonishments had any effect. The ambassadorial committees of COREPER, could not agree terms to implement his proposal for the European centre for the Development of Education.

For the Commission in contrast, as both guardian of the treaties and initiator of policies, it was incumbent on officials to think about policy capacity, when advancing policy ideas. It was rapid to implement a bureaucratic solution which would ensure that education became an established domain. That is not to say that the degree of Community competence was unambiguous. But as we see from the actions of Spinelli, the Commissioner, working in tandem with Noël, the Secretary-General, the point had been reached where both agreed that it was important to set up 'an embryonic bureaucracy'.

This lock-in to institutional processes within the Commission – with the help of policy entrepreneurs among the Italians, the French and the Commission – and the parallel commitment to ministerial meetings, significantly stabilised the issue of Community action on education. Education – including higher education – acquired three characteristics seen as essential in policy-making. (1) Education was accepted as an agenda issue for EEC policy makers and decision-makers; (2) it was given its own venue; and (3) a rudimentary bureaucracy in its support was brought into being. In short, a policy domain for education was created, re-creating an EC domain for higher education.[83] In putting Mercereau in charge of two Commission groups on education questions, and in getting the Commission to resource the Janne committee, Spinelli was preparing the ground for a new policy cycle in which his successors would develop decisions on a Community basis.

6
Stabilising the Policy Domain, 1973–76

From 1973 to 1976 education was explicitly recognised as a policy domain in which the Community action had some role, both as a sector in which there was a developing law and – not coterminous and rather ambiguous – a developing common education policy based not on binding law, but on public international law or Community 'soft law'.[1] But on the basis of this account they can more accurately be seen as the years in which for the first time a resource-based policy could be designed. This chapter shows how and why it was possible to develop policy-making in a form which broke new ground in Community governance.

Presenting a Community policy

On 27 February 1973, barely six weeks after the Community's first enlargement, the new Commissioner for education, the German sociologist, Ralf Dahrendorf, received a report on what a Community policy on education might be. The report was compiled by Professor Henri Janne, whose name had been proposed by the outgoing Commissioner for education, Spinelli, and who was assigned the task by the Commission in July 1972. Janne's report presented the thoughts of major intellectuals and educationists on a Community policy for education[2] – the culmination of Commissioner Spinelli's strategy of developing the 'embryo' of cooperation in education.

Spinelli and his official, Mercereau, had intended that Janne would present something more ambitious than either the project for an EC centre for intergovernmental cooperation in education, under study within a Council working party, or any project that emerged from the strict application of the European Economic Community (EEC)

Treaty – i.e. educational action within vocational training (derived from Article 128), action on the mutual recognition of diplomas (Article 57), or action on the education of migrant workers' children, which, in 1968, had become an issue of jurisprudence (derived from Article 7).

One of Spinelli's last words on the subject before changing chairs in the Commission was that education should have a 'real' Community dimension, and an impact on the global thinking of the Commission – it should not be a mere sectoral policy.[3] A background note issued by the Commission had stressed that 'educational Europe' could bring two benefits to the Community, signalling both a 'change in dimension' and a 'change in direction'.[4] The domain of education, it was argued, could boost the global image of the European Community (EC), as well as drawing attention to the diversity of cultures signed up to a common desire for European union.[5]

In drawing up his report on EC education policy, Janne – himself an eminent sociologist, dean of the Université Libre de Bruxelles, and a leading player in the futurology exercise *Europe 2000* – travelled to a dozen European cities in eight countries, holding discussions with intellectuals and experts in the field. Those interviewed included many of the great educational names of the time: Eric Ashby, former vice-chancellor of University of Cambridge, who had written widely on university issues; Helmut Becker, director of the Berlin-based Max Planck Institute for Educational Research; Asa Briggs, vice-chancellor of the innovative University of Sussex; Hendrik Brugmans, rector of the College of Europe; Michel Crozier, author of the influential *Blocked Society*,[6] and a specialist on the sociology of cultural organisations in the French research organisation, the CNRS; Alfred Grosser, professor at the Institut d'Etudes Politiques in Paris; Richard Hoggart, assistant director-general of UNESCO and author of the *Uses of Literacy*; H. Leussink, former minister of national education and science in the German Federal Republic; André Lichnérowicz of the Collège de France and *rapporteur* at the Grenoble conference of 1970; Albert Sloman, vice-chancellor of the University of Essex and a well known British Europhile; and Aldo Visalberghi, professor of educational sciences at the University of Rome and closely connected to the OECD's Centre for Educational Research and Innovation. The list also included three non-EC citizens: the Norwegian, Jan Tinbergen, a Nobel prize-winning economist; Alexander King, director-general of scientific affairs at the OECD; and James (Jim) Perkins, president of the International Council for Educational Development in New York and a good friend to senior

figures in the European Cultural Foundation (ECF). Indeed, Janne described Perkins as a 'single leading figure playing an outstanding role
through his international initiatives'.[7] If Mercereau, had had his way
the list would also have included Daniel Cohn-Bendit, an initiator of
the student protests in France in May 1968.[8]

A contemporary English commentator, John Pratt, suggested that
given this method, no one should have expected policy recommendations to emerge from Janne's investigations. 'The very idea that it is
possible to "formulate the first principles of an education policy" by
asking 34 "authorities" is bizarre'.[9] Stuart Maclure, who at the time was
editor of the *Times Educational Supplement*, took the same view. Maclure
remembers Janne 'as a genial Mr Fixit who obviously knew the ins and
outs of the Commission well' but Maclure was not left with the im-
pression of a man aware of the important policy dimension to his
work.[10] 'We had arranged to meet at a big educational conference and
were chatting about this and that over a coffee when Janne dug some
notes out of his brief case and asked some general questions and
I answered,' Maclure recalls.[11]

An aspect of Janne's report was that it was framed in grandiose
and abstract terms – like those which the British prime minister,
Margaret Thatcher, came to hate. A Community function in education 'may have fundamental consequences for our civilisation'[12] in a
context of education in crisis. 'The state of western education in
Western Europe', 'the cultural revolution and the problem of values',
the 'profound change' and cultural 'revolution' rocking Europe',[13] the
'de-schooling' debate and other signs of 'democracy in danger' were
presented as the justification for the report.

Yet on the core judgement that a Community policy was inevitable,
and the core question of the instruments the Community might use,
Janne argued concretely. The Community could not, in his view,
expect to implement the vocational training articles or to pursue its
economic and regional policies, or scientific and technical development, without calling on 'education and training'.[14] He pointed
to extensive activities already undertaken at a European level. The
College of Bruges for postgraduate European studies; the EC Institute
for University Studies created by Monnet and directed by Max
Kohnstamm; the 1971 meeting of EC Ministers of Education; and the
place of education in the new Commission, confirming 'the Commission's power with regard to education'. There were also the intergovernmental measures such as the convention establishing the
European University Institute in Florence, signed on 19 April 1972,

and the work of Council officials in following up the Minister's meeting of 1971. These suggested the opportunity for some coherent policy-making.

Janne's conclusion was that a Community policy would need to go beyond what existed under the Treaty. He suggested four criteria: no interference with national structures and educational traditions proper to each country; 'compensatory' community action, with member states the first to benefit;[15] and the safeguarding of academic freedom.[16] Furthermore, EC education action or policy should make provision for association to include other European countries. Janne reasoned that education had intrinsic qualities binding it to the wider world of culture and science. The education-culture link was essential at Community level, since 'education cannot be conceived of without the fundamental values which alone confer a meaning upon it and define its fundamental aims',[17] while the Community was in a position to promote its culturally diverse character. At the same time, science policy – in which universities were key players – was perceived to be at 'a turning point'.[18]

According to the clumsy English translation provided at the time, this thinking amounted to a recognition that 'a whole education-culture-science sector ... must tomorrow be covered by a Community policy rendered indispensable by the requirements and consequences of the developments of economic policy with its social aspects'.[19] The activities advocated followed the broad outlines of propositions made a decade previously: promoting the mobility of teachers and students; knowledge of languages; cooperation between scientific and technical establishments; joint experiments; information and documentation – these were the issues which needed the Community to put 'effective procedures' in hand.

However the experts disagreed over the instruments necessary to create the Europe of education. At least one believed a global or Community policy of harmonisation was required. At the other extreme, the Briton, Maclure, was alarmed at the idea of the EC assuming more powers over education than those enjoyed by Britain's own minister for education (this was before the system operating in England and Wales became centralised). Most others supported action-based programmes, in some cases limited to exchanges, or targeted only at teaching staff, and in the case of at least one discussant, the promotion of permanent education, in recognition that the essential needs of the individual are now long term.[20] In general the British and Germans preferred to focus future policy on 'action strategy'[21] and 'concrete developments',[22] rather than on wide-ranging policy-making.

More seriously for Janne, he was reporting to a new commissioner, and furthermore, one who was averse to the idea of Community policy in education. The first commissioner to have education as a portfolio. Ralf Dahrendorf, the German Federal Republic nominee, and a survivor from the previous Commission, was a relatively unwilling recruit to the 'difficult inheritance' of education.[23] A junior minister for foreign affairs in the German federal government, a rising star in his liberal party, and a famous sociologist, he had expected to keep the external relations dossier. He was foiled by British entry.

> I had talks with François-Xavier Ortoli,[24] who told me the foreign portfolio was going to Soames,[25] but I had the choice of the rest. I took research. Taking science, too, was logical ... On education, I was the only one with something to give – I'm not sure how important it was. A mild form of working together is all right but education is a matter for national governments.[26]

Although some accounts have attributed the developments of 1973–76 as coming from Dahrendorf, Dahrendorf himself in interviews and in documents of the time was explicit in his belief that the only approach which made sense was to regard the treaty framework as defining the limits of the possible – and indeed desirable – role of the EC in education. It 'assign[ed] only very limited tasks in the fields of education, training, and cultural activities'. He argued that 'not everything is improved by being on a European scale ... the main problems of education are shared by all developed industrialised countries' – the example of the time being managing mass higher education. As he put it,

> The Community was not necessarily the appropriate political framework for solving the problems.... Harmonisation of the European educational systems was neither realistic nor necessary.[27]

He robustly admitted, 'My chief job at the time was suppressing paper.'[28] For Dahrendorf, even exchanges of teachers within the EEC, as well as cross-frontier projects to link educational establishments which 'deserved to be encouraged ... exceeded the capabilities of the directorate-general for research, science and education'.[29] He was also against having a council of ministers consisting of education ministers. It would be sufficient to appoint a high-ranking European personality to advise the Commission on education and training questions, along with a request to member dates to name advisers on whom the Commission could call.[30]

However, in at least one area, Dahrendorf's attachment to an inter-governmental line was uncontroversial. This was in respect of the recognition of qualifications, the thorniest educational issue of the time.[31] Dahrendorf's concern was the Commission's determination to implement Article 57, as it affected the medical professions and architects, in terms of hours of training. This had created conster-nation, not least among university organisations, who dropped their opposition to working with the Community in order to become players, and national professional bodies.[32] Dahrendorf's successful alternative was to worked for a system in which the professional bodies of the member states had the decisive input.

Those working under Dahrendorf came to understand that he was immovable on the idea that the EC could promote a common policy or 'harmonisation' of education.[33] He had, he told an interviewer, found 'a hopeless dossier on harmonisation'.[34] There may have been a misun-derstanding. The word 'harmonisation', meaning convergence, contin-ued to be used by educationists in the 1970s,[35] and as we have noted before subject to different interpretations. Janne himself, introducing the word with the utmost caution, and in predictive rather than prescriptive mode – and writing in French – almost certainly meant voluntary convergence by member states. Years later a French minister defined harmonisation as 'difference in harmony' (Allègre, 1999). But some English language users, in the Commission and the British government, interpreted the word as implying use of the law.

Given Dahrendorf's interpretation, the outcome in the context was predictable. The Commissioner damned the Janne report with faint praise. In his foreword to the report published in the course of 1973, he wrote that the new Commission attached 'so much significance to the questions of education policy it has to deal with' and was aware, as the Paris Summit conference had put it, 'that economic expansion is not an end in itself', that the report was to be commended to the general public. As 'a report by a non-Commission expert' the Janne report did 'not simply indicate the directions which a future Com-munity education policy might take, but goes beyond this to state ways and means in which the Community might achieve this aim'.[36] The Commission could (only) consider the report in relation to Com-munity procedures. Dahrendorf had taken the report off the policy making agenda, the one dimension that mattered to Janne.

Generating a winning vision

However, the political climate favoured action. The communiqué to the Paris summit of heads of state was a constant reference for ambitious officials. In Neave's version:

> Economic expansion ... must as a priority help to attenuate the disparities in living conditions. It must emerge in an improved quality as well as an improved standard of life. In the European spirit, special attention will be paid to non-material values.[37]

In Dahrendorf's directorate-general, there were many who opposed Commissioner's minimalist line. One such was the director-general, Gunter Schuster. Schuster, a German, is described by Christopher Layton, a member of Spinelli's cabinet, as an activist, and likely to counter his fellow countryman, Dahrendorf, if he were so minded. As Layton put it, 'a determined DG like Schuster could continue to push something forward, buttering up the national officials as he went'.[38]

Another key enthusiast was the head of the new education and youth division, Hywel Ceri Jones.[39] Jones, a Welshman, was very different from the Commission officials who had previously worked on education. He arrived in Brussels in May 1973 with hands-on experience of managing educational change. He came from a post at Sussex University, as assistant to the vice chancellor for planning and development. His political baptism had been as president of his student union in Aberystwyth, a college of the University of Wales, where he had studied languages at the beginning of 1960s student radicalism. He also had experience of the theory of education. He held a postgraduate diploma in education from the University of Wales. At the University of Sussex, his political and policy experience combined. Sussex boasted that it was 'redrawing the map of knowledge'.[40] Among its innovations, the university had developed European studies, and made a study year abroad compulsory for these students, as was already the practice with language students. Such commitment prompts some academics to claim – not altogether convincingly – that Sussex was at the origin of the European Community action scheme for the mobility of university students (Erasmus) programme.[41]

For Jones, the greatest benefit of his time at Sussex was that it offered him a seat at the side of the eminent historian, Asa Briggs – a man who was to have a profound influence on Jones:

> Asa Briggs taught me that you cannot achieve change unless you have achieved trust,[42] Jones later recalled.

Briggs was also responsible for recommending Jones for Brussels through a strong political network. George Thomson, a former Secretary of State for Commonwealth Relations in a Labour government, and one of the two British commissioners to take up office with UK accession, was seeking advice on 'the exciting task of putting together a team from the UK to bid for the various senior posts in the Commission following British accession'.[43] Thomson recalled that

> Asa Briggs[44] originally mentioned Hywel Jones to me.... My main link with Hywel Jones was undoubtedly through Gwynne Morgan[45] who came with me as my *chef de cabinet* ... I attached a great deal of importance to the education dimension in the building of a united Europe ... I felt that in creating a consciousness of a common European identity it was important to bring about wider exchanges between students within the European Community. The Commonwealth, despite great differences of economic development and of historical background, enjoyed the advantage of a common language. In Europe there were underlying common values of European civilisation but great barriers of language. It was against this background that I was glad to help persuade Hywel Jones to join the European Commission.[46]

Reflecting on his sentiments at the time, Jones said, 'British entry into the EEC was hugely symbolic,' adding that he, Morgan and another Aberystwyth friend, Aneurin Rhys Hughes, a Foreign Office diplomat, 'applied for our jobs because of British entry. "Europe" was the chance to be at the cutting edge.'[47]

Once in Brussels, Jones had line responsibility to another Briton, Alan Bath, the director of education, training and youth. According to Jones, Bath, a former senior official of the UK Committee of Vice-Chancellors and Principals, was not an activist.[48] Nor did Jones expect much active support his fellow division heads. Two of them operated in the treaty areas – the mutual recognition of professional qualifications, the co-ordination of vocational training, and the training of adults – a third in external relations in research, science and education, and in the fourth in similarly emerging domain of culture. As Jones describes their relations, there was a mutual agreement not to impinge on each others' territories.[49]

Thus when Jones inherited responsibility for preparing the policy papers for the next ministers of education meeting to follow up on action taken following the first meeting in November 1971, he claims 'I was left to write the Commission communication entirely on my

own, with some interaction with Dahrendorf and our shared understanding of national sensitivities, and some negative reactions to
Janne.' He claims neither Alan Bath, Director for Education and
Training, nor the Director General, Gunter Schuster, got involved.[50]
The Jones claim is plausible, given it is Commission practice to get
desk officers to develop policy. It is clear that the Commissioner and
his cabinet would give the issue only spasmodic attention, given the
range of their responsibilities. Their big issue was mutual recognition.
In any event Dahrendorf had decided that he preferred academic life.
In October 1974, he stepped down from the Commission to become
director of the London School of Economics, having achieved advances
on draft directives and a clearly education-oriented resolution on the
Council's desire for a 'flexible and qualitative approach'.[51]

Jones thus felt relatively free to view his work as encompassing
crucial issues of strategy and tactics. But while he understood the
Commission strategy as being to gain Community competence for
the new domain of education, the Commission could not credibly
make recommendations that were at odds with the desire of ministers
to proceed by cooperation rather than by anything approaching
common policy. As far as he – and the Commission in general – was
concerned, a first tactical requirement was to avoid the Guichard
model of intergovernmental cooperation.

It so happened that the Guichard proposal had collapsed as Jones
took up his post. National representatives in the Council working
party, along with the one Commission representative, could not agree
on a blueprint for 'a permanent team with contacts between different
administrations and with the power and means to make recommendations to responsible ministers' – let alone a 'strong ... flexible body
which would prepare and eventually execute decisions of ministers of
education in the Community.' The representatives had laboured at the
task since April 1972, winding up a year later without any plan of
future action. The group's sole achievement was a declaration for
the record that representatives were 'unanimously in agreement on
co-operation from a practical point of view and as a supplementary
contribution to the construction of Europe'.[52]

The other tactical requirement for Jones was that he avoid the Janne
model, as he and Dahrendorf understood it. On a personal level, Jones
found this reality hard. Looking back, Jones recalls Janne with great
warmth.

[He was] such a nice man, so full of energy and eminent in his field.
I remember his wife Betsy, a wonderful woman, complaining in

front of us at a dinner that Janne in older age had worked harder on his report than on anything in his career. Janne replied: 'Mais Betsy, je prépare l'avenir' (But Betsy, I am preparing the future).[53]

Politically, however, Jones had no difficulty in following the Commissioner. Jones, like Dahrendorf, took Janne to be thinking of long-term standardisation rather than voluntary convergence. As he put the issue in a retrospective speech to a major education conference in 1983:

> There was a common concern, fully shared by the Commission, under the strong influence of Professor Dahrendorf, to avoid any harmonising or standardising forces and modes of operation appropriate, maybe, to legislation about agricultural products, but certainly both undesirable and unrealistic in the education field.[54]

Jones also shared the sense, common in Britain at the time that culture was a dangerous issue for the EC to be getting into.[55] In the 1970s, references to central control of the curriculum were frequently followed, in British education circles, by references to the rise of Hitler and Nazism, if not to traditional British jokes against Napoleon.

By the time the Commission statement on education was formally approved by the College of Commissioners for transmission to the Council of Education Ministers, Jones had found a line which was neither 'Guichard' nor 'Janne'. In an innovation which deserves to be better known, he had solved the conundrum of how education could be both a sovereign issue and one in which the EC could intervene in ways that were likely to add quality.

The new strategy was to extend EC action by involving large numbers of practitioners: a strategy of 'common action' – rather than the more familiar Community method of 'common policy.' The Commission Communication, *Education in the European Community*[56] – a noticeably less ambitious title than Janne's *For an EC Policy in Education* – for the first time provided ministers of education with concrete proposals for action in the education domain. In marked contrast with the Dahrendorf formulation presented to Commissioners in March 1973, the 1974 Communication interpreted the treaties and recent political decisions as dynamic, 'laying emphasis on the place of education in the process of development towards European Union'.[57] It suggested mechanisms for EC co-operation both through the university community and through links with other EC policy, such as the environment, industry and social affairs, and future regional policies. In addition, the

Communication picked out potential areas for action that illustrated opportunities for intervention with a variety of instruments, treaty and non-treaty, in collaboration with other policies (e.g. the European Social Fund), and through more dynamic forms of co-operation, and the use of Commission facilities to get initial movement.

Two examples illustrated how higher education problems could be effectively dealt with at EC level. The first was university admission for non-national students, an issue on which the Commission proposed public hearings:

> At a time when pressure on available student places from nationals has been rising, the particular arrangements for the admission of foreign students ... has given rise to difficulty in some member states. It will therefore be necessary ... to establish the position, to examine the specific arrangements in force ... and to consider what steps might be proposed.[58]

A second example related to opportunities for the EC to strengthen and extend traditional cross-border links between universities. The communication noted that the universities had already made considerable progress, for example in establishing consortia and setting up collaborative programmes of study and research, and proposed the Community should liaise with the universities to assess how it could most usefully be of assistance.[59] As Jones later recalled

> Our analysis was that for the Community to play a catalytic role, there had to be opportunities in the first instance for practitioners to meet their opposite numbers in other member states and to compare experience on specific issues and to work out for themselves ways in which they could work together. That is to say, the routine contacts with ministers and officials had to be complemented by 'field' experience.[60]

The 'common action' envisaged would be the outcome of a 'broad pooling of information and exchange of views between the competent authorities'.[61] There was no conception of harmonisation: indeed, the communication specifically stated that the special objectives and requirements of higher education (and education in general) 'made harmonisation undesirable as well as unrealistic'.[62] Instead, there was a bold attempt to cut through the issues on which the Council working party on the Guichard centre had been blocked.[63] The mechanism proposed was a European Committee for Educational Co-operation, to be established by a Decision of the Council – a policy instrument binding on those to whom it was addressed – which would advise the Council on the elaboration and development of action in the field of education, prepare opinions, make reports and raise questions of interest to the EC. From Jones' perspective:

> These were ground rules designed with careful ambiguity, offering safeguards to reluctant Europeans yet confirming a degree of Community commitment to develop educational co-operation.[64]

In fact, ministers of education were ready to support a non-regulatory and dynamic vision of EC higher education and education action, in which there was an explicit conceptualisation of 'Europe' as a complement, rather than a competitor to national action, and hence as providing opportunities for innovation. No member state wanted supra-national control in place of co-operation.[65] However, in 1974, the ministers did not want to follow on from the Guichard initiative with another failure. Their position was thus that they needed to find a favourable outcome. The domain might be one that caused political difficulties and one on which they, as representatives of national governments, could be easily divided. But their heads of state or government had signed up to important summits that expressed the political desire for the Community to be active in domains that were not entirely driven by economics: six governments in the case of the Hague (1969), nine for the Paris summit (1972).

On receiving the communication, Council secretariat advisers responsible for preparing ministers' meetings developed a text, taking account of the Commission's paper. The advisers did not dissent from the Commission's recommendation for an EC domain for action, despite the fact that such action might take in both non-treaty and treaty issues. They also backed the proposal for a strong policy advisory structure. As a result, the Council position combined the Commission's 'policy expert' model with Council control – though not precisely as the Commission had advocated. The Council document proposed an education committee that would foster the immediate action on which ministers were prepared to agree.

The breakthrough was that the Council group – and later the ministers – accepted the innovative principle of dual membership of Council and Commission. While member states would be represented, as normal, by government and professional representatives of the national policy community, the Commission would be an equal member. As Jones recalled:

> Even those of us who had worked so hard to negotiate agreement ... could not have dreamed at that time that the unique formula which was invented to promote co-operation in the field of education at Community level would have withstood the test of time so well.[66]

The ministers of education met on 6 June 1974, once more on inter-governmental terms 'within the Council,' but not as the Council. 'Taking account,' as they put it, of the Commission's communication of March 1974, the ministers agreed that co-operation in higher education and education should be initiated 'by progressive stages' and 'in accordance with a procedure to be laid down'.[67] They also approved the innovative structure of the Education Committee a committee structure unique to the Commission until a Culture committee was set up almost a decade later.

The resolution adopted at the June 1974 meeting reflected an effort to strike a balance between, on the one hand, the belief that higher education and education were integrally linked to both national culture and to the aims that had led member governments to join the Community and, on the other, mechanisms that respected both the spirit of cooperation and the need for dynamism. Hence:

o the programme of co-operation ... whilst reflecting the progressive harmonisation of the economic and social policies of the Community must be adapted to the specific objectives and requirement of this field
o on no account must education be regarded merely as a component of economic life
o education co-operation must make allowance for the traditions of each country and the diversity of their respective educational policies and systems
o harmonisation of these systems or policies cannot therefore be considered an end in itself
o this co-operation must not hinder the exercise of the powers conferred on the institutions of the European Communities

The resolution made no reference to the 16 November 1971 resolution – disliked by the British – that EC education action should be brought about in order to strengthen Europe's cultural identity.

The priorities for cooperation outlined at the meeting included a number of higher education issues:

o The promotion of closer relations between educational systems in Europe
o Increased co-operation between institutions of higher education
o Improved possibilities for academic recognition of diplomas and periods of study
o Encouragement of the freedom of movement and mobility of teachers, students and research workers, in particular by the removal of administrative and social obstacles to the free movement of such persons, and by the improved teaching of foreign languages

Other objectives included better facilities for the education and training of nationals and the children of nationals from both member and non-member states of the Communities, and equal opportunity for free access to all forms of education.

With these goals agreed, the education committee was asked to report within a year – providing Jones with an opportunity to test the body as a platform for Commission innovation.

Obtaining Community funding

The achievement of a governing formula for educational policy-making was a major step in allowing the idea of higher education to progress within an EC domain. The new Education Committee extended the network of those committed to advancing education. The education committee usually consisted of one national official and one academic from each member state, who made the visit to Brussels for meetings held every four to six weeks – and in cases of difficulty, more often. A member of the UK permanent representation probably spoke for many colleagues when he linked the Education Committee more strongly to the Commission than the Council. 'We always thought of the Education Committee as "them".'[68]

Jones later savoured the success with which a new forum for co-operation had been established. 'At a stage when governments thought of the OECD and the Council of Europe as the natural venues for co-operation, the Community was succeeding with 'a new-fangled'[69] education committee which:

tarnished the sacred Community process ... by introducing an intergovernmental element' and seemingly ignored the European Parliament completely.[70]

The negotiations between the Commission and the education committee illustrated how the Commission wanted to package the diverse
issues which would demonstrate the principles of cooperation and
allow Community funding because elements were linked to EC law.
There needed to be 'soft' European topics such as mutual understanding of educational systems in the Community and language teaching,
and a range of 'social' topics such as the education of migrant workers
and their families, and the transition of young people from education
to working life.[71] As Jones put it, 'This wasn't theology. It was a way of
ensuring we could get Community finance for a popular cause'.[72]

By the autumn of 1975 the Education Committee had approved an
ambitious 22-point package for an action programme in education,
with the *EC Bulletin* recording that the Commission had taken an
'active part' in the work.[73] Italians played a particularly important role
during their presidency in the second half of 1975. On 22 September
1975, MEPs passed a resolution stressing the importance of the Community's activity in the field of education.[74] This was the first step
towards the Parliament deciding to give education the budget line
the Commission and the Education Committee wanted. Within the
education committee, the Italian presidency also smoothed over
difficulties that had prevented earlier approval of the action programme package.[75] Ministers finally agreed at a meeting in December
to support the Jones mixed package in principle.

On 9 February 1976, Ministers sat for the first time as both Council
and Ministers of Education meeting within the Council, to agree a
package that had inter-governmental and EC elements.[76] Taking their
rhetorical lead from the support for 'non-material' policies recorded in
the Paris summit communiqué of 1972, the ministers reaffirmed:

> their desire to achieve European co-operation in education, aware
> of the contribution such co-operation can make to the development
> of the Community.

The decision was approved in the form of a non-binding resolution,
and affirmed the mechanism by which ministers wished to act on
higher education and education matters – through the education committee consisting, as before, of representatives of the member states
and the Commission, and under the control of the Council. The Commission was to act at all times in 'close liaison' with the education
committee in undertaking appropriate measures to be implemented at
Community level. It was for the Education Committee to co-ordinate

and have oversight of the implementation of the programme and to report to the Council and Ministers of Education meeting within the Council.

Higher education co-operation by now occupied a pre-eminent place in the package, with proposals including joint programmes of study and research in which institutions set the rules for co-operation between themselves. This idea built on several existing varied programmes, such as a joint degree scheme linking four institutions providing business education Middlesex Polytechnic, the Ecole Superiéure de Commerce de ll'administration des Entreprises at Reims, the Fachhochschule Reitlingen in the German Federal Republic and a college in Spain.[77] Others included the study abroad schemes of Sussex University. All were perfect examples of 'bottom-up' co-operation, carried out on an entirely voluntary, decentralised basis – the Commission, according to Neave, operating with a 'facilitating' policy 'style' called into play out of respect for academic autonomy.[78]

Similarly, the Action Programme did not have to specify regulation. Domenico Lenarduzzi, later the senior official responsible for the Erasmus programme, looked back on the Action Programme resolution on that account as 'one of the most beautiful documents in EC history'.[79] Furthermore, the promotion of 'mobility' had been honed to allow officials to hold discussions on the obvious obstacles to co-operation arising when bridges needed to be built between nine very different systems – teachers and students were outside the freedom of movement legislation. Admission and funding headed the list of obstacles. There were a number of schemes in existence.[80]

Developing informal capacity

Outside the Commission, resources critical to the development of higher education policy ideas had been available since 1973, from an informal group describing itself as the 'Europe of Education'. One of its members, Gabriel Fragnière, wrote in 1976: '[It was] primarily a small community of research. It includes many inter-governmental organisations – UNESCO through its regional programmes, OECD, the Council of Europe and, more recently, the EEC Commission – together with non-governmental organisations which have carried out particular programmes or studies, such as the European Cultural Foundation (ECF)'s *Plan Europe 2000*.'[81]

Within weeks of his arrival in Brussels,[82] Jones was in touch with this grouping of Europe-minded education experts. A conference on the future of universities in the European Community, held at the College of Europe in Bruges, assembled several big names associated with the ECF, which was completing the important prospectives project entitled *Plan Europe 2000*. The ECF group included several 'graduates' of the Grenoble conference of 1970: the Commission's expert, Professor Henri Janne, who chaired the education section of *Plan Europe 2000*, Ladislav Cerych, director of higher education at the OECD, who was scientific director of the education project, James (Jim) Perkins, a former president of Cornell University, and director of the New York-based International Council for Educational Development (ICED), and Raymond Georis, active on higher education within the West European Union,[83] and at the time director for education at the ECF.

The leitmotiv of the *Plan Europe 2000* thinking – and the eventual report – was that Europe must strive for innovation not harmonisation. The members of the ECF network strengthened Jones' view that a common EC policy on education would be inappropriate; instead, the Community's role in education should be to encourage joint innovative action. 'There is no such thing as an institutional or political Europe of education,' wrote Fragnière. 'What does exist is an educational dimension to European problems and a European dimension to educational problems.' Hence 'Europe must encourage experiments, new approaches and risks'.[84]

The alliance between Jones and the ECF was sealed when Georis, strongly backed by Perkins and Cerych, came up with an idea for developing policy capacity to undertake joint and innovative action in education at a European level. Described by his friends as a man of vision and intuition,[85] Georis had a driving belief in the innovative capacity of foundations. As he put it later:

> Foundations serve best when they are prepared to experiment and to take risks on the frontier of thought and action. Their function is to be counter-cyclical. They are there to remind governments that they can't do everything. They have to consider new themes, new values, to inject a sceptical attitude into mainstream research. Above all they need to spend a lot of time and money on actually doing things.[86]

In 1974, opportunity played into Georis' hands. He had just been promoted to the post of ECF Secretary-General. He proposed to his Council that the ECF set up an institute to perform a Europe-wide collaborative role, possibly as envisaged by Guichard. Indeed, the politically astute Georis believed that if the idea were linked to Guichard, the French might back it too. Georis' case was that such an institute would be a logical and a fruitful development of the ECF-sponsored work for *Plan Europe 2000*. The ECF already had the benefit of a network of high-level collaborators that had allowed it to develop a medium-term strategy for research and development based on innovation not harmonisation.[87]

The reasoning, publicly expressed in the *Plan Europe* report two years later, was the need:

> to develop a European institute, independent of governments, entrusted with comparative research and the formulation of innovative projects.

And a foundation, it was argued, was ideally equipped to fulfil that role:

> ... independent non-governmental organisations can still play a vital part in exploring new ideas and promoting novel projects. It is their vision and creativity which will determine future progress.[88]

... we feel *Plan Europe's* proposals must be backed by some institution offering the prospect of practical action.[89]

On 29 November 1974, Georis got the approval he sought for an institute from the council of the Amsterdam-based ECF, headed by Prince Bernhard of the Netherlands. The Commission, represented by Hywel Ceri Jones, and Perkins of ICED, agreed to be founder members, with Janne as honorary president. Within a year the French Government had honoured the link to the Guichard proposal and provided offices free of charge within the University of Paris-Dauphine, in the building that had housed NATO until the French expelled it in 1967.

So while Georis' own office was based in Brussels, the European Institute of Education of the ECF moved to Paris at the end of 1975.[90] And from there, its development took off.[91] Members of the Council included names familiar from the 1970 conference in Grenoble and the Janne report, supporting Cerych's claim that the 'Educational or University Europe' was quite largely formed of a network of researchers and policy specialists. Among the ex-officio members of the original Council were the EC Commissioner for Education, Guido Brunner, who had replaced Dahrendorf in 1975, and the Director for Education and Cultural and Scientific Affairs of the Council of Europe. Among the members were Janne and Gaston Deurinck, who had chaired a University of the Future study for *Plan 2000*.[92]

With the ECF-backed Institute – which later became known as the European Institute for Education and Social Policy – Georis had opened up exactly the opportunity for policy research and development that Jones was looking for, as he started to formulate a Community programme. In Cerych, whom Georis had persuaded to leave the OECD to become the institute's director, the institute had a respected and productive name in political science and education. Czech by origin, Cerych had left Prague after the Communist coup of 1948 and spent some years in the US. He therefore brought with him an important trans-European and trans-Atlantic network as well as a capacity for policy-oriented development work and diffusion, as attested by the early issues of the *European Journal of Education*, which he founded and the ECF backed. As Jones quickly realised, Cerych would have easy access to policy specialists in education and employment, well thought-of in the research and development world.[93] Furthermore, the European Institute of Education as envisaged could act rapidly on related issues: the organisation of conferences and seminars, the mobilisation of consultants and the dissemination of results.

Within three to four years there was evidence that the Paris-based institute was an active organisation in policy areas other institutions were not touching. Under the chairmanship of the historian Asa Briggs (Jones' admired boss as vice-chancellor of the University),[94] and with other Council members drawn from the networks of the ECF, OECD, the Council of Europe and academics, some of whom, like Janne, were widely known in European university circles, the institute grew to a staff of 15 full-time equivalents, including support staff and researchers by 1979. One of its staff was Alan Smith, future coordinator of the pilot activities leading to the Erasmus programme and thereafter director of the technical agency managing the programme, and as such known to thousands of academics throughout Europe. In the early stages, the institute's research activities included the topics of trends in national higher education reform, student mobility (both the statistical issues and policy issues such as admissions), an international comparison of barriers to reform, the relationship of higher education and regional development, and access to higher education in Eastern Europe and Western Europe.

By 1979, demonstrating the speed of reaction of which Georis had boasted, the Institute was running the *European Journal of Education*, which disseminated the activities of this research world. By 1979 it was also engaged in two important development projects for the Commission designed to develop European co-operation in higher education. One was the management of the Office of European Associations of Higher Education, which provided common services for start-up associations in this domain.[95] The other was the management of grants on behalf of the Commission to develop university co-operation across the EC: the set of programmes that would come to be known as the joint study programmes.

Jones and his allies had carried off a triumph, selling all the key ideas built up within Jones' networks during the previous three years, in terms of the substantive issues and the policy instruments.[96] This was the founding act, says Luce Pépin, in her official history of the development of education and training policy in the EC[97] Jones had built up substantial formal and informal policy capacity. But implementation, as we shall see, was a different process.

Crafting a governing formula

Decisions of fundamental importance for later EC policy-making in higher education were taken in 1974–76. The issue of governance, innovation and support for educational activities, as delineated in the Action Programme, found favour with the Commission and Council. Ministers were prepared to break from the normal policy advisory group pattern to back the 'dual' Education committee, of which the Commission was a member. They were also prepared to approve the mixed process of decision-making.

Analysing the remarkable trajectory of the idea of Community policy-making in education from 1973–76 provides an insight into how organisational capabilities evolved in line with a policy vision, in a favourable political context – and without immediate external constraint. A significant factor behind this smooth evolution was that in 1973, for the first time, the policy makers inherited an established policy domain. The issue was no longer whether the Community *should* play a role in higher education/education. Rather it was 'what the appropriate mechanisms were for advancing cooperation?' The 1971 agreement that the Community should play a role in educational cooperation was confirmed by organisational changes within the Commission that took office with enlargement. Furthermore, the establishment of a policy-making venue in which the decision-makers were knowledgeable and likely to be sympathetic – ministers of education as opposed to ministers of foreign affairs – also helped stabilise the notion of a Community role.

But distinctively, here was a moment in which the vision matched the situation. A vision in which the issue of the Community contribution was framed as a source of resources rather than as regulation, offered two opportunities. One was to present a proposal for a policy advisory committee in which the Commission would have a role. The other was to find a way of making educational cooperation eligible for treaty-linked Community funding. As we have seen, the institutional factors that allowed this strategy to proceed were, first, the fact that there were small areas of treaty-linked regulation and a law of education that had emerged in the late 1960s – as with the children of migrant workers, the recognition of qualifications and vocational training. Second, there was the reform that gave the European Parliament (EP) the right to allocate resources for pilot projects. MEPs gave their support willingly.

The organisational decisions indicate confidence on the part of decision-makers which went beyond the general desire for the Community to be concerned with more than economics, as they had stated at the Paris summit of 1972. It has been said that in all political systems, issues are a resource as well as a problem,[98] and this was indeed the case with the issue of education in the EC in 1973. The challenge was to match, at European level, ideas for a policy domain that touched on cultural identity and, in many cases, state building, while creating mechanisms that were neither binding nor, on the other hand, meaningless. The structures played into the hands of the Commission. In a contemporary study, Helen Wallace maintains that the hybrid decision-making had escalated to the point where ministers of education were not sure whether they were Councils or not.[99]

A further factor to explain the innovative solution for Community policy activity in higher education and education is that Jones effectively enjoyed a policy monopoly, a situation in which there was no external political interference.[100] He was able to exploit the opportunity to develop linkages with the ECF and for the OECD working on the same themes, and willing to network. The linkages were strengthened by friendships, especially that of Jones and Geöris. The particular form of Community action matched the mood of the practitioners who wanted the opportunity to network on a European scale but who were viscerally opposed to supranational interference. That was a major achievement for the Commission, and a significant – if ambiguous – step for the ministers who believed they had agreed to a funded intergovernmental structure. All understood the nature of the bargain: without policy capacity, policy ideas could not flourish – and at this stage, all wanted to act.

7
Implementing the Action Programme in Education, 1976–84

The implementation of the Action Programme marked the beginning of serious conflict between the Council and the Commission, though this was mostly played out behind closed doors. Even Neave has only a brief mention of it, though his text exudes the sense of officials living dangerously, a common attitude within the education service of the Commission at the time.[1] The issue was Community competence. However in an unstable climate, strategies to engage higher education in European Community (EC)-wide activity – well down the Commission's priority list for the Action Programme – emerged politically strengthened. This chapter explores how and why.

Facing conflict over competence

The effect of the Action Programme resolution was immediately felt on EC educational activity. The Commission launched straight into action – but not in higher education. In the months between the February decision and the November meeting of the ministers of education, the Education Committee was working on two issues,[2] neither of which was purely educational. One focused on training, helping young people make the transition from school to work and the young unemployed prepare for working life – an aspect of the Action Programme to which the Commission attached special urgency. The second issue concerned the rights of migrant workers' children to be provided with intensive teaching in the language of the host country, as well as access to teaching in their mother tongue.

Hywel Ceri Jones, promoted in 1979 to be director for education, vocational training and youth policy, considered the focus on these two issues as evidence that 'education was a component of social action.'[3] He described himself later as having been 'deeply committed to using Community dynamism to generate equal opportunity In the face of rising unemployment and the recession which followed the 1973 hike in oil prices, those hardest hit were the young leaving school and trying to get work. It was agreed they were the most deserving cause'.[4]

In addition to the intrinsic merits pointed to by its supporters, the action in favour of migrant workers' children was strategically attractive to the Commission as a potential building-block towards strengthening the law of education and ultimately a 'soft law' common education policy for the Community.[5] The treaty link enabled the Commission to aim at a draft directive on migrant workers' children. Well before the formal signing of the Action Programme resolution in February 1976, the Committee had accepted a Commission proposal that a small group of experts and liaison officers appointed by each member state prepare a draft report on the education of migrant workers' children. The Education Committee, with a majority of national representatives, agreed to support the development of a draft directive. The aim was to have a report and draft measures agreed by 1 July 1976.

The issue of higher education took third place in the priorities for implementation although few universities, while claiming to be European, were exploiting their European potential. And very few students were studying in the universities of other member states.[6] Generations of Europe-minded academics and politicians had favoured increased academic mobility especially for advanced or postgraduate students. But Jones's view was that '[h]igher education was embedded in the rest. I was not prepared to accept the argument that the Community should focus primarily on higher education issues. It would have been easy. But there were so many more things the Community could do. We needed to demonstrate that the Community could add value to the education of those who were not part of an elite.'[7]

This is not to say that higher education was being ignored. At the meeting of the Education Committee in March 1976, the Commission obtained its agreement to developing the idea of joint study programmes (JSPs) between higher education institutions, as defined in the Action Programme.[8] The development work was to be carried out by the staff of the European Institute of Education set up by the European Cultural Foundation (ECF).[9]

At a meeting of ministers of education eight months later, on 29 November 1976, the Dutch presidency was able to report progress

on all three issues.[10] The most striking achievement on higher education in that period was the creation of JSPs between higher education
institutions in different member states, from the academic year
1976–77 – i.e. immediately following the Action Programme resolution. There had also been important policy discussions. An April
meeting with academics and administrators had discussed how to
finance mobility in the joint study programmes. The Commission had
then convened a meeting with national experts in public service
and social security on the knotty problem of seniority and pension
entitlements for professionals working in higher education.[11] At the
same time, the Members of European Parliament had added their
support, considering that efforts were needed to bring education
systems more closely into line.[12]

Ministers, meeting in November, backed the Education Committee
proposals for extending measures of cooperation in higher education.
In the committee's view, the joint study programmes needed to be
broadened and a new scheme launched for the benefit of teaching and
administrative staff and researchers, in the form of short study visits
(SSVs) between volunteer universities in the different member states.[13]
This programme of professional development was strongly supported,
not least in institutions that had only recently assumed university
status as a result of an expansion in higher education.

Christopher Price, a former Labour MP, well known in education
circles, who was director of Leeds Polytechnic in England[14] in the
1970s maintains:

> The short study visits were an inspired piece of professional up-
> grading for teachers in new universities. In the old universities acad-
> emics got around, thanks to their research grants. There was none
> of that in the 'polys'. I encouraged Leeds Poly staff to use the
> opportunity. I'd say 'Europe is there. Make the most of it!.[15]

However ministers were more equivocal. Two incidents generated a
conflict over the use of policy instruments during 1977–78 to the point
that a meeting scheduled for November 1978 was cancelled. In the
first incident, the Commission was successful in getting a directive
approved to make better provision for the education of migrant
workers children. Some of those who remember the era think the directive was a logical step. The Council had approved a social action programme in 1974 and established a social fund. There had already been
a regulation [12/68] demanding that member States make provision for

the education of the children of 'migrant' workers – meaning EC citizens who had crossed frontiers. The issue of such children and their language needs had been accepted as a theme for the 1976 action programme in education. Jones himself says 'the social policy context of education was the reality of that period.[16]

However governments were more equivocal once the decision had been taken to approve a directive – i.e. binding legislation – in relation to the education of migrant workers' children arose under a British presidency. The chair had been taken by an internationally known and respected politician, Shirley Williams, the UK Secretary of State for Education and Science in the period 1976–79. Jones' view was that 'We were fortunate to have the enlightened Shirley Williams as president of the Education Council. She was prepared to mount the necessary fight for the Article that 'Member states shall, in accordance with national circumstances and legal systems, and in cooperation with states of origin, take appropriate measures to promote, in coordination with normal education, teaching of the mother tongue and culture of the country of origin.'[17]

But in backing this position, Shirley Williams – or her advisors – were almost certainly deviating from the traditional British line, though several of the British actors centrally involved do not remember any sense of a big issue.[18] After this, the member states who were doubtful about EC action on education – this included the UK, Denmark and Germany – started making their criticisms of EC policy-making in education explicit. They feared that the Commission in trying to build 'a common policy', was adopting 'the Community method by stealth' in what was basically an intergovernmental sector.

A British official, John Banks, basically sympathetic to Community aims, was intensely sceptical about the means.

> When Education Ministers met in 1975 and 1976 there was a good deal of looking over their shoulders at the dangers the Commission might present if they went too far towards writing education into the treaty. After all, with a Court of Justice to back the Commission up – and likely to be willing to decide doubtful cases in their favour – caution was justified.
>
> Yet within two years of the Education Ministers steering a clear course away from statutory means in education, the Commission had obtained the approval of the Social Affairs Council for a directive establishing some educational rights for migrant workers and obliging Governments to 'promote' development for them. The

Ministers who thought the 1976 plan did not go far enough were no doubt pleased.... Others thought differently and wondered why economic union could lead to obligations so far from economic objectives.

Harmonisation – that concept again – of systems or policies could not, he concluded be considered an end in itself.[19] The British – as Jones and Dahrendorf – saw harmonisation as forced conformity.

Thus, when the Commission tried its next major education policy initiative in the autumn of 1978, there was so much bad feeling that Jones and his team came face to face with a refusal to approve even *non-binding* legislation on education issues. The immediate crisis was precipitated by the Commission sending four communications to the Council on 27 and 28 September 1978. One, initially developed by Ladislav Cerych and Alan Smith of the European Institute, made recommendations on a common policy on the admission of EC students to higher education in all member states. A second proposed a Community scholarship scheme to supplement national schemes. Two sets of proposals affected schools: one on the teaching of modern languages, the other on instilling a European dimension to curricula.[20]

The Commission, pushed by Smith and Cerych, was becoming enthusiastic about organised mobility for building Europe. But the immediate aim of the admissions proposal was to overcome the institutional barriers of moving from state to state. The Commission proposed that EC students should be exempt from the count from Germany's *numerus clausus* scheme. It proposed the scholarship scheme to give an added boost to the joint study programmes by encouraging students to study abroad.

But the use of the term 'common policy' was unfortunate, given the growing hostility to educational activity in some member states. Banks again:

> The conclusions of [a Commission analysis] are likely to be labelled by some as 'common policy' though it is to be doubted whether the Ministers established the programme with anything of the kind in mind. Their aim was to use the facility of the Community to improve their national capacity to tackle the problem: in other words, they thought they were engaged in inter-governmental co-operation backed by the resources of the Community budget and the expertise of the Commission.[21]

The Danish government maintained that it was only challenging the Commission over issues that they believed exceeded its mandate,[22] and in education it was the Commission's incursion into schools rather than universities that drove the Danes to action.[23] Furthermore, the detail of the admission communication – largely drafted in the Paris-based European Institute[24] – made it clear that there was no intention to impinge on member state sovereignty, that there was no question of harmonisation, and that the document was consultative. The reason that the authors envisaged the mixed formula of the Council and Ministers of Education was, the document made clear, in order to access to Community funds. The Commission was not seeking to 'enter into consideration of ... national policies [on admissions] ... but to establish a common set of principles to guide future policies.... [T]he very diversity of existing national admissions systems makes it impracticable to seek a solution by way of an identical method of treatment of incoming university students across all member states. The need ... is to guide the policies ... and the broad manner of application of those principles in each main problem area.'[25] The 'problems' referred to were (i) numerical restrictions on admission, such as the German *numerus clausus*, (ii) academic and other criteria for selection, (iii) financial conditions of admission, (iv) linguistic requirements and (v) administrative procedures for admission.

The Commission's preferred solution to these issues was that reciprocal arrangements be reached between member states. It argued that in any event, EC students should be admitted to institutions in a host country on a basis no less favourable than that country's own students – a principle of non-discrimination which was to become policy seven years later.[26]

A week before the meeting of ministers 'within the Council' scheduled for November 27, the session was cancelled. Banks maintained that by this time, there had emerged 'an inherent divergence in the underlying interests of the Commission and the individual Member States.'[27] Although the Education Committee had been supportive of the Commission proposals,[28] officials from the national delegations in Committee of Permanent Representatives (COREPER), preparing the Council agenda for 27 November, could not give the Danes the guarantee they demanded – that these communications fell within the treaty. The British wanted the same guarantees, but let the Danes making the running.[29]

The conflict between the Danes and the Commission was of sufficient magnitude to prevent other Community institutions from being willing or able to break the deadlock, either in 1978 or in 1979, although efforts were initially made by both the Education Committee, which had approved the documents the previous week, and the European Parliament (EP)'s Committee. Meeting on 12 December 1978, the Education Committee rescued what it could, issuing a recommendation that existing work should not be affected by the breakdown – specifically, the pilot joint study and short study visits programmes. The education and culture committee of the EP also lent its support with a support.[30]

However the crisis remained unresolved for over a year. A key factor preventing its resolution was that the Commission leadership was itself uneasy about various efforts within the Commission to expand its competence. This sentiment was made explicit in September 1978. Roy Jenkins, President of the Commission and a former senior minister in UK Labour governments, had summonsed his fellow Commissioners to an informal meeting at Comblain-la-Tour.[31] The prime purpose of the get-together was to seek his colleagues' contribution to the programme address, delivered each year by the Commission President. But Jenkins was also concerned about Danish opposition to all 'new' policy areas, manifest in the challenge launched earlier that month, and wished to explore the matter further. Two questions were predominant: (1) Was the Commission creeping into policy sectors in which Community competence had been explicitly assured by the treaty at the foundation of the Community? (2) Was it active on non-economic policies in sectors in which action was geared to other than exclusively economic ends?[32] Both were 'grey areas' in which Jenkins and his cabinet considered it risky for the Commission to meddle.

As the minutes of the secretary-general, Emile Noël, show, there had been a tough debate with several Commissioners who argued strongly for developing policy in the new areas of activity which had emerged since the Paris summit of 1972, where the EC's leaders had used the famous formula 'Economic expansion ... is not an end in itself. As befits the genius of Europe, particular attention will be given to non-material values'.[33]

This group of Commissioners argued that the new policies were needed in order to give a 'human face' to the Community. But Jenkins' response was that these needed to be very carefully selected, lest the Commission be accused of over-administration.[34] Indeed, on 17 September 1978, Jenkins issued an announcement to the press to the effect that the Commission's overall priority was to do fully and effectively what the Treaty required of it, and that it would adopt stricter criteria for legislative proposals and its future programme of work.[35]

After Comblain-la-Tour, action passed into the hands of the secretary-general, Emile Noël, whom the Commissioners asked, on 22 November 1978, to create an inter-departmental working party and to produce a fact-finding report on Commission activity in the 'Grey Areas'. This opened up opportunities to refine the Jenkins view, on the strength of evidence from a largely hostile group of officials working in the new policy areas. One director-general refused to attend.[36] For Henri Etienne, one of Noël's informants from within the general secretariat, the first meeting got off to 'a very bad start'.[37] This was a state of affairs which Etienne blamed on the chairman, the British deputy secretary-general, Christopher Audland – the British Foreign Office high flyer who joined the Commission with British entry.[38] Audland, said Etienne, was 'very House of Lords', and had 'made up his mind in advance'.[39]

In fact Audland's working party emphasised Community achievements in the new policy sectors. But it matched the Council criticisms, finding fault with officials who had not respected procedures in certain policy areas – education and training among them. The working party report reproached the directorate of education, vocational training and youth policy for not envisaging 'the possible implications of some of the actions [in the Action Programme]. Good intentions had not been enough to surmount practical difficulties,'[40] the report said. Furthermore, normal procedures had not been adhered to.

> The fact that the education service had by-passed the working paper procedure and gone straight to the European Parliament with communications early in 1978 must have had some bearing on the hardening of positions which led to the cancellation of the Council meeting.[41]

However on the question of whether the Community could continue to act in non-treaty areas, the report favoured development into new areas since the Paris summit of 1972. One relatively widely held view was that '[m]ovement into new policy areas had helped resolve old problems'.[42] Here education was expressly cited for praise – specifically, Commissioner Dahrendorf's success in negotiating the principle of mutual recognition of diplomas in place of an imposed schema in 1973–74. Jones, ready for this and covered by his immediate boss, Bath, had provided the working party with three justifications for continued EC activity in the education policy area compatible with Community economic and social aims.

First, education was central to Community concerns. Jones claimed it was a tenet of public policy in all member States to promote integrated measures on behalf of young people and adults, and that distinctions between 'education' and 'training' were fast disappearing. That, in his view, should be the starting point for the Commission's role in education.[43]

Second, higher education and education were components of many other Community policy sectors, including employment, environment, research, consumer protection, overseas development and co-operation, information, industrial affairs and aspects of social policy.[44] The inter-sectoral aspects derived from a combination of treaty reference and expressions of political will in favour of co-operation.[45] Jones gave the examples of the European Atomic Energy Community (Euratom) treaty articles on research and the European University; the EEC articles on free movement and recognition of qualifications, and Council resolutions in favour of a social action programme as examples of the first, co-operation in the field of education as an example of political will.[46]

Third, in the directorate's view, decision-making mechanisms *were* adapted to this particular policy area. There had been a measure of agreement with ministers of education 'which allowed the Community to enter areas of high national sensitivity'.[47] Jones argues that this was in part because his directorate were also convinced that legislation 'is rarely appropriate to activity in the education field given the nature of educational policy and the structure of responsibilities within member states.' He also believed networking with other international organisations on European activities – OECD, the Council of Europe, and the Standing Conference of European Ministers of Education – had extended Community influence, and established confidence in its role.

However such interventions did not turn the authors of the report from a prudent outcome. This was in any event consistent with the view of the Commission president, Jenkins. The completed Audland report of 19 December 1978 concluded that the new legislative measures should be explicitly linked to the main objectives of the treaty. In the version approved by the Commissioners' *chefs de cabinet*, the report maintains that clear distinctions should be made between measures requiring legislative action and those based on cooperation. In addition, it was agreed that the Commission should be ready to withdraw measures if the political will for them should wane.[48]

Jones and his close colleagues chose to interpret the Audland conclusions optimistically. The working party had upheld the idea that there was scope for activity on higher education and education not exclusively linked to the common market – i.e. through Community-backed cooperation.[49] But the report had also made it clear to those who wanted the Community that the criteria for Community action were likely to be restricted in non-Treaty areas. It was a situation which invited reflection of alternatives.

Evolving a new strategy

The 'Grey Areas' crisis had lasting institutional consequences for Community activity in education and training. As Jones read the situation, the Danes 'and the British sheltering behind them' were never prepared to trust in the Commission. 'There was never any question of harmonisation. That had been made clear in 1974. The trouble was Britain and Denmark did not believe us.'[50] This is a view which to this day infuriates British officials who worked in this area. As one former official put it:

> Those involved in 1974 or even 1978 may not have had plans for harmonisation. But the point about Community competence is that once granted it becomes part of the *acquis* and can never be rolled back ... One doesn't know what future generations might do with something which seemed innocent enough at the time. Jones was asking for a leap of faith. If the British couldn't make the leap it does not amount to bad faith.[51]

In November 1979 the situation remained deadlocked. Ministers had once again refused to meet. MEPs however kept the issue alive by adopting a resolution regretting the difficulties caused to the Community's educational activities by the cancellation of the ministerial meeting.[52] But in this atmosphere a breakthrough was difficult to achieve. Even Domenico Lenarduzzi, the senior official who had heralded the Action Programme resolution as 'the most beautiful document in the history of the European Communities because it demonstrated that the Community was not simply a 'merchant' body',[53] was hard pressed to maintain his optimism.

The first signs of a breakthrough came in 1980, brokered by the education committee, under the Italian presidency.[54] The Italians had been consistently supportive of an EC dimension to education policy.

Only four years previously, the Italian presidency of the education committee had negotiated the final agreement for the action programme.[55] Now it was the Italian MEP, Mario Pedini, who was chairman of the parliamentary education and culture committee, and his colleague, Giatto de Biasi who jointly took the procedural initiative to ensure that the European parliament used its new powers in relation to the budget to make second reading appropriation on non-compulsory policies.[56] They worked with Jones to develop the idea that ministers could meet without taking any decisions, to open the way to agreeing new policy initiatives and to enable the EP to resume budgetary support. They also suggested that the Education Committee should report on what it had been doing to monitor progress on existing initiatives since the collapse of the Council process. This work was substantial and included a re-examination, on 19 March 1979, of the three Commission communications to which the Danes had objected in November 1978.[57]

The Italian proposal was successful to the extent that, in June 1980, ministers met to consider the Education Committee's general report.[58] This report – a 25-page document – indicated that higher education had emerged as the educational policy sector on which action was most developed. The cooperation section recorded that 212 institutions had been involved in 121 joint study programmes. On the admission of students from other member states to higher education institutions be adopted, the report supported the proposals of Cerych and Smith, to adopt 'a common approach'. It also advocated the concept of reciprocal arrangements for the exchange of students between institutions, as a way round the problems posed by national selective mechanisms – competitive entry, *numerus clausus*, etc. The report also drew attention to an expert report, submitted in June 1978, which detailed all existing arrangements on the recognition of academic diplomas, and recommended a Community policy on the issue.[59]

Council officials were responsive to the ever-determined Jones' efforts to develop educational activities within the parameters of the working party report. Jones' line was to suggest that *any* meeting of ministers ought to deliver the authority for the EP to resume financing educational development. The Council's legal advisers helpfully suggested that 'agreement in substance' had the 'substance of a decision'. But this did not carry weight with the national diplomats meeting within COREPER. The French and Danish representatives rejected this mediating move on the grounds it was not in *'bonne et due forme'*. They insisted that further negotiations and any budgetary implications could only be dealt with within COREPER.[60] Consequently, the Commission's usually steady allies in the European Parliament, while supportive of existing activities refused to finance new activities of the education and training directorate within the 1981 budget. Jones was disappointed. But MEPs were only playing by the rules.

Jones reacted to such constraints by trying to develop new institutional resources. 'The one acceptable option was to try and develop a complementary base for action,' he later recalled.[61] Given the warning contained in the Commission's Grey Areas enquiry that officials should be clear whether they were taking treaty-based action or simply organising coordination, Jones' judgement was that he should get the directorate for education, vocational training and youth policy transferred from the directorate-general for science, research and education, which had never had much synergy with other directorates,[62] to the DG for social affairs, where there were likely to be many opportunities to link education to treaty-based activities.

In terms of jurisdiction, this DG and its Council of Ministers (employment and social affairs) dealt with the aspects of higher education which were treaty-linked: vocational training, freedom of movement, and the issue that had dogged higher education since the 1950s – the recognition of diplomas, a crucial instrument for mobility. But as Jones described it, the real difference lay in the individuals operating the rules. He maintained that the social affairs ministers 'expected to deal with Treaty matters. They therefore expected to make decisions.'[63]

Jones argued that there were procedural precedents to attach education to social policy. Thanks to a Council Decision of 22 July 1975, resources in the social area – European Social Fund grants – could be used for some educational purposes.[64] There had already been significant education activity, born of the treaty-based Community process, which the Commission initiated, the Council approved and the Commission implemented. The proposals and decisions that Jones regarded as important included many on social policy issues:[65]

o 1973: Commission proposal for a social action programme, followed by a Council resolution[66]
o 1974: Commission proposal for setting up a European centre for vocational training (CEDEFOP). Established by Council regulation[67] and set up in Berlin
o 1975: Commission proposal for a Council directive on the implementation of the principle of equal treatment for men and women; Commission guidelines for a framework for EC Committee on safety; Council decision on the use of European Social Fund grants

o 1976: establishment of Eurydice, the education information network of the EC; the creation of the first programme on transition of
   young people from school to working life
o 1977: Council directive on the education of children of migrant
   workers, and implementation of Commission pilot schemes
o 1978: Commission proposals for action programme on language
   learning and on equality of education and training for girls
o 1979: European Council request for study of concrete measures in
   areas linking work and training, followed by Council decision[68] and
   Council resolution[69]

Jones maintained that such a move would strengthen Community educational activity by bringing it closer to mainstream Community concerns –
the argument he had used to the Grey Areas enquiry. He did not believe that
a move to the social affairs directorate-general would change the vision of
education within the EC. As he described the situation, '[t]he concept
of Community education policy as a continuum with training was well
established'.[70] The higher education activity already agreed and/or implemented was consistent with this view – for example the Commission communication, *Education in the Community*, the ministers' resolution of 6 June
1974, the resolution on the action programme on education, 1976, followed
by the first meeting of the Education Committee, and the 1978 proposal for
a common policy on higher education admissions.

From the perspective of the new Commissioner for social affairs, Ivor
Richard – a former junior minister in a Labour government – who took
up the commissioner post in 1981, referring to education as 'training'
had proved a successful strategy:

> Jones' effective – some would say devious – tactic was to present DG
> activities as training. Anything educational had to be done by
> stealth. I don't remember taking anything specifically educational in
> my period of office to the Commission. But that did not stop the
> DG being effective. The funding of pilot projects and encouraging
> educational networks were very important.[71]

Furthermore, Jones' efforts appeared to be in line with the concerns
of the university community. As Cerych observed at the time: '[T]he
general orientation of higher education towards professional [vocational]
studies ... makes it less difficult to introduce into higher education
another training preparing for practical professions.'[72] Given the 1970s
expansion in universities and the backdrop of rising unemployment, this
was a reasonable position to hold.

However, speaking from a member state perspective, Banks, the British official, had a different interpretation of what strengthening links with the social affairs council would do for a policy area that member states by now viewed as purely intergovernmental. Banks warned that if the Commission could not advance, as it wished, with the ministers of education, it 'would be likely to stick to an 'indirect approach', using the social affairs council'.[73] Banks went on to describe the social affairs council as providing a 'cover' for education-linked proposals under the treaty.[74] Such a statement signalled a view among some member states that Jones was adopting a 'semi-clandestine' or 'devious' approach – the same phraseology employed by Commissioner Ivor Richard.[75]

Events played into Jones' hands – and those of others wanting closer treaty links for all Commission activities. The Community calendar favoured change. The last months of 1980 were marked by the juggling of people and portfolios for the new Commission. Gaston Thorn of Luxembourg was to succeed the Briton, Roy Jenkins. Jones' strategy was to get approval before Jenkins stepped down, both for the Directorate to move to DGV Social Affairs and for him to remain Director.

The situation was complicated by the rivalry as to which commissioner would be responsible for education. Was it to be Ivor Richard at social affairs, or the francophone Belgian diplomat, Etienne (Stevie) Davignon? Davignon, whose experience went back to the earliest days of the Community, when he served as *chef de cabinet* to Spaak, had been the Commissioner responsible for the internal market, customs and industrial affairs under the Jenkins presidency. But his ambition under Thorn, to whom he was going to be a vice-president and an evident strong man,[76] was to drive the key policies of industrial affairs, energy and research policy – the old Spinelli portfolio. Davignon also viewed education as a necessary part of that portfolio.[77]

In the event the portfolio went to Ivor Richard, a Welshman, who adopted the arguments of his fellow Welshman, Jones, in order to secure the post – although he later conceded: 'I had to fight hard to get education back from Stevie.'[78] Richard had followed Jones' lead in declaring that co-operation in education would take on a new significance if it were more firmly linked more firmly to the overall political and economic development of the Community. Hence, went the argument, it made sense to have education and training under the Commissioner for social affairs.

A member of Jenkins' cabinet, Nick Stuart, also remembers the difficulties. 'It was quite difficult' to put the package in place. 'We needed to fight off the Italians and the French'.[79] Jenkins' British-staffed *cabinet* also favoured the argument which Jones was putting forward for bringing education closer to training. The fact they all knew each other helped. 'We backed Hywel', says Stuart. There were other contenders for the job of director backed by France and Italy. But Jones, as many colleagues recognised, was nothing if not persistent.[80] On 4 January 1981, in the last act on the last working day of the Jenkins Commission, the deal was done. Jenkins gave his agreement to the directorate of education and vocational training and youth policies moving to the social affairs DG.[81] Jones was appointed to the directorship.

Jones made the shift in emphasis public, stressing the strategic role education had to play in the Community's *social* policies. Thus two years later, making the keynote speech at a major UK conference, Jones said that 'As a direct result of our evident incapacity to cope with the damaging effects of the economic crisis,' higher education and education had moved 'from the periphery to a more strategic location in the spectrum of Community policies.'[82]

Developing support for higher education

It might have been thought that the Community's higher education activities would take a back seat once an education and training directorate had been established in the DG for social affairs. In 1981, the DG's most visible efforts were devoted to developing proposals to use the social fund for measures to create jobs in disadvantaged regions as part of a Community-wide fight to reduce youth unemployment.[83] The EC budget for education for the period 1976–82 showed the credits for the whole of the Action Programme lagging behind those for the programme for the transition to working life until 1982. Other credits obtained for further education and training – for a centre for information on vocational training in Berlin known as CEDEFOP, and the scheme for the exchange of young workers had a combined total of almost twice the Action Programme budget.[84]

Domenico Lenarduzzi, in charge of higher education in the Education and Training Directorate, remembers a period of 'stagnation' until 1983–84.[85] Alan Smith, at work with Ladislav Cerych at the European Institute of Education in Paris, caught the mood in an article for the *European Journal of Education* entitled 'From Europhoria to pragmatism'.[86] But higher education was much better resourced than these statistics would suggest. This was not just a question of budget, though the EC budget for education and training had grown from 460,000 ECU in 1976 to 11.5 mn ECU in 1982, of which the Action Programme was getting 3.4 mn ECUs.[87] The Community's higher education activity generated alliances. The European Institute for Education in Paris had consistently engaged in development work useful to the Commission. By 1982, the European Cultural Foundation (ECF) which funded the institute was paying the salaries of a director, a deputy and several others, maintaining the institute and contributing to various publishing projects, including the *European Journal of Education*, an essential source for those interested in monitoring EC activity in education. Cerych, the director of the European Institute, had focussed on developing the intellectual resources and databases for the development of EC education policies, including the first surveys on mobility. An important part of his work was the initial development on policy papers needed by Jones in the Commission. The 1978 communication on a common admission policy was an example of such work.[88]

The main responsibility of Alan Smith, by all accounts an indefatigable worker, was to assist Cerych in the development of policy papers, as well as running the pilot programmes for the joint study projects and the short study visits. These pilots were crucial in building up networks. But the policy papers were also an opportunity to extend contacts. The 1978 common admissions policy draft, for example, was tried out on university representatives at a conference in Bonn. Another such occasion came on 3–5 April 1979, when Smith assembled the 86 directors of joint study programmes at a conference at the University of Edinburgh, organised by the Commission and chaired by Jones' former boss at the University of Sussex, Professor Asa Briggs.[89]

Smith described the Edinburgh event as 'a famous occasion. It institutionalised a network of pioneers.'[90] The literature of networks and other forms of university cooperation also started to build up,[91] with Smith himself producing one of the early EC studies in education '*Joint programmes of study, an instrument of European cooperation in higher education*'.[92]

At the same time, greater political interest in higher education was being kindled in larger policy forums, as the grass roots developments of pilot projects became better known and cultural cooperation became an issue on the main Community agenda, for the first time since the mid 1970s. Policy proposals for cultural cooperation within the EC had originally derived from the Tindemans report of 1975 – Leo Tindemans, a Belgian, and former Prime Minister, had been charged by the European Council to make recommendations to advance European integration. His recommendations included the establishment of a European Foundation. Raymond Georis of the ECF was tempted when approached for the job, but decided against it.[93] Jones, who was developing the Action Programme at the time was deeply opposed. The foundation, despite lengthy and extensive discussions, never materialised. Tindemans speaking at a 1986 conference was still bitter.[94] His only consolation in this regard was to repeat publicly that the EC activity on education could have been much more ambitious than the Action Programme of 1976.[95]

In the 1980s, high level Council initiatives aimed at advancing integration renewed political interest in cooperation, and gave higher education a prominent place. First, the German and Italian Foreign Ministers, Hans Genscher and Emilio Colombo, put forward proposals for establishing European political cooperation on a legal footing – an effort that failed to make much progress. However, a German presidency initiative to get heads of government to sign up to a 'Solemn Declaration on European Union', launched in June 1983, had considerable success.[96] Even the highly sceptical British Prime Minister, Margaret Thatcher, went along with the majority, arguing that in any case the 'grandiloquent language' had no legal force and she 'could not quarrel about everything'.[97]

The Stuttgart Declaration had direct implications for higher education, especially once the Commission interpreted the declaration as committing member states to seeking the fullest range of co-operation between themselves in a wide range of areas not covered by the treaty establishing the EC. EC leaders agreed that nationally they would promote closer cooperation between higher education institutions, including exchanges of teachers and students; intensify exchanges of experience, particularly among young people; and further develop the teaching of languages of the member states; improve the level of knowledge about other member states, including the promotion of European awareness through history and cultural activities. They would also develop the activities of the projected European Foundation and the existing European University Institute.[98]

In 1984, EC leaders returned to the higher education issue, under the umbrella of bigger questions facing the Fontainebleau European Council under the French presidency. The French concern at the time was that 'Europe had had a breakdown',[99] one symptom of which was an apparent inability to resolve the long-running British budget dispute. On this issue the French president, François Mitterrand, reached a deal with Thatcher, enabling the EC to move onto a new strategy. There was thus a potential for new EC action. The immediate opportunities for higher education, however, derived from a different symptom of breakdown. The 1984 French presidency of the EC proposed the establishment of an *ad hoc* committee on a People's Europe to find ways of countering the lack of public interest for the EC. For Jones and his deputy, Lenarduzzi, this project represented another opportunity to make the joint study programme model much more widely known as a response to European leaders' general concern for 'citizens'.

The education ministers also came out in support of action to promote higher education mobility and, in particular, the joint study programmes. In 1982, they had agreed on the need to find a solution to the academic recognition of diplomas and to collect data on students studying in other member states, including information about their 'social and material conditions'.[100] At a meeting on 2 June the following year, ministers convened as the Council and Ministers for Education to draw up 'conclusions' on how to extend mobility in higher education, recognising that mobility was 'one of the most important objectives of EC educational cooperation'.[101]

The ministers concluded that they wished to see an extension of the joint study programmes, recognising that they had 'proved to be particularly suitable in overcoming obstacles to mobility in higher education'. They also wanted to see more twinning of institutions, and measures to reduce the financial difficulties faced by students. But they stuck to the intergovernmental formula: the nearest ministers would get to action was to undertake a commitment to 'be guided by the principle of greatest generosity and flexibility' on the recognition of courses and periods of study abroad.

Ministers had thus accepted an argument long put by Jones that 'the direct inter-institutional co-operation of the type promoted by the Community's grant scheme has increasingly proven to be an efficient instrument for overcoming some of the most intractable problems related to student mobility within the Community.... In many cases, such as high tuition fees, restricted admission quotas and difficulties regarding academic recognition of study abroad, [the difficulties] can be successfully surmounted through the direct participation of higher education institutions themselves in addressing the problem.'[102]

As the Commission recorded events, the EP had pointed to a more specifically Community approach to higher education. In 1984, having adopted a resolution 'on the substance of a preliminary draft Treaty establishing European Union [it] proposed that the Union shall have concurrent competence to adopt the following regulations for

(i) Union-wide diplomas ... other qualifications ... and recognition of periods of study (ii) the promotion of common or comparable training programmes through training establishments ... and the higher education system, through the ministries or universities of the Member States.'

Just as the widening political interest in EC education provided Jones with an opportunity to make his repositioning of EC education policy public,[103] so too were new opportunities for the EC to develop higher education coming from sources over which neither Jones nor the Commission had control. Following the low turnout for the second set of direct elections for the EP in 1984, for example, heads of state and government were looking for solutions and thinking again about the 'human face' of the Community, developing a renewed interest in cultural cooperation.

Technological change was also on the way. As Jones had explained to the Standing Conference of European Ministers of Education, a Council of Europe body, at around this time,[104]

> Whereas in the period 1976–82, attention had been strongly focussed on the links between education and social policy, especially in measures to combat growing unemployment, in the past two years a new and growing emphasis had been given to the contribution of education and training in the task of modernising the economies and of exploiting the potential of the new technologies.[105]

The French director-general of the DG for social affairs, Jean Degimbe, had already suggested the role of IT in education as an issue worth working up for the 1984 Fontainebleau Council. In what turned out to be a decision with important implications for the development of higher education, the Council did indeed back the idea of further work on the questions of how to integrate information technology into higher education, and on the transfer of technology.[106]

Thus in 1984, thanks to the combination of events and institutional opportunities outlined here, higher education was the education policy area most firmly ensconced in EC political opinion. How and why higher education became the subject of a full Community decision in the space of the following two years is the subject of the next chapter.

Resolving conflict

The sequence of events recounted here helps solve the puzzle, as to why – given the dynamic and cooperative approach to educational cooperation agreed by ministers of education in 1976 and the directive of 1977 – no use was made of Community instruments during the late 1970s or early 1980s. The immediate answer is that the implementation of the Action Programme revealed the essential fragility of the process. Its innovative deals on policy making and its packaging of actions raised suspicions among some member state governments – notably the Danes, the British and the French – that the Commission was using treaty procedures in domains where these did not apply.

Such a charge from a member state took the issue away from the policy specialists and into a political policy venue. With the Danish intervention, education ceased to be the virtual monopoly of a small section of the Commission and a policy committee within the Council, closer to the sector than to the diplomats who made up the permanent representation of the Council. This charge involved the highest levels of the Community institutions – the permanent representatives, the Council secretariat and the highest levels of the Commission, both within the general secretariat and for the president and the commissioners, and the ministries of foreign affairs. The ruling of the Commission president – guarantor of the treaties – gave the officials at Jones' level no choice but to obey their hierarchical superiors. A case might have been made for a different and more flexible interpretation as the Commissioners' own discussions, illustrated. But not under its British president Roy Jenkins. The outcome might also have been different for education, if the education and training directorate had not been shown up by the Audland working party as failing to follow the correct procedures. Hence the fears of suspicious member state representatives were fuelled.

However the fact that no decisions were being prepared was not a sign, as the Commissioner Ivor Richard seemed to suppose, that nothing was happening. The almost invisible action was significant. Jones was working to find a less conflict-ridden venue for decision-making and saw that in the DG social affairs and working for a maximum of activities that could be backed by the Council of Ministers for social affairs, as being more Community-minded than education ministers. But this outcome also has to be explained by Jones' conviction that education would be more solidly anchored within the Community if it could be viewed as at the service of the Community's strategic aims. That, too, was easier if the directorate could develop policy proposals which allowed to the Council of Ministers for social affairs.

From then on, the contingency of a developing and more ambitious Community played its part. In 1984 an energetic French presidency was looking for new ideas. Heads of state and government began to get concerned about the potential of IT. The French director general of social affairs responded with a suggestion for a programme which the following year became the Comett project. The EC leaders' other preoccupation in 1984 played to Commission's readiness to present its higher education cooperation as a response. The leaders were concerned that the European elections of the previous year had revealed growing public indifference or hostility to the EC. In this context, the developing joint study programmes and university cooperation and student exchange looked to the European Council's policy advisers as not just a good example of making Europe 'closer to the people', but an admirable 'solution' to their 'problem'. Hence the idea that the Community should act on higher education emerged from the events paradoxically the stronger for the conflict. It was linked to two Councils or decision-making venues and it had been brought to the attention of EC leaders – in large part thanks to Jones' persistence.

8
Attaining a Goal: The Erasmus Decision, 1985–87

If there was one event that greatly enhanced the chances of cooperation in higher education becoming enshrined in European Community (EC) law, it was the installation in January 1985 of a new Commission, under the presidency of the dynamic French politician, Jacques Delors. But that event was itself the culmination of many others. This chapter recounts the process by which broad support for a full EC decision on higher education was gained, and how the issue was refined by obstacles and events, expected and unexpected.

Developing the Commissioner's programme

An immediately precipitating factor was that breaking with a pattern, education gained a new and energetic commissioner. This was Peter Sutherland, a former Irish Attorney-General and future president of the WTO. Sutherland succeeded Ivor Richard, whose main interest had been social policy, leaving education – as indeed he had no hesitation in saying – 'to Hywel'.[1] But Sutherland took the job under rather special conditions. His prime interest and prime responsibility was as commissioner for competition. He held the portfolios of social policy and education 'in trust' for one year, pending the accession of Spain and Portugal.

In some respects Sutherland was similar to Richard in that he also had no specialist interest in education. But notwithstanding the scepticism of some of the staff of his *cabinet*,[2] he interpreted the European Economic Community (EEC) treaty – and its jurisprudence – as giving the Commission had some powers in the field of education.[3]

Sutherland sent for the key officials, Jean Degimbe, director-general of DGV, social affairs, and Hywel Ceri Jones, director for education, vocational training and youth policy within the Directorate General (DG). As Jones remembers, they were called in on a Friday. After a weekend spent reading the relevant files, 'on Monday Sutherland wanted to see us again to discuss his assessment of possible action.[4] Given Sutherland's confidence in a legal base, the key question was whether the commissioner had the resources necessary to carry through the action. On reading the dossiers, he concluded that both the joint study programmes and the university technology-transfer project could be worked up as draft decisions.[5] Both initiatives had already received favourable comment from the European Council. Sutherland also liked the symbolic parallel between contemporary student exchange and 'the fine medieval European tradition of mobility of scholars between centres of learning'.[6] However, he wanted evidence that there was sufficient support and experience in the directorate to do the preparatory work and to make the linkage to current EC strategic aims.

Degimbe, the French director-General of DGV, had been pushing for policy development to encourage universities to act as 'knowledge poles' for the economy of their regions.[7] He had become interested in the issue a year earlier when the 'sherpas' preparing the French Presidency and the Fontainebleau European Council of June 1984 were trawling for ideas to be put forward for Council approval. At the time Degimbe had suggested that the education and training directorate should build on work that had resulted in 1983 in a resolution from the Council (social affairs) on vocational training measures to meet the challenge of new information technologies.[8]

In early 1984, André Kirchberger, another Frenchman working in DGV, had been given the task of exploiting the opportunity, provided by the French presidency, to write the first draft of a programme on technology transfer and training.

> Degimbe had suggested that we should play to French interests in education and employment. We could produce a paper on the theme 'Technical change? Social change?' We should focus on the deficit in qualified manpower.[9]

Jones was already a powerful advocate on human resource issues, and in particular for the case that, in order to take advantage of a skilled technology-based economy, Community commitment to education and training was essential. To other officials initially involved, this marked a new and exciting departure. Kirchberger described the atmosphere in the office as an 'intellectual Wild West', in which 'adventurers' could innovate:

> Nothing was ruled out, nothing ruled in.[10]

The title he and Jones came up with the possible programme – Comett – reflected their sense of the Community moving into new space.[11]

Jones also saw his contacts with Sutherland as an opportunity to present the joint study programmes (JSPs) as a successful solution to the problem of enabling students and staff to move freely between the Community's universities. Firstly, they had been tried and tested for almost ten years, between volunteer academics from more than two hundred universities. The JSPs had solved all the technical problems posed by Europe's diverse traditions in higher education. The fact that these programmes were based in contracts between academics, backed by their institutions, to exchange students and to develop elements for joint courses, was an agreement which overrode the different national rules. Indeed the scheme was initially engineered as a way round the problem of different admission systems.[12] Secondly, they matched Sutherland's and Delors' skill-building concerns. But the JSPs needed Community funding, at a time when just one per cent of university students were studying abroad.[13] And above all this academic bridge-building created goodwill.

There was one other key education player at this stage – Michel Richonnier, another Frenchman, who had previously worked in the office of the French national 'plan' (*Commissariat au Plan*) on issues relating to educational strategy at the national and European level. Richonnier was the official responsible for education within Sutherland's *cabinet*. By the time Sutherland met Degimbe and Jones, Richonnier claims he had already been 'softening up' the Commissioner.[14]

It was with some authority that Richonnier pressed Sutherland to take the lead on a co-operative approach by the Community to the technological revolution[15] and the importance of training young people to acquire the new 'technological culture'.[16] He also supported Jones' contention that a strong Community line on educational cooperation would provide a common base from which to combat the crisis of unemployment and the change in the nature of work – and, furthermore, reduce the drain on social security funding.

But Richonnier, in a tradition that had faded since the Janne and Tindemans reports were issued in the 1970s, strongly believed that the Community should back educational co-operation for the political benefits it would reap.[17] Unlike Jones, but like his fellow French citizen

Jacqueline Lastenouse in DGX, Richonnier was an enthusiast for the cultural role of education. Indeed, in his view education was a necessary instrument to counter political cynicism about the Community.

> There will not be a second generation of Europeans – as opposed to the heroic first generation – if the youth of today does not acquire a sense of Europe, the reality and the usefulness of the Community construction.[18]

From Sutherland's vantage point, it was essential to ensure that the core argument in making a case for education was in tune with the new Community strategy to complete the single market, taking shape under Jacques Delors. For Sutherland, everything fitted. He was convinced that the proposals could be 'dovetailed with the Single Market focus of the Commission.[19]

It quickly became clear to Sutherland and his officials that the new president of the Commission had a highly developed idea of education and the part it could play in his strategy for advancing European integration via the single market. Delors, a politician who personally would have given priority to economic and monetary union as the energising 'big idea' for his mandate, was willing to go along with the preferred option of the member states for completing the single market. Having emerged from the Christian socialist tradition, he had been active for years as an advocate of economic growth as a condition for strengthening of social cohesion.[20]

Delors made this conception of the single market explicit, at the European Parliament (EP) session of 14–15 January 1985, convened to discuss the thrust of Commission policy. There was a need, said Delors, to make national economies more flexible to achieve the goal of a single market. Linking his ideas to Jean Monnet's concern that Europeans had lost their ability to live together and to combine their creative strength, Delors also stressed the human dimension of a single market. He saw the benefits of enlargement to Spain and Portugal. This meant that the Community would encompass 'almost every current of European humanism'.[21] There were also benefits of scale and the 'multiplier effect' within the Community. The challenge lay in convincing individual Europeans that economic reform was worthwhile. Hence the declaration that:

> I wish to be part of the attempt to rebuild confidence in the importance of human resources and skills which they contribute. Our policies on education and training must help everyone to a better

understanding of the way the world is going and enable everyone to make best use of his talents and resources in the service of society.[22]

Sutherland did not hesitate a moment longer. His *cabinet* and the DG would devise programmes and draft decisions modelled on the joint study programme and technology transfer programmes, which he would then present to the Commission. This was a milestone. For the first time since the 1960s, the Commission could begin work on drafting full EC decisions in the higher education domain that did not derive from the 'law of education', as did legislation on academic recognition, derived from Article 57. Furthermore, as all involved knew, work had to be carried out quickly before Sutherland's term as education commissioner ended in December 1985.

The immediate response to Sutherland's decision from within the education and training directorate was to give the new programmes a reality by naming them. Not only was there Comett thought up by André Kirchberger and Jones,[23] Alan Smith, running the technical agency for the joint study programmes, is widely seen as the individual who came up with the acronym Erasmus – the European Community Action Scheme for the Mobility of European Students.[24]

Sutherland's decision also brought about an immediate procedural change in that responsibility for managing the issue shifted from the specialist bureaucracy of the Commission to the Commissioner's *cabinet*. It was for Michel Richonnier to negotiate on resources and jurisdiction, and to liaise with Jones and the technical services on the development of the draft decisions.

Jones recalls the first stage of programme development as one in which he and Sutherland had regular contact,[25] while Sutherland remembers his own involvement as small in time terms but highly targeted: 'I was personally concerned to see that the proposal was well crafted'.[26] Richonnier underlines the sense of a team. He recalls that his task became 'to help the dynamic and creative team led by Hywel Jones to transform a pilot project approach initiated at the end of the 1970s by Hywel into major programmes such as Comett and Erasmus.... Jones, Lenarduzzi and Kirchberger[27] were supportive ... [making] immense efforts to have the programme proposals approved by the Commission as early as 1985.'[28]

In this context, Richonnier's aim was to achieve a highly ambitious budget for the programmes. Jones says: 'Richonnier goes down in history for daring to think the unthinkable. He kept saying to us 'Think Big!'[29] And he did. Jones' working budget for Erasmus had projected a 10–30% increase on the joint study programmes. Alan Smith did those calculations for the years 1984–88, on the basis of a 1983 grant of 500,000 ecus. A 20% increase would have brought the sum to 1.3 million ecus by 1988. In the event, the Erasmus programme received 10 million ecus in 1988.[30]

In fact, Richonnier had started his budget calculations from a different perspective. Instead of starting with the joint study programmes representing 1% mobility among existing students, he settled on a mobility target of 10%.[31] He later explained that his thinking was framed by what he perceived to be the shortcomings of the Action Programme. 'Too few individuals were affected. Of the 1,000,000 students in French universities in 1981, only 10,000 were from the Community.'[32] Improving on that low point thus became his goal.

Facing the unexpected

In February 1985, a ruling from the European Court of Justice (ECJ) – the so-called *Gravier* ruling[33] – changed the way Sutherland's *cabinet* and Jones viewed the legislative basis of the Erasmus programme. The ruling has subsequently been the subject of much commentary, with the general conclusion being that it was the Gravier judgement that enabled the Erasmus decision to be taken.[34] The case had been brought in 1983 by a student who was a French national wanting to pursue a course in cartoon design at a Belgian art school. She took the Belgian authority, the City of Liège, to court, on the grounds that as an EC national she should have been given a place on the same terms as Belgian students, and that she should not have been charged the foreign students' fee, the *minerval*.

The ECJ judgement was constructed around two concepts. One was the principle of non-discrimination between EC nationals in access to training. This drew on Article 7 of the Regulation 1612/68, which was itself derived from the rights of workers to freedom of movement, as embodied in Article 49 of the EEC treaty – i.e. non-discrimination between Community nationals.[35] The second concept underpinning the ruling was Article 128 of the EEC treaty, which enabled the Council to lay down general principles for implementing a 'common training policy' in vocational training. A Council decision of 2 April 1963 on the subject had laid down the general principles involved,[36] but it had remained a dead letter.[37]

The Court had thus accepted the argument of the Advocate-General, Gordon Slynn, that there should be no discrimination between EC nationals in terms of access to training and that the word 'training' should be deemed to cover university education, from which it followed that:

> Any form of education which prepares for a particular profession, trade or employment, or which provides the necessary training and skills for such a profession, trade or employment is vocational training, whatever the age and the level of training of the pupils or students, or even if the training programme includes an element of general education.[38]

From an ECJ perspective, the Gravier judgement was plugging a gap in the jurisprudence on education, which the Court had begun to develop with the 1974 *Casagrande*[39] case (case 9/74). According to the 1974 ruling, the functional aims of the common market could not be obstructed by national legislation in policy areas that had not been transferred to the Community.[40] By extension, the 1983 *Forcheri*[41] ruling made it clear that education and training policies were not, as such, part of the policy sectors for which Community institutions had been given competence. In this light the *Gravier* ruling afforded the Court the opportunity to define what it meant by 'lawfully established', a term used in the *Forcheri* case, and to give substance to the concept of vocational training.[42] Accordingly, the Court argued that access to vocational training would promote the free movement of persons throughout the Community, by enabling them to seek qualifications and complete their training or develop their particular talents.

From the point of view of Sutherland's cabinet, the *Gravier* ruling was a godsend. As a member of his cabinet recalled, 'We took the work on Comett and Erasmus far more seriously after that.'[43] This was not just for the procedural advantage of Article 128 of decision-taking by simple majority, though that helped. The alternative legislative procedure in reserve was far more onerous to operate. The Article 235 'reserve powers' procedure required unanimity. It states:

> If action by the Community should prove necessary to attain, in the course of the operation of the common market, one of the objectives of the Community, and the treaty has not provided the necessary powers, the Council shall, acting unanimously on a proposal from the Commission, and after consulting the European Parliament, take the appropriate measures.[44]

The *cabinet* needed the judgement to be watertight, and they were reassured to see the Article 128 linkage between university education and the EEC treaty being made on the highest authority.

Jones subsequently maintained that he had not thought the legal basis of education was a problem, saying, 'You could afford to be pragmatic. Something would turn up'.[45] In his view, political support was the key. In that respect, Article 235 had the advantage in that its use demonstrated the strength of collective political will attaching to any action taken under it. Article 128, on the other hand, would secure a large budget more easily, with Mediterranean states outvoting those who contributed most to the budget. However, as indicated by Jones' contributions to *Social Europe* in 1983 and 1984, his confidence lay essentially in the fact that the link between education and training had become a well-established part of the conventional wisdom – a link further strengthened in relation to the EEC treaty by the new Community emphasis on skills and technology.

Sarah Evans, legal officer in Jones' directorate, and close colleague,[46] says the issue was also one of the informal rules and procedures which underpin an ambitious bureaucracy:

> In our service, our job is to get decisions. Article 128 made getting a decision seem relatively easy. It not only provided for treaty competence, but also established the unusually straightforward procedure of simple majority voting. This appealed to the Commission, since the smaller states that were often enthusiastic about education would outnumber the often reticent larger states such as France, the UK and Germany.[47] We saw the link to Erasmus and Comett would come in the Council Decision of 2 April 1963, laying down general principles for implementing a common vocational training policy, based on this Article.[48]

In fact, by June 1985 there was an opportunity to pursue a double strategy in order to secure a decision. Whilst the directorate and Sutherland's *cabinet* continued to work on the draft programmes on the basis of Article 128, there were also signs of a more favourable political climate in the Council working groups, where the idea of building a recognisable EC strategy on higher education increasingly came to be perceived as a logical offshoot of efforts to build a European identity. This shift in political climate followed the Fontainebleau European Council of 1984, which had left its mark on citizenship issues, and which promised far more dynamic developments than anything likely to emerge from the education ministers.

The Fontainebleau communiqué contained a plea that was passionate by diplomatic standards, 'considering that it was essential that the Community should respond to the expectations of the people of Europe by adopting measures to strengthen and promote its identity and image both for its citizens and for the rest of the world'.[49] The EC called on the Council of Ministers to take a series of specific measures before the middle of 1985 – the culmination of the Italian presidency. An *ad hoc* committee on 'A People's Europe' was established, chaired by an Italian, Pietro Adonnino.

The Fontainebleau request provided two opportunities for Jones' directorate to get their ideas straight to the heads of government. First, the Italian, Domenico Lenarduzzi, head of the directorate's higher education unit, drew on his national network to invite his fellow Italian, Adonnino, to work with him in drawing up drafts that would form part of the Commission submission and the eventual report.[50] In his account of events, he pointed to the large table in his office, declaring 'That is where the report's passages on education were written!'[51]

The education and training paragraphs of the Commission's input to Adonnino, communicated on 24 September 1984,[52] even though built on ten years of the directorate's experience, contained new ideas for European leaders. The heads of government were encouraged to see that the issue of academic recognition for study abroad was as important as the mutual recognition of diplomas – the Article 57 issue that was itself far from satisfactorily resolved. Over a 13-year-period, the Council had refused to take a single decision on draft directives for professional freedom of establishment – when Dahrendorf was struggling to find a solution which would provide freedom of movement and establishment for doctors, pharmacists and architects.[53] As a result, the Commission now has adopted an alternative tack, proposing that instead of trying to establish detailed equivalences for study abroad, a general system for the mutual recognition of university degrees should be initiated.[54]

Political leaders were also made aware of the achievements of the joint study programmes. By 1984, more than 500 universities and other higher education institutions had devised and carried out such schemes. The Council had agreed that the Commission could now award institutional grants to support faculty mobility as well as a limited number of scholarships in support of student mobility. The Commission was now working to advance co-operation in education and higher education by securing Council approval for measures aimed at stimulating European scientific and technical cooperation and interchange.[55]

With the Commission communication on *A People's Europe* in the public domain, the Commission continued to press education ministers on the European dimension to education, and dropped the first hint that Erasmus and Comett were in the pipeline. They persuaded the Council to convene two meetings of education ministers, on 3 June 1985 and 13 June 1985, and for the second meeting, repeating Jones' idea that employment ministers should be invited too.[56] Ministers were told that the Commission expected to be presented with a proposal on higher education and technological change within two months, and further proposals on cooperation before the end of the year.[57] But the nearest ministers got to any decision was to agree conclusions that they should act to make their domestic curricula 'more European'. They also 'discussed' forms of European higher education cooperation, but were not willing to put on the record anything more precise[58]

Meanwhile, at the political level, the Commission's celebrated White Paper, *Completing the Internal Market*,[59] published on 14 June, had made a clear reference to the Commission's intention to extend activity in higher education cooperation, saying the Commission 'intends to increase its support for cooperation programmes between further education establishments in the different Member States, with a view to promoting the mobility of students, facilitating the academic recognition of degrees and diplomas, and helping young people, in whose hands the future of the Community's economy lies, to think in European terms'.[60]

Other aspects of EC policy relevant to higher education were being developed in parallel, notably by Etienne Davignon, with a particular focus on research. Davignon is widely seen as the most impressive figure in the 1981–84 Commission. Having taken a lead on many EC issues over the years, this time he was mainly concerned with issues relating to the EC's industrial performance and competition, and the question of how to strengthen a Commission-industry alliance to complete the single market programme. In 1980–81, he had launched the European Round Table, a forum for discussion and action, bringing together twelve of Europe's biggest industrial companies. This successfully opened up a process of policy discussion which had previously been bogged down among officials.[61]

In 1982, Davignon moved a step further in trying to ensure Community research was more strategically oriented, in the form of the Esprit programme – the European Strategic Programme for Research and Development in Information Technologies (ESPRIT) – and viewed in many quarters as the model for Erasmus, though this did not emerge in my interviews.[62] Davignon would have liked the education portfolio to link to his main portfolios of research and technology, as in Dahrendorf's time,[63] – as seen earlier. But he nevertheless moved to attract university engagement in EC-wide research by establishing the fist of the 'framework programmes'. This ran from 1984–87, and set the pattern of defining priority themes, for which universities in transnational partnerships could bid for EC-funded projects.[64]

This significant Community backing for higher education was reinforced at the Milan European Council of 28 and 29 June, 1985, which accepted the *People's Europe* report. Adonnino's committee had effectively matched the forward-looking mood, fuelled by the agreement on EC enlargement to include Spain and Portugal, the Commission's ambitious White Paper proposing to complete the single market by 1992, and the agreement of all Europe's leaders, except Margaret Thatcher, at Milan itself to consider European political union as well as the single market – a context of expectation about the Community's advance not seen since the Hague summit of 1969.[65]

Stating that it was 'essential to involve and interest young people in the further development of Europe,'[66] the Adonnino committee, in an energetic turn of phrase, called for a 'comprehensive' programme of European inter-university exchanges and studies, open to a 'significant' section of the Community's student population. The committee also reached out for the first time to a non-technical audience, proposing a European academic credit transfer scheme (the future ECTS), establishing bilateral or multilateral higher education partnerships to devise the credit transfer arrangements for their institutions on the basis of the ECTS model.[67]

However the difference between rhetoric and action was evident, once the Milan summit was over. Right from the start, the previous January, Sutherland, Degimbe, Jones and Richonnier had anticipated the Comett programme decision as a test of Article 128, hopefully leading the way for Erasmus. In September, when the Comett draft decision and explanatory document were presented to the College of Commissioners, there was little euphoria at this apparently timely proposal. There had been no follow on from the Adonnino report, which the education and training directorate had hoped would be a building block for both Comett and Erasmus. The Comett proposals, although also apparently in tune with the prevailing Community mood, did not go through the Commission easily.[68]

Peter Sutherland recalled the informal negotiations with the Council which preceded the presentation to the Commissioners as 'difficult' because of the budgetary issue – a factor of particular concern to the Germans who were wary about extra financial commitment at Community level. Sutherland said:

> I had a tough time getting the Comett programme through the Council largely against German finance ministry opposition. But I had seen how the Commission could make and win the argument politically and I knew that a similar powerful case could be made for Erasmus.[69]

But Sutherland was able to achieve his goal. Comett was approved by the College of Commissioners during his 'trusteeship' at their meeting just before Christmas 1985. The draft decision was transmitted to the Council on 3 January 1986.

The difficulties with the Comett proposal presented a problem for Erasmus, which was much less directly linked to the treaty or to the Community's single market objective. Sutherland, Degimbe, Jones and Richonnier had anticipated the Comett programme decision as a test of Article 128, hopefully leading the way for Erasmus. The lessons Sutherland drew was that it would be essential to demonstrate support from key players and, given the sensitivity of some member states to education issues and the potential difficulties presented by budgetary issues, 'to make sure that the Erasmus proposal was well crafted'.[70] At this stage the sentiments of the Adonnino report, in favour of integration, and which the education and training directorate had hoped would be a building block for Comett and Erasmus, had been forgotten.

Reaching the decision agenda

In the parallel work of preparing the Erasmus draft decision, and its supporting documentation, the drafting team had for the first time to spell out the justifications for the decision and the objectives of the Erasmus programme. This was where good 'crafting' showed. Until this stage of the process, the directorate's priority had been to get the action launched, not to justify it in legal detail.

The challenge during the writing of the explanatory document and the draft decision had been to reflect the multiple reasons that the events of the year had thrown up for supporting the Erasmus programme. In an early draft for the explanatory document, Alan Smith of the technical agency summed up the objectives in terms that closely reflected the joint study programme's experience. The Erasmus

programme would meet 'the need for people to be able to communi-
cate, cooperate and to comprehend each other, for future decision-
makers to regard joint ventures as natural and a positive line of action
rather than a potential source of danger. Mobility was an effective
means of combating emotive campaigns aimed at promoting narrow
national interests to the detriment of the Community as a whole'.[71]

By the end of the year, the draft decision had been written up, budgeting for a 10% take up by students. The communication or explanatory memorandum largely reflected the views of A People's Europe that
there was a cultural case for the programme – that Europe needed 'the
mentality of co-operation ... among young Europeans before they have
completed their studies'. Furthermore, that mobility was a crucial
element in policies aimed at ensuring the economic and social development of the Community as a whole'.[72] In the draft decision which,
in contrast, had to demonstrate the legal link to the treaty of a
Community-funded activity, the recitals gave pride of place to links to
the treaty via a Council Decision of 1963 on vocational training policy.
The objectives of the programme gave priority to securing an adequate
pool of manpower. This double approach enabled the proposal to go
through the Commission in time to be forwarded to the Council of
Ministers on January 1986.[73] The programme was described as

(i)   enabling a growing number of students (at least 10% by 1992)
        to acquire first hand experience of life in another Member
        State through a recognised period of study abroad
(ii)   ensuring the development of a pool of graduates with direct
        experience of intra-Community cooperation, as a means of
        providing a broader basis for intensified economic and social
        cooperation in the Community
(iii)   strengthening ties between citizens of the various Member
        States, with a view to consolidating the concept of a People's
        Europe

Nevertheless the cultural argument remained explicit, reflecting the
way Richonnier had problematised the issue of new generations of
Europeans at the beginning of the year. 'In an increasingly competitive
world it is vital that persons in positions of responsibility recognise the
crucial need for increased co-operation with partners in other Member
States. Such a mentality of co-operation can and must be encouraged,
in particular among young Europeans before they have completed
their studies.

This is one of the best ways of ensuring that future generations of decision-makers will regard joint ventures with other EC countries as a natural and positive line of action rather than a potential source of risk and danger.

By the same token, it is a particularly effective means of combating emotive campaigns aimed at promoting narrow national interests which are to the detriment of the Community as a whole.

For all these reasons a higher level of mobility among the 6mn students at 3,600 institutions must be regarded as a crucial element in policies of ensuring the economic and social development if the Community as a whole.[74]

In terms of what the Erasmus proposals wanted from the Community, it was primarily the resources for grants for the students who would follow courses in other member states, as well as financial support for the organisation of intensive short-duration seminars on specific subjects for students from different member states. The Commission had envisaged that to stimulate student exchanges, the Community would set up a network involving 600 universities by 1987, and that this would be expanded to 1,700 institutions by 1989. As the academic recognition of diplomas and periods of study abroad was an integral part of the overall strategy to encourage the mobility of students in the Community, the Erasmus programme would also need to provide financial support to three schemes: the introduction of an experimental scheme for the academic recognition of diplomas and transferable course credits; intensification of the activities of the current network of twelve national academic recognition information centres; and the joint development of curricula by different universities in the Community. Community financial support also needed to be available for a number of complementary measures (preparatory visits, contacts between university teachers; introduction of a Community dimension into the activities of teachers' and students' associations; annual award of European prize). The proposed budget allocation for the first phase (1987–1989) was estimated at 175 mn ecu.[75]

The Commission proceeded at this stage on the basis that the principles of the programme were acceptable to all member states in the form presented to the Council, but might face difficulties on the scale envisaged and the legislative instrument.[76] Furthermore ministers of education were decision-averse. As Jones put it: 'Remember, ministers of education had not been willing to make any type of Community decision – even the non-binding instruments used in education'[77] – since the directive of 1977 on the education of migrant workers children.[78]

The informal consultations that got under way while the Commission was drafting the decision exposed the specific concerns of various member states. The Commission proposal that the issue be decided under Article 128 and thereby simple majority voting was known to be as a disadvantage for the net contributors to the budget – Germany and the UK – who had previously acted as brakes on EC activity in education. The net contributors' reticence might however be offset by the Mediterranean states' enthusiasm. They stood to gain most from forms of exchange which insisted on reciprocity rather than leaving student movement to the market, which historically favoured only the British, the French and the Germans. The Dutch, net contributors, were also in favour of the proposal, as were the Luxembourgeois.

The Commission decision

The draft decision on Erasmus was presented to the College of Commissioners on 5 December 1985 as a programme for cooperation in the field of higher education set up in 1976,[79] and aimed at taking Community action in this field beyond the experimental stage.[80] The commissioners approved its transmission to the Council of Ministers under the terms of Article 128.

The proposal was forwarded on 3 January 1986 with a recommendation for a budget of 175 mn ecu for the period 1987–89, to cover the mobility costs of 10% of students and the establishment of new cooperative frameworks between universities. Sutherland was thus able to sign off the Erasmus documents, having achieved his objective as Commissioner for education. Both the issues selected the previous January for transformation into potential Community legislation had reached the Commissioners during his short term of office. Furthermore, it had been easier to get fellow commissioners' support for Erasmus than for Comett and the future augured well. 'The European rectors were most enthusiastic supporters and a key positive influence on the ministers of education'.[81]

From then on, the future of the programmes lay with the Council of Ministers where, so Jones and his colleagues estimated, officials were likely to be supportive but member state governments divided.

The Council takes over

On 3 January 1986, when the draft decision on the Erasmus pro-gramme was formally received by the general secretariat of the Council of Ministers, the focus of attention shifted to different actors and processes. In asking for a Council decision, the Commission was asking for legislation binding in its entirety upon those to whom it was addressed (Treaty EC Article 189). In order to secure such legislation, Article 189c required a proposal from the Commission, an opinion from the European Parliament and a decision from the Council. Hence the Council was the ultimate decision-maker.[82]

Formally, the draft decision's progress through the Council involved three stages. First was an initial examination of the text by an expert Council working party representing the twelve member states, who cleared particular issues as necessary with national authorities. Second was an assessment by members of the diplomatic missions, rep-resented in the committee of permanent representatives, COREPER, who decided whether a proposal was ready for enactment – acting as a filter for ministers' meetings, COREPER working parties clear as much common ground as possible before ministerial meetings, leaving the most sensitive matters for ministers to resolve in their discussions.[83] In the third and final stage as approved by the appropriate level national officials – deputy ambassadors in the case of Erasmus.[84]

Those concerned with the issue in the various EC institutions – the Commission, the Council and the EP – expected that the Erasmus decision would be approved within a year. This was true of, even the Council, which had not made an educational decision until it approved the technology-transfer programme, Comett, in July 1986,[85] and where was it was predictable that some permanent representatives would be anxious about breaking away from the inter-governmental aspect of the 'mixed' process. Alan Forrest, head of the education secretariat at the time, recalls:

> We thought that with Erasmus we were dealing with an issue which would go through the Council processes within a year. The Dutch presidency in the second half of 1985 had strongly sup-ported the Commission's drafting of the proposal. We foresaw dis-cussion by ministers in Council in June under the Luxembourg

presidency, and the decision taken in November under the UK presidency. But it took the Belgian presidency of the first half of 1987 to deliver agreement.[86]

In the spring of 1986, the new Commissioner for education, the Spaniard, Manuel Marin, proposed some classic 'softening up' to help the process along. He proposed that the forthcoming tenth anniversary of European educational co-operation – the Action Programme resolution of 1976 – should be celebrated.[87] The obvious idea was an informal 'ministerial'. An informal ministerial occasion was a tactical bonus for the Commission. It created a channel to ministers, away from the bargaining considerations inherent to meetings of national diplomatic missions to the EC, where diplomats and finance ministry officials dominated. For ministers themselves, the informality of such Community proceedings provided those rare occasions when they felt Europe came together. Robert Jackson, a British minister for higher education in the late 1980s and a former academic, was at an informal ministers' meeting later, in Segovia and found the experience unforgettable:

> It was an extension of the informal lunches we would have during Council meetings, always the best moment. These informal meetings were wild and wacky. People would talk at the level of ideas they had in the bath.... The informal ministerial was the same, only it went on longer and more splendidly. I remember a great feast of sucking pigs cut up by armies of chefs. Menus were in the most flowery of languages. On that occasion Paris was described as the capital of Europe. My companion in the coach on the way back was the French minister, Lionel Jospin. He was inordinately pleased.[88]

Jackson was well aware of Jones' strategy. 'There was this twinkling Welshman,' Jackson recalls, 'networking away like mad. Very Tafia.[89] He was clever. He took the opportunity to embark on some intense lobbying for his project'.[90]

National officials, however, were nervous about such occasions. A British education ministry official who had accompanied several successive ministers to the Council, remembers some informal ministerial meetings:

> We thought them downright dangerous. The Commission was always trying to get ministers to take a position on an issue which would be coming up on the formal agenda. So we'd have to step in

to say we weren't working under Council procedure and that no decisions could be made, no commitments given. We were firm with the Commission that nothing said at an informal meeting could be used on the record.[91]

The informal ministerial meeting took place on 16 May 1986, to consider the Commission's projects, Erasmus and Comett, as well as a youth programme the directorate was developing. Ministers were reminded that support for Erasmus was gaining ground in Community institutions. On 23 April, the Education Committee had praised the design of the envisaged programme and welcomed the Commission's evident resolve in trying to overcome the serious obstacles to mobility.[92] Furthermore, the European Parliament had supported a resolution that welcomed the proposal as a way of bringing about voluntary convergence in higher education and assumed the proposal would go through rapidly.[93] According to the record, ministers discussed possible new programmes – Erasmus and the youth programme – as well as the proposed youth programme, Yes for Europe, and Comett.[94] But they had all been briefed not to take any decision.

On 9 June 1986, it became clear that, despite the best hopes of Marin and Jones, the informal meeting had not significantly advanced the cause of Erasmus. On that day, ministers of education met in a session which officials at both the Council and in the Commission had pencilled in as the date for indicating support for the draft Erasmus decision,[95] in preparation for formal approval in December 1986. But in fact ministers meeting 'within' the Council, failed to reach agreement on even the principle of a programme. A harsh instruction to the education committee urged it 'to focus its attention on the possibilities of extending agreement between universities within a European network, and on ways to avoid the creation of further cumbersome structures in this sphere'.[96] The best that could be done by the Luxembourg presidency – which favoured Erasmus – was to get the Erasmus draft decision referred to the next meeting of ministers.

The brakes had been put on the Erasmus programme within COREPER, at the level of the deputy ambassadors – diplomats whose background is usually in the ministries of finance or trade. In this diplomatic forum for presenting national governments' views, and negotiating consensus, education could not expect the specialist attention it had had in the Council working party. 'We used to think of education under its budgetary classification, as part of 'other matters',' recalled one former deputy ambassador.[97] And indeed budgetary questions and issues of sovereignty appear to have dominated the discussions.

Governments which had approved the rhetoric of, for example, Adonnino, were deeply divided once faced with a concrete proposition for a higher education programme.[98] Beyond the divide between the net contributors to the EC budget and the net beneficiaries, there were also specific national concerns. The UK, traditional destination for a large number of Greeks, feared an influx of students from the new Mediterranean member states,[99] though some claim such a factor inclined the UK to favour the concept of organised, and thus controllable, mobility being developed by the Commission.[100] For their part, the Belgians stressed that they did not want their relatively open medical schools to be inundated with yet more Scandinavian students. As for resources, several member states thought the Commission's recommendations looked expensive, and possibly difficult to contain. In France ministry officials feared any Community funding for education would lead their ministry of finance to claw back part of the national grant for the sector. Others feared that a jump in student mobility from around 1% to 10% not only looked expensive but unfeasible.[101]

Before a Council meeting ministers are given a final briefing from the national diplomatic mission. 'It was to make sure we did not deviate' recalls Jackson. who thought of COREPER as 'the real chaps'.[102] 'They took you in charge. They told you what to think. There was no question of discussing the issues.'[103] As an intellectual, he remembers with frustration that an issue which was a minor matter for the diplomats could be a major matter for the minister of education. As many sources concur, the Council meeting procedures were not conducive to discussion either. Ministers would once more be expected to speak to national positions.

In the months that followed, as the issue went between the education committee, which was looking for solutions, the council working party, and COREPER, which was defending a variety of national lines, it was clear that there was no consensus to be found. Ministers, like Jackson, who thought that 'Erasmus was like apple pie and motherhood. You couldn't be against it,' were mistaken.

Jones, getting the feedback that the Council meeting of education ministers scheduled for 28 November, was not certain to approve the Erasmus proposal, struck upon an opportunity to rally influential support. The rectors of universities in existence in Erasmus' time – generally not only the oldest but the most prestigious – were meeting in at the Catholic University of Leuven (KUL)[104] on 27 November, at the initiative of the Leuven rector, Roger Dillemans.[105]

Educated in philosophy and law at Leuven and Harvard, Dillemans, like Jackson, was an academic inspired by the idea that the Community was at last taking education seriously. Dillemans however had more opportunities than a junior minister. As rector of Leuven university, a jewel in the Belgian crown, he had been instrumental in getting the Dutch EC presidency of 1985 to support the Erasmus idea. He later said: 'I saw its value as promoting the mobility of the intelligentsia, changing a situation in which the mobile were mainly the rich.'[106] In his speech to his fellow rectors from 29 of Europe's leading institutions, Dillemans proclaimed:

> University education contains much more than just training for the practice of a profession.... After 30 years of Europe's existence, the public thinks the study of other peoples' language, culture, religion, scientific achievements is relevant to every one of us and a necessary part of university education, of common interest to the peoples of Europe.
>
> The Erasmus programme could introduce an ever-increasing number of students to European realities, to strengthen relations between citizens of Member States of the European Community and, in the end, to create a true European university network. One of its strengths would be that it would attract brilliant, but otherwise ordinary students, and researchers of whatever social origin, language, creed and opinion.[107]

Dillemans described the 30 rectors at that meeting as initially believing that they should 'go carefully, but firmly, on how to improve opportunities for undergraduate and research students under existing national laws, mindful of the fact that the Community was going beyond its traditional sphere and that was still an issue within the Council'. Then Jones arrived.'[108] It was the first time Dillemans had met Jones – and he was greatly impressed.

> He made a very great speech. He entirely changed the spirit of the meeting. His address on the dangers of the Erasmus programme not being agreed the following day gave urgency to our own idea that the Community should be supporting mobility which did not depend on social class, but intelligence. Here in our panelled halls,

we instantly agreed to send a telegram to national ministers of education.[109]

Dillemans achieved his wish that rectors give a strong impetus to Erasmus. The rectors' telegram urged ministers to recognise that 'the provision of substantial direct support for students is the key to the success of the Erasmus programme'. The proposed Erasmus budget 'would enable some 50,000 of the 6 million students in the 12 EC countries to become mobile' – a figure that was still, they emphasised, 'a small proportion of the total student population.'[110] The rectors' message also informed ministers that:

> The Conference has given its unanimous support for the pro-gramme which it regarded as providing the means for a vital break-through in achieving an appropriate level of student mobility within the European Community, as called for by the heads of state and government. For their part the universities are ready to respond to the challenge of implementing the programme.[111]

At the meeting at the Council in 28 November 1986, ministers of edu-cation had to consider whether they would approve the full Community procedure of Article 128 as the basis for Erasmus, and the draft budget drawn up by Richonnier. The rectors' lobbying had no impact at this stage. The ministers were not concerned with the issue but with the procedures. They could not even agree to meet under a full Council procedure, as required by Article 128. The annual report of the Council records a meeting under the mixed process devised in the 1970s. 'At its meeting of 28 November, the Council and Ministers of Education meeting within the Council engaged in a long and detailed examination of the programme for a Decision adopting a Community action scheme for the mobility of university students (ERASMUS).'[112]

An important issue for the ministers was that approval of the Comett decision, in July 1986, had, contrary to Jones' hopes, failed to set a precedent for a broad 'Gravier' interpretation of university education as vocational training and thus consistent with Article 128. Comett, much more genuinely vocational than was Erasmus, was finally approved on the basis of Article 235 alongside Articles 128.[113] Ministers of employment and social affairs, for all their commitment to Community decision-making, had nonetheless judged aspects of the proposal to fall outside the treaty.[114]

At the meeting of 28 November 1986, ministers divided into three camps on the issues of jurisdiction and resources. The Commission proposal that the Erasmus programme be approved under Article 128 pleased Spain, Portugal, Greece and Italy, as well as Luxembourg.[115] For the Spanish, Portuguese and Greeks, all of whom had suffered under dictatorships, Erasmus was perceived to provide a means of upgrading their universities and underpinning their autonomy.[116] Furthermore, under the 'free market' movement of citizens, their students went north while few came south. For the Italians, who had seized every opportunity to strengthen a European dimension to higher education – both through the EP committee concerned with education, and through the European University project – organised student mobility represented a way forward in terms of university reform. None of these countries was a net contributor to the EC budget.

The second group – the Germans, Dutch, Irish and Danes – believed that Erasmus should be approved on legal grounds, on the double basis of Article 128 and Article 235. Net contributors to the budget, including Germany and the Netherlands, were against the sole Article 128 procedure, which meant they could be outvoted by the Mediterranean countries. A third group, consisting of Belgium, the UK and France, insisted that Article 235 should be the sole legal foundation for the decision, relying on the Article's requirement for unanimity to act as a brake on budgetary demands to fund the programme.

There were other national concerns. The Belgians, like the British, feared an uncontrolled influx of students, and held out little hope that the ECJ would help them.[117] France was reticent given its long-standing position, evident since the 1950s, that co-operation needed to be seen as a political choice. But the French also had tactical reasons for rejecting Erasmus, associated with the 'claw back regime' operated by its Ministry of Finance. Ministry officials had persuaded the minister concerned, Michèle Alliot-Marie that Erasmus was not worth its price. Furthermore, there were fears that Erasmus was 'an Anglo-Saxon' programme.[118]

The British, meanwhile, who had chaired the meeting as holders of the presidency in the second half of 1986, had a complicated domestic agenda which vied with the traditional wish of a presidency to succeed. Officials within the British department of education appreciated that organised exchanges based on reciprocity, as proposed under Erasmus, was advantageous because it was predictable.[119] The pro-European minister for higher education, Christopher Patten, was in favour of Erasmus for wider reasons. But the secretary of state, Kenneth Baker, was not. Baker, who was close to Margaret Thatcher, shared her suspicion of EC measures that could be a 'can opener' for more expensive EC projects.[120] Furthermore, Thatcher had expressly forbidden ministers to approve any new expenditure. Patten was therefore ruled out as unsafe, and another junior minister, Angela Rumbold, was sent to chair the meeting, assisted by the director of higher education in the education ministry.[121]

This change in chairmanship contributed to the meeting's chaotic outcome on 28 November and when it reconvened on 1 December. Faced with divisions over the legal basis for Erasmus, the senior British education official, Tony Clark, decided to focus his efforts on getting a deal on resources for the programme, which, if successful, could prepare a deal on the legal base. When the Council resumed its session on 1 December, Clark announced to his minister that he had a deal on a major point of contention: the budget reserved for Erasmus. As against the Commission's proposed budget of 175 mn ecu, the Council proposed 50 mn ecu, to set up a European university network. The Council would also 'save' Community money by excluding grants. This suggestion by the chair appeared to be a response to the French minister present, Michèle Alliott-Marie, who explained her opposition to the Erasmus programme by saying that 'we cannot let students loose with a grant but no prior guarantees on recognition for their studies'.[122]

At that point Commissioner Marin withdrew the proposal on behalf of the Commission, maintaining that the Ministers' offer no longer corresponded to the aim or method proposed. The Commission's programme had designated 100 mn ecu of the total 175 mn ecu to be provided over three years to go towards direct financial grants. According to Marin, reducing the programme to a university network without providing grants 'would be like buying a cookery book to assuage one's hunger. How can we promote students' mobility without giving them the means to be mobile?' he asked.

Marin, a former student leader, then left the meeting to address the press with the memorable words that

> In the EC we accord more importance to a cow than to a hundred students....

As he explained

> The budget for Erasmus requested by the Commission amounted to four days of farm spending. This is why Europeans think we are mad: we can spend enormous amounts for our agriculture, but we are incapable of spending anything to educate our young people. If Erasmus of Rotterdam had been present at the Council he would have been tearing his hair out.[123]

Several officials from the education and training directorate thought Marin's decision to withdraw an item from the agenda was a high-risk strategy. 'We wondered whether Marin had forgotten which political arena he was in', remembers Lenarduzzi.[124] However the directorate's legal officer, Sarah Evans, maintained that such manoeuvres 'happened the whole time when the Council introduced new material'.[125] The immediate question for all the policy-makers committed to Erasmus was how to rescue the draft decision.

The European Council to the rescue

Just four days after the failed meeting of ministers of education, the London summit was due to be held, presided over by Margaret Thatcher. It was an occasion Thatcher herself remembered for her 'housekeeping', and for the beginnings of her dislike of Jacques Delors.

> I took a close interest in the physical as well as the diplomatic preparations for our big summits.... On this occasion I took care to have the battleship-grey walls of the Queen Elizabeth II Conference Centre covered with beige hangings and pictures, deliberately having some drawings by Henry Moore opposite President Mitterrand, who I knew loved Moore as much as I did.

Politically Thatcher saw the summit as memorable in three respects. 'Undoubtedly the main achievement of the British presidency was the adoption of, or agreement to, a record number of measures to implement the single market. This was the sort of solid progress the Community needed, rather than flashy publicity-seeking initiatives which came to nothing or just caused bad feeling.'[126] It was also the meeting at which she perceived Jacques Delors to be 'a new kind of European Commission president, tough, talented, demagogic on occasion – and a major player',[127] and for her prediction that even the veto, legal safeguards and declared exemptions might be overthrown by the emerging Franco-German bloc.

Yet for those concerned with the Erasmus issue, the European Council was memorable in a different way. By 5–6 December, the rectors who had been present at Leuven, and whose universities had educated many of Europe's political leaders, had done their work. They had called on their national leaders to support a scheme aimed at securing 'the mobility of the intelligentsia'.[128] For example Dillemans had briefed the Belgian prime minister, Wilf Martens, a fellow Leuven graduate. He believed that Mitterrand had been briefed by Déréchat of

Poitiers.[129] In any event, Mitterrand, according to his closest adviser, Jacques Attali, had come to the meeting determined that 'We will have Erasmus', and to return with the issue settled.[130]

A detailed account of the extensive pressure that built up at the meeting is provided by Garret Fitzgerald, the Irish prime minister who had been alerted to the Erasmus issue by an Irish Leuven graduate, Paddy Masterson, President of University College, Dublin. Masterson told Fitzgerald that Erasmus might fail because education ministers of the bigger EC countries were reluctant to approve spending at the level recommended by the Commission.[131] As Fitzgerald recounts the story:[132]

> Paddy Masterson ... asked me if there was anything I could do about it; I said that I would see if I could raise the matter without notice at the European Council.

> I decided the best way to approach the issue was informally; accordingly during a break in the discussions I spoke to [the French prime minister] Jacques Chirac. He responded enthusiastically, clearly concerned that his minister for education should have taken a negative view of the proposal, and he suggested that we jointly approach Hans-Dietrich Genscher, because the German minister for education was another of those opposed to it. We went across the room to speak to Genscher and secured his immediate support.

> I told my officials at once about this, and the project was then successfully pursued at other levels, with the result that the Erasmus programme, the survival of which had seemed threatened, got off the ground quite soon thereafter.[133]

Such are the agendas of statesmen that Chirac, the French prime minister, had to fly back to Paris early on the Sunday, to a crisis: a young man had died during student demonstrations after being beaten up by riot police. Meanwhile Mitterrand, the French president, was able to breakfast with the German leader, Helmut Kohl, to discuss French monetary problems, as well as the situation in the Soviet Union, Libya and Iran. He had dinner with Felipe Gonzales of Spain. According to Jacques Attali, the special adviser who spent the weekend at Mitterrand's side – and who was also keeping a diary for later publication – the two leaders discussed 'delicate dossiers' like agriculture, and the prospect of concerted action against terrorism. But the weekend was also notable for settling the Erasmus issue. As Attali noted, the communiqué stated that 'The European Council desired the rapid adoption of Erasmus'.[134] Erasmus was back on the decision agenda, despite the conflicts of the previous week.

The solution for a quick settlement on Erasmus was to put the issue on the agenda of the General Affairs Council of 15–16 December, i.e. the Council of ministers of foreign affairs. Two key procedural issues remained to be addressed. The first was to get the Commission to re-present the proposal that had been withdrawn at the 28 November/ 1 December session of the Council of Ministers (education). The second was to give the incoming Belgian presidency the opportunity to make a commitment that it would settle the issue before the next meeting of Council of Ministers (education) scheduled for June 1987. The embattled tone, however, remained in press at the time:

> The General Council took note of the letter by Mr Marin, Com-missioner, to Sir Geoffrey Howe, Council president, in its Tuesday session. The letter states that the Commission is pleased with the political commitment shown by the European Council in London which asked that 'the Erasmus programme on mobility of students be studied again so that the Council can reach a decision at its next session.

> The Commission presented its original proposal again because it feels that now the conditions are present for the Council to make a decision respecting the core of the proposal – grants to allow greater mobility for students in the Community – as well as respecting the quantitative and financial scope of the programme.

> After Mr Marin's remarks, President Howe said that he took note of them and added that the Council will reflect on the European Council's view and will decide on the Erasmus programme at its next session. As a result, the file was sent to COREPER.[135]

The pressure on the Council to sort out the problem mounted significantly within days. At the customary EP session that follows Council meetings, and at which EC presidents and the President of the Commission give their assessment, Delors himself raised the issue of Erasmus. The Commission had been 'very disappointed' by the London discussion on the co-operative strategy for growth, the research programme and Erasmus – 'this little student exchange programme'. An Irish MP, who probably knew of Fitzgerald's intervention at the European Council, echoed Delors.[136] On 11 December 1986, a compromise amendment moved by four groups of including the two largest, the Socialists and the EPP (Conservative) asked the Council to adopt the entire Erasmus programme with the credits planned, and that it be implemented quickly. The Parliament welcomed the Commission's statement that it was ready to present the programme to the General Council on 15 and 16 December. It 'deplored' the education Council's failure on 28 November to approve the project, especially since the Council representing finance ministers had written the necessary credits into the 1987 budget, just three days previously.[137] Margaret Thatcher was enraged, blaming Delors for the Parliamentary amendment[138] – it was the beginning of their mutual hostility.

As for Erasmus, Mitterrand followed up the issue, addressing an audience of students on the theme of Europe as the way forward, and committing to the programme. It was a speech that members of the Commission's education directorate and officials in the Council secretariat in post at the time judged to be very important.[139] The French Minister of Education, René Monory, resolved the particular French problem over Erasmus by working out the financial deal between the education and finance ministries, 'an act which turned the balance in France'.[140] But even then, when Erasmus should have been close to agreement, the French produced another suggestion. In April the French government celebrated the 30th anniversary of the signing of the Treaty of Rome by issuing a Blue Book (*Un Livre Bleu*). This statement on Community cultural policy as a matter for political cooperation rather than Community regulation appeared at least implicitly to include education.[141] The Commission and the Belgian Presidency, trying to keep Erasmus within Community processes, rejected this 'piece of intergovernmentalism'.[142] However the Belgian presidency, with the aid of the Education Committee, delivered agreement on Erasmus. On 14 May 1987, the date of the subsequent Council meeting of ministers of education, it was clear that there was a deal. The Belgian presidency announced that all delegations had agreed that Erasmus could go ahead on the double basis of Article 128 and Article 235. A final recital added to the draft decision achieved the compromise on jurisdiction – and on the same basis as Comett. The final recital reads:

> Whereas this action programme includes aspects relating to education which, at the present stage of the development of Community law, may be regarded as falling outside the scope of the common vocational training policy as provided by Article 128 of the Treaty; whereas these aspects of the programme can, together with the vocational training objectives to which they are closely linked, contribute to the harmonious development of economic activities

throughout the Community; whereas to the extent the Treaty has not provided the necessary powers, and action for this purpose appears necessary to attain, in the course of the operation of the common market, one of the objectives of the Community.

One of the officials in the working party, devising the deal, remembers Domenico Lenarduzzi, Jones' deputy in the directorate for education and training, being 'furious' at the suggestion that Article 235 had to be added.[143] But it was that suggestion that got approval from the member states. The fact that another part of the Commission – its legal services – were threatening to take the Council to the European Court for misusing Community processes in seeking the double legislative base – was ignored for the moment. What ministers wanted was a political deal. Process could be dealt with later.[144]

At the Council of Ministers meeting (Education) of 14 May 1987, the double legal base was agreed, despite the fact that the Commission would probably appeal. So was the proposal for a budget of 85 mn ecus over three years – reduced from 175 mn ecus – but with provision for the EP to review the programme budget after two years. The funding would be released in blocks – 10 mn ecus for the first year, 30 mn ecus for the second and 45 mn ecus for the third. By the third year, the proportion of funding reserved for scholarships would be double that reserved for building a network of universities and the broader recognition of diplomas.

The Italians were disappointed that the budget was not larger. But it was estimated that 29,000 students from the Community would benefit from Erasmus scholarships during the first three years, and that there would be about 3,000 grants to universities to allow them to organise exchange programmes for students and teachers. Commissioner Marin recorded his satisfaction on all aspects but one procedural issue.[145] And it was all much more than Jones, Lenarduzzi or Smith had dreamed of at the drafting stage.[146]

On 15 June 1987, the formal agreement to the Erasmus programme was given by the Council of Ministers, on the double basis of Articles 128 and 235, and approving that it should come into effect immediately.[147] For the first time full Community authority was being exercised for higher education cooperation, with the agreement of Member States. The Decision records that they needed:

(i)   to achieve a significant increase in the number of students from universities ... spending an integrated period of study in another Member State in order that the Community may draw upon an

adequate pool of manpower with first hand experience of
economic and social aspects of other Member States

(ii)   to promote broad and intensive cooperation between universities
in all Member States

(iii)   to harness the full intellectual potential of the universities in the
Community by means of increased mobility of the teaching staff,
thereby improving the quality of the education and training provided by the universities with a view to securing the competitiveness of the Community in the world market

(iv)   to strengthen the interaction between citizens in different
Member States with a view to consolidating the concept of a
People's Europe to ensure the development of a pool of graduates
with direct experience of intra-Community cooperation, thereby
creating the basis upon which intensified cooperation in the
economic and social sectors can develop at Community level

History had been made. With the decision of Erasmus, the idea of
Community-sponsored higher education cooperation had completed a
trajectory that could be traced back to the original, unexpected proposal at the Messina meeting of 1955 signalling that the new Europe
needed close links with universities – both as an indication that this
Europe wished to be defined at least partly in terms of 'learning', 'intelligence' or the 'intelligentsia', and to draw on the intellectual firepower
of European universities to support Community policies.

However, by the time of the events covered in this chapter, ideas for
the Europe of Intelligence had been significantly restricted. The issue
had become a question of a programme only – and 'a little programme'
at that, in the words of Delors – for organised exchange and cooperation between Community universities. Moreover, there was a wide gap
between what the Commission had proposed and what the Council
had accepted. The Commission had proposed that the programme
should aim at 10% of Community students, and should cover such
cooperation activities as joint curriculum development, for which it
had budgeted 175 mn ecus. The Council, one the other hand, refused
to set a target for the number of students, insisting only that most of
the funds went towards top-up funding for student exchange and
mobility, and reducing the total sum by over 50%.

Explaining the decision

This account shows that it is simply not plausible to think the EC decision to create the Erasmus programme was made because of a single

cause – be it the Single European Act, the Gravier ruling of the ECJ or the chaotic way in which a deal was stitched up between the European Council and the Council of Ministers, and the Council and the Commission, and certain member states to approve the programme.

The Council Decision creating the Erasmus programme completed a policy cycle that had begun in the late 1960s, with the problem of not just *what* the Community might do in the higher education policy domain, but also *how* it should do it, and the cycle was influenced by what had gone before. If member state governments were all, more or less, attracted to the idea that the Community should have a university dimension – and ideas for the Europe of Intelligence resurfaced regularly over these years – there was a real problem about how such an idea could be translated into policy in ways which respected university autonomy and national sovereignty, and yet was more dynamic than anything hitherto achieved under pure intergovernmental processes. Over the thirty years a number of different combinations were tried.

In general this account confirms a causal link between an agreed definition of the issue and the existence of a viable policy 'solution' before a decision is made. Getting agreement to the issue can be a long process. As we have seen there was no progress as long as the issue was seen as the creation of a European University. Once the issue was reframed as using Europe for reinforcing cooperation, the higher education policy-making took off. With the 1970s and 1980s development of university networks and joint study programmes, the Commission was able to demonstrate that it had a solution when the issue which interested ministers became one of student mobility. The higher education 'solution', moreover, had a wide appeal. It showed how much could be achieved by using non-binding law and political will, backed by some structured cooperation. And this was long before this became a generalised EC approach in areas of social policy.

However issues and solutions have to be brought together and consensus achieved if there is to be a decision. But while the efforts of policy entrepreneurs had contributed to both issue definition and solution over many years, the decision – in contrast – may be taken, and was in this case, by office holders able to pay only limited attention to the issue. In ways which were characteristic of modern theories of limited rationality and rule following, the ministers of education involved lived with the constraints of the demands on their time, the particularity of the rules under which they operated and the changing combinations of participants – and brought to bear their identities, their judgements about consequences and appropriateness.[148]

In such circumstances decision-making becomes damage limitation. The aspects of the Erasmus decision which attracted ministers' attention were those of financial resources and legal backing. The idea of Europe of the Intelligence took second place.

In the immediate situation it took the leadership of the epistemic community leadership of the rectors – and the un-diplomatic outburst of a Commissioner able to reach the press – to reassert the idea of *why* Erasmus was important. But from then on Erasmus could prove itself in practice – and, in the way that the decisions do, it immediately opened the door to new developments. One policy cycle had ended, but another had already begun.[149]

Part III

The Europe of Knowledge – Why the Idea Recurs

9
Policy Entrepreneurship in EU Higher Education: Process, Actions, Identities

Introduction

The idea of the Europe of Knowledge is recurrent, as we see from the preceding account. What kept bringing it back to the policy-makers' agenda? This account of policy change on higher education within the European Community (EC) institutions draws attention to a factor in the higher education literature. There were almost always well-placed individuals playing an innovative and entrepreneurial role to advance the idea of Community role in higher education. This happened over almost every policy cycle accounted for here since 1955, regardless of the very different historical circumstances. The evidence invites us to make the generalisation that *there are almost always politically skilled individuals to respond in specific contextual and institutional circumstances to the opportunity to advance policy ideas.*

This chapter wishes to advance our knowledge of policy entrepreneurship in considering *how* and *why* some of these individuals acted as they did. I have set out to answer the question by focussing on those working in or around the Commission, including ministers present on the Council. These are not the only individuals to have played an entrepreneurial role in the development of higher education policy, as will be clear from the narrative. But the entrepreneurs in national administrations or in the foundations lie outside the initial research concern which inspired this book. It was my interest in the Commission which generated the questions of how do position and procedure create resources for individuals who want to influence the course of an issue or the course of a policy? How is the 'career' of an issue related to the a career of an individual, as they have emerged in this historically oriented research.[1]

As discussed in the introduction, many commentators on European Community politics view policy entrepreneurs as institutions. There is nevertheless a significant literature of individual policy entrepreneurship. Within the last decade Roberts and King have produced a typology of entrepreneurs based on change agents in a study of American schooling, to widen the concept of policy entrepreneurship to other stages of the policy process.[2] Schneider, Teske and Mintrom, revisited the work of Schumpeter, who famously proclaimed that entrepreneurs are innovators and their function is innovation, for their study of American local government. Having conceptualised 'public' entrepreneurs – public policy entrepreneurs – in terms of a neoclassical economic model, their view of entrepreneurs was as agents for change in the local market for public goods.[3]

Germane to this study is the work which builds on an institutional literature as applied to the European Community and/or Union. As I suggested earlier, two examples stand out as relevant to this work. Dudley and Richardson, in looking at the history of the European Coal and Steel Community, identify individuals over several policy cycles as instrumental in changing 'policy frames', alongside 'power brokers and political heavyweights'.[4] Dyson and Featherstone, in their study of the negotiations that produced European economic and monetary union (EMU), identify 'creative agents' – and among them the promoters of ideas, as well as the *'animateurs, ingénieurs*, and the more or less skilled strategists, the more or less skilled craftsmen'. The insight for this study is that they found personal beliefs functioning as 'road maps' in explaining the behaviour of these agents.[5]

But Kingdon in adapting the original Schumpeter concept to the political arena, and specifically the pre-decision process, remains a reference which others complement but do not replace. His study, in generating core propositions where the goal is to explain the linkage between ideas, identity and function in the evolution of a policy sector, has a continued relevance. Hence the first, and Kingdonesque, proposition of this study is that policy entrepreneurs are identifiable individuals with particular characteristics. They have a claim to a hearing – expertise, an ability to speak for others, or an authoritative decision making position. Such a person is known for political connections or negotiating skills, and more than likely to be persistent.[6] A functional proposition arising out of the Kingdon study of the pre-decision process is that policy entrepreneurship provides a *necessary* though not *sufficient* explanation of policy change in higher education. Policy entrepreneurs have a function to perform in advancing a policy idea towards decision. They characteristically perform this function with an exceptional degree of tenacity and skill. But even the most wily and the most charismatic entrepreneur is at the mercy of events. As Kingdon puts it, the window opens because of some factor beyond the realm of the policy entrepreneur, but the individual takes advantage of the opportunity. In an era before the word 'tsunami' entered the language of horror, he could write 'They are the surfers who wait for a wave'.[7]

However Kingdon does not develop an understanding of beliefs, and is little concerned with institutions. This latter point is no doubt evidence of the stability of American governmental institutions, as contrasted with those in Europe. But the European Union (EU) studies referred to earlier are persuasive in suggesting the importance of the cognitive dimension and the instability of institutions. Dyson and Featherstone make the case persuasively, on the basis of their evidence, that it is the cognitive dimension of normative beliefs about economic policy and historical memories, and by the transmission of knowledge, which create the 'road maps'.[8] Noting that the EMU negotiations had their own process of development, their own particular rhythm and shape, specific to the subject matter and the precise historical context, the factor which gave 'the negotiations ... a life of their own' were 'the flesh and blood people whose motives were very complex and preferences by no means fixed, whose likes, aversions, ambitions and manners played an important part in the dynamics of the process'.

This study, in attempting to deepen our understanding of policy entrepreneurs by using these insights, incorporates the March model which looks for a match of situation, identity and action, into the explanation of policy entrepreneurship. My default model is thus that individual beliefs and identities are likely to play an important part in explaining the effort a policy entrepreneur will exert, and that the wider context and institutional rules explain the opportunity. Hence the following sections examine those policy entrepreneurs, who were closest to the pre-decision process at European level, in terms of their biographies and their opportunities. It starts with a presentation of the selected policy entrepreneurs as linked to one of two policy cycles: the first in 1955–71/72 – the period before it was agreed that ministers of education would cooperate on education under intergovernmental rules but according to EC procedures, a decision that created a policy domain; and the second from 1973–87 when the domain had been established and policy entrepreneurs were working to secure policy decisions.

The policy entrepreneurs: who they were and what they did

Around 1990–91, when, as a journalist, I was reporting on EC education, Jones was widely seen in the Commission as synonymous with
the domain. In the general view, he was the person who made education a policy area, bringing it from nothing in the 1970s to treaty
recognition 20 years later. However, it was satisfactory from a theoretical point of view to discover, through a historical narrative conceptualised on the basis of agenda-setting, that there were always individuals
who could claim to have 'made a difference' to the development of an
EC higher education policy throughout its history – and even more satisfactory that many of them were known names, but not known for an
interest in higher education.

This analysis focuses on the seven officials and politicians associated
with one of four outcomes: the 1957 Euratom treaty agreement to
create a university institution; the 1971 double agreements to cooperate on EC education and higher education[9] and to establish the
European University Institute;[10] the 1976 mixed intergovernmental/
Community agreement to create the Action Programme in education;[11]
and the 1987 Community decision creating the Erasmus programme.[12]
I also include the ambitious 1960 Interim Report on the European
University, on which decision-makers never agreed, as an ambitious
example of policy design and failed entrepreneurship.

To recapitulate who these individuals were. In the policy cycles in
which neither higher education nor education were recognised as a
Community policy domain, they were *Walter Hallstein*, head of
the foreign ministry of the German Federal Republic, who worked
closely with Chancellor Konrad Adenauer. As we have seen, in 1958
Hallstein became the first president of the European Economic Community (EEC) Commission; *Etienne Hirsch*, President of the Euratom
Commission (1958–61); *Olivier Guichard*, French minister of education 1969–72 and *Altiero Spinelli*, Commissioner for industry and
technology 1970–72.

In subsequent policy cycles, the main policy entrepreneur was *Hywel
Ceri Jones*, who holds the record for longevity as an entrepreneurial
individual in higher education and education. He was successively
head of division for education and youth policies within the directorate for education, training and youth policy in DG XII research
(1973–78), director for education and youth policy (1979–88), situated
within DG XII until 1980, and DGV social affairs until 1988. He then
became director of the task force human resources, education, training
and youth (1989–93), which he left to become deputy director-general,

and acting director-general of the DGV social Affairs in 1993. Of the two additional individuals who played a critical role in securing the Erasmus decision, *Peter Sutherland* was Commissioner for education and social affairs in 1985, in addition to his main portfolio as Commissioner for competition, a post he held from 1985–89. *Michel Richonnier* was the cabinet official working to Peter Sutherland on education and training questions in 1985.

In terms of what they did, if we go back to 1955–57, Hallstein's task was to ensure that an issue proposed by the government of the German Federal Republic reached a successful conclusion: this was the proposal for the Community to establish a European University. I claim that it was his advocacy that helped change events and get the European University inscribed on the decision agenda of the six foreign minister members of the European Coal and Steel Community (ECSC), and that it was his work that led to the inclusion in the treaty of an article establishing the European Atomic Energy Community (Euratom), allowing the Community to create a university-level institution. Once the Treaty of Rome was enacted, Hallstein, as president of the Commission, continued to act as advocate for the European University.[13]

Etienne Hirsch emerged as a policy entrepreneur at the stage the Council was making its second attempt to implement the Treaty of Rome European Atomic Energy Community (EAEC) article on the creation of a university institution. His task was to produce a policy design that would demand general assent. He, and the committee he chaired, came up with an ingenious plan to present the European University as one of several higher education issues on which the Community could play a role, producing a map, or even a charter, for a Community-related higher education strategy. The challenge, as in any process of policy modification, was to build up shared beliefs. But one consequence of Hirsch's work was that General de Gaulle demanded that education be removed from Community competence.

Olivier Guichard emerged in 1969, as an advocate for Community on education in general. His task was to change the agenda – an operation that won broad assent. Altiero Spinelli initiated the institutional transition that led to the formation of an educational bureaucracy within the Commission from 1973.

Once there was acceptance for some kind of Community education policy, Jones was the key official on education within the Commission from 1973–93. His task unofficially was to try and get Community competence for the non-Treaty sector of education. He was thus deeply engaged in the pre-decision policy making which produced the 1976 Action Programme on education and, in 1987, the Erasmus programme – the years under study here. From 1973–76, he was both advocate and fixer, in getting recognition that the Community could lead the way in supporting educational innovation, for example for early school leavers, or for the children of migrant workers (children of EC citizens working in member states) – both groups which tended not to rate as a high national priority. At the same time he played a critical role in securing political agreement for two innovative institutions which recognised the primacy of national sovereignty in education but at the same time institutionalised a Community role. These were the advisory structure of the Education Committee and the 'mixed' process of decision-making for education which worked, as appropriate, to both inter-governmental and Community rules.

From the late 1970s, Jones was effective as the strategist who manoeuvred education policy-making ever closer to Community goals – an objective ruled out in 1971 by ministers seeking to define the benefits for education of a Community dimension – and into the social affairs domain, in parallel with cooperation activities in which ministers of education were the decision-makers. Jones was then a key member of the team that secured the programmes of 1988–92, starting with his work with the Commissioner, Peter Sutherland, and the cabinet member, Michel Richonnier, to get approval for Comett (1986) and Erasmus (1987).[14] Jones was thus important in playing a key role in all stages of stabilising and then advancing the higher education – and education – issues, from policy idea (1973) to policy design (1976) to decision (Erasmus, 1987).

I suggest here that Peter Sutherland took the critical steps in 1985 that ensured that the Erasmus project reached the decision-makers' agenda, in a form that he expected would be approved by the Commission and, eventually, the Council of Ministers. During the same period, it was Michel Richonnier who secured the agreement of the Commission bureaucracy for the legislative framework and for unexpectedly large resources.

The explanatory framework

A way of interpreting the questions of how and why policy entrepreneurs act they way they do, is to understand the questions as requiring an explanation of policy entrepreneur effort and policy entrepreneur effectiveness. I have already argued, interpreting Kingdon as a method for structuring a process in which many factors interact over time, by thinking of the situation facing decision-makers in terms of the agenda and alternative choices with which they are presented, we are part way to an explanation. We can see how the process of agenda-setting and alternatives can be analysed, alongside the events recounted in the historical narrative, to provide an explanation of why and when the identity and the opportunities of policy entrepreneurs impinge on the trajectory of an issue. James March goes one further in creating models of decision-making as driven by a 'logic of consequences' or a logic of 'the logic of appropriateness'.[15]

In order to understand policy entrepreneur effort, I have taken an analysis of policy entrepreneurs' prior life experiences as an explanatory factor for the beliefs they hold, to be set alongside character traits such as tenacity or ambition, and the skills needed for the political situation they faced. This use of life experience has been a characteristic of several successful case studies of policy change, and is consistent with an historical approach.[16] Life experience may be interpreted here to include national identity, professional identity and experience of historic events. Linked to events – or in Barzelay's phrase, 'context-in-motion'[17] – the use of biographical information enables us to draw inferences about the past to use in parallel with archives and other evidence to explain policy entrepreneur action. This approach leads to the formulation of topic-related questions: Why did policy entrepreneurs do what they did? How did biographical (and, indirectly, historical) factors affect individual identity and action?

A second set of topic-linked questions – why were the policy entrepreneurs effective or less effective? How did opportunities for change in EC higher education policy emerge and disappear? – is linked by Kingdon to the opportunities the policy entrepreneur has the political skills to exploit. In my view, the concept of opportunity needs more explanation than Kingdon gives it. The way in which Kingdon presents the concept of opportunity, which he projects mainly in terms of events,[18] is no doubt explained by his research in the comparatively stable American political system. Applied to the unstable institutional framework of the EC, however – and underlined by the historical narrative presented here – the concept of opportunity must include the positional resources available for the policy entrepreneur to exploit at the time of intervention.

The following sections discuss these questions in relation to individual entrepreneur's contributions to the policy cycles, or partial policy cycles, that led to the 1971 agreement to co-operate, the 1976 decision to agree a policy design, and the Erasmus Decision, 1987. The chapter

concludes with a survey of what this understanding of policy entrepreneurship identity and policy entrepreneur effectiveness adds to our
understanding of policy entrepreneurship.

Policy making outside a recognised domain, 1955–72

Why life experience led policy entrepreneurs to intervene

Walter Hallstein the first to intervene on the issue of higher education
in the Community, has been dogged in the past by the pejorative
judgement that he was an intransigent technocrat. Ralf Dahrendorf,
the German Commissioner in charge of education from 1973–74, was
one such critic.[19] General de Gaulle in 1965, and the German rectors
also shared this view. Hallstein's own account reflects how deep was
the mutual antipathy on the European University.

> How much further would we have advanced if an unholy alliance of
> reactionary and backward sections of the academic brotherhood –
> which unfortunately exists also in Germany – had not steered the
> original plan for a European University ... into a blind alley.[20]

Recent scholarship, however, has been sympathetic to Hallstein with
some commentators suggesting that he was one of the key, and under-
appreciated figures of European integration, worthy of the title of a
'founding father of the Community'.[21] His book *Der unvollendete
Bundesstaat*, published in German in 1969 and in English under
the title *The Unfinished Federal State* in 1972, epitomised the view that
on Europe rules could never be made, cut and dried, for all eventualities. The book was a plea for a strategy of 'reconciling the necessary European unity with the protection of diversity ... the basic
rule by which Europeans can live together'. European integration was
not 'a static state: it is a process, a continuous creation ... The
European challenge is continuous.[22]

There had been much in Hallstein's experience to make him a passionate believer in an ultimately federal Europe. Born in 1900, he had
lived through the First World War as an adolescent. By the time of the
Second World War, he was an experienced professor of public law
appalled to see his country under a Nazi government. His personal
choice was to keep as far from the government as possible, preferring
to leave a post in the prestigious University of Frankfurt for the relative
isolation of Rostock, on the Baltic Coast. He was also marked by his
experience as an American prisoner-of-war. The Americans encouraged

Hallstein to set up a university within the PoW camp, for which he was enduringly grateful. They also saved him from a Nazi assassination attempt.[23] This period provided Hallstein with enduring contacts, and led, for example, to an invitation from President Eisenhower for the Communities to make a state visit to the US, and to the Ford Foundation's offer to help fund the European University.

After the war, when Hallstein returned to Frankfurt to take up the elected post of rector, he soon came to the notice of Konrad Adenauer, Germany's first post-war Chancellor. Many believe that without Adenauer, Hallstein would never have had a historic role in Europe. The evidence is that the view that the post-war 'German question' needed a 'European' answer, was as much Hallstein's as Adenauer's. It had to be a prime objective of German policy to return to the international stage.[24]

Hallstein's interest in education, which has not been studied, appears coherent with his view that rules cannot be made, cut and dried, for all eventualities. But the Community could do much to set up the framework which would benefit the young, the universities and the economy. It was a vision of a European Higher Education Area. In *The Unfinished Federal State*,[25] Hallstein argued that the Community would need a common market of the intelligence' to exploit the electronics-based industries of the future and to close the technology gap with the US. A free market, liberating the movement of workers as well as that of students and academics, could make a reality of the Community's decision to strive for competition rather than protectionism. But beyond that

> Would not such a market – more than anything else – accord with the concept and the tradition of a university, the most magnificent form of cultural institution created by the European mind?[26]

In that context, the speech that Hallstein made at Messina, emphasising the German desire that the Community should be seen to be doing something for the young, and proposing a Community-created European University as the solution,[27] can be explained as entirely consistent with the beliefs that had formed him.

Etienne Hirsch In his unstinting effort to get a workable plan for the European University, Etienne Hirsch was also driven by the personal beliefs of a fervent European who wanted a federal solution. Like Hallstein, he had been made 'a European' through the events of World War Two. He had been a member of the French Resistance, joining de

Gaulle's Free French Government in Algiers. But Hirsch's life had been even more painfully marked than Hallstein's. Members of his Jewish family and his in-laws had perished in Nazi death camps. He wrote in his memoirs that in the post-war years, even shaking a German hand was difficult though, 'naturally', he did it.[28]

Hirsch was the model of a high-flying technocrat who helped stabilise French Fourth Republic policies and administration as governments came and went, succeeding Monnet as head of the French planning commission. Jean Monnet and the Commission's first secretary-general, Emile Noël, both greatly admired Hirsch. Monnet said that whatever Hirsch decided to do, he did well,

> mastering and simplifying the most complex problems. That came with his engineering training. But I think that above all it was his moral force, his legendary calm which enabled him to resolve problems which are wrongly described as technical since in reality they are responsive to good sense.[29]

In December 1961, when Hirsch had an extension of his period of office vetoed by de Gaulle, the young Nöel wrote to Hirsch, saying, 'I am saddened and disappointed by the decision the six governments have just taken, saddened by the injustice, disappointed that the six governments have so easily torn up the most precious of institutions, the independence of the men who compose the Executives.... [A]lthough I have never worked for you I will always be grateful for the lessons of *sang froid*, and courage given simply and quietly and with a sense of humour. Mr President, and *cher monsieur*, I offer you my deepest sympathy and respect.'[30]

Given his training as a chemical engineer, Hirsch might have been expected to back a scientific university. But although a senior servant of the state, attracted to the European University as an educational resource for training a future elite,[31] it was consistent with his wartime experience that Hirsch should see it as crucial to give priority to the humanities. Hence the hard work to secure the agreement of foreign ministers and diplomatic delegations that any future European University should be a place where the young would be educated together as being in part an instrument of reconciliation.

Hirsch's passionate commitment, and the energy he was prepared to commit to the projects he took up, emerges through the pages of his autobiography. But so does his disappointment. He said of his work for Europe, 'of all the jobs which fate had handed me it was the one which aroused in me the greatest enthusiasm.'[32] In this context, the European

University was a project into which he had put 'all his heart' and about which, he said, he felt 'bitter'.[33] But the question remains, should he not have seen conciliation with the rectors as essential?

Olivier Guichard The personal factors that encouraged Olivier Guichard, the French Minister of Education in 1969, to take an initiative to make higher education – and, for the first time education – an issue for the EC policy agenda, included a 'de Gaulle' factor. But whereas Hallstein and Hirsch had been destroyed by de Gaulle, Guichard had been formed by him. He became the General's *chef de cabinet* in the post-war coalition government designed to help France re-emerge as a great nation after the Occupation, and to close the rift within France between Nazi collaborators and those who had chosen to resist. The Gaullist experience of the 1940s' near destruction of the French nation, inclined them to want a European Community at the service of the nation state – an ideal of *'L'Europe des patries'* – not a federal superstate. Hence, like de Gaulle, Guichard believed that the Community offered institutional resources and common knowledge that member states should share.[34]

Events played their part, too, in developing Guichard's educational vision and, we can assume, his determination to act. As minister of education in 1969, Guichard dealt on a daily basis with a still greatly unsettled university community after 'the events' of May 1968. At the same time, he was frustrated by a lack of action in the one common venue for EC ministers, the Council of Europe. His proposal – picking up on the Bonn Summit agreement of 1961 – that the EC ministers of education should co-operate reflected his no-nonsense pragmatism that effective solutions were needed.

Altiero Spinelli Altiero Spinelli, the man responsible for establishing a basic Commission bureaucracy for education and hence the moving force in institutionalising education in the EC, is another giant of Community history. One well-placed European commentator says of him:

> Few men have appeared and re-appeared at so many different stages in the history of European integration, seeking to stimulate and influence the process from such a variety of vantage points as Altiero Spinelli.[35]

Spinelli propagated his federalist thinking from Mussolini's prisons and the resistance movements. He was the founder and long-time leader of the European Federalist Movement. He was adviser to successive Italian governments. And he was a member of the Commission, an MP and, finally, an Member of the European Parliament (MEP) – a role he combined with the position of leading advocate for a treaty of EU.

Spinelli's European action spanned five decades and helped shape Europe as we know it today.

With such convictions and life experiences, it is not hard to see why Spinelli was ready to take the initiative on behalf of Community higher education and education. Beginning his professional life as a political journalist, followed by his wartime internment by Mussolini, Spinelli turned into one of the earliest theorists of a federal Europe, which he viewed as a rampart against the excesses of the nation state. By the time he arrived at the Commission in 1970, he had been Secretary-General of the European Federalist Movement for more than a decade, the kind of senior lobbyist and counsellor that prime ministers and presidents took seriously. Spinelli was a man of action, a politician determined to make an impact. He writes that one of his heroes was Sir Francis Drake, the 16th century circumnavigator of the globe. Spinelli identified with Drake's prayer:

> Oh Lord God when thou givest to thy servants to endeavour any great matter, grant us also to know that it is not the beginning, but the continuing until it be thoroughly finished, which yieldeth the true glory.[36]

In becoming a Commissioner – a development that surprised his friends – Spinelli was adopting an alternative approach to implementing his belief that 'the purpose of the EC is to unite progressively the destinies of several nations by the development of a body of laws and institutions common to them all, obliging them to face certain great tasks with a common policy and to adopt a common position and responsibility towards the world outside.'[37]

Spinelli believed that, by the 1970s, the EC should be working on an ambitious scale in new policy areas – for the reform of the common agricultural policy, the creation of a European monetary fund, regional policy, an agenda for industry, technology and the environment, and a strengthening of the European Parliament (EP). The book he wrote to coincide with Community enlargement was not 'a vague programme but as an agenda' for the extended construction of Europe by peaceful means. He also placed a strong emphasis on individual rights.[38]

Although Spinelli was highly critical of the extreme nationalism projected through many school systems, education was not part of his core strategy. Indeed, education gets no mention as a possible Community policy in *The European Adventure*.[39] His decisive action to get his hands on this policy sector, in 1971, – *'porteur de l'avenir'* – is most

plausibly explained by his recognition, as the Commissioner concerned with research and technology, of the way such a policy could
serve the Community.

Why policy entrepreneurs were effective (or not), 1955–72

Exploiting supportive procedures In the period before higher education
and education acquired their own policy venue, individuals working to
advance EC higher education issues operated within a framework
determined by the central project for European integration. They could
not deploy their skills or exhibit their tenacity until they had identified
the opportunity for action or had the problem thrust upon them. The
opportunities consisted of events and procedures.

Messina was an opportunity for the Germans of the Federal Republic,
who had been nursing the idea of a Europe of the Intelligence, as the
account by the former professor, Alfred Müller-Armack, makes clear.[40]
Influential figures in and around government believed German universities had become isolated and inward-looking. This group was seeking
an opportunity to win support for their view, and the Messina meeting
was just such an opportunity. The prevailing political mood – both at
the meeting and back in the Member State chanceries – favoured new
ideas to advance European integration, taking it beyond the ECSC. The
six member state governments had been humiliated by the failures in
1953–54 to achieve a European political or defence community, and
badly wanted a success. The German proposal put forward at Messina
had the additional advantage that a project aimed at Europe's younger
generation would play well on the international stage, and was consistent with the Adenauer-Hallstein strategy of making post-war Germany
diplomatically visible.

The institutional and procedural structures available to the policy
entrepreneurs were in themselves resources for advancing a policy idea.
Hallstein and his colleagues would have identified the opportunity to
place an item on the agenda, and, as experienced diplomats, no doubt
calculated that the Messina meeting was the kind of occasion that typ-
ically had an overcrowded agenda. That meant many issues would be
carried forward for lack of time for discussion, rather than rejected out
of hand. That is what happened. As we have seen Paul-Henri Spaak,
foreign minister of Belgium and initiator of the Messina meeting, was
to write in his memoirs:

> So many ideas had been advanced and so many problems examined
> that the ministers were unable to make an altogether rational
> choice.[41]

In negotiations thereafter, ministers – and their governments – agreed that not every proposal had to be defined in detail before the signature of the treaty: their attention was focussed on the big issue of how to get a successful outcome on European integration.

The fact that proposal for the European University went forward to the treaty to be incorporated as Article 9.2, albeit in an ambiguous form must have reflected the judgement of Hallstein, as head of the negotiating team, not to cause an unnecessary showdown with the French before the treaty was signed. For he would have discovered in May 1956 that the European University had been switched from the draft EEC treaty to the Euratom treaty. Nor did he apparently object to the ambiguous formula that went into the draft Treaty of Rome (EAEC), according to which the Community would create 'an institution of university status'. It allowed the Germans to interpret this as the European University and the French to believe that they had avoided it.[42]

But thereafter the situation changed. By the time the treaty was signed and ready to be implemented, Hallstein was President of the EEC Commission. On the one hand, he could bring to bear new institutional resources, in support of his Euratom colleagues and his own personal prestige. For example, the contacts he had developed as one of America's elite prisoners of war, had enabled Hallstein to approach the Ford Foundation for support in funding the European University, should it be agreed.

At the same time, Hallstein's greatest ambitions were focussed on other fields, once he was EEC Commission President. The responsibility for steering the representatives of the six through the debate on what such a university should be had passed to the Euratom Commission. He was in a characteristic situation of a policy entrepreneur. The issue remains but participants change.[43] Hallstein's camp had even lost the support of the West German foreign ministry's cultural department, which had chosen to back his old enemies in the West German rectors' organisation. This situation may have resulted from the arrogance that Dahrendorf argued typified senior public servants in the post-war period. But it is equally likely that different institutional pressures meant Hallstein no longer had to be, or wished to be, entrepreneurial on this issue, in order to fulfil his essential goal of advancing European integration.

Facing a hostile context Hirsch was in a much more difficult position than Hallstein over the European University. He was faced with a problem for which decision-makers wanted a policy solution, and on which there was a previous record of failure. Hirsch did not have a 'solution' ready for the 'problem' though he recognised the need to produce an alternative.[44] Furthermore, he was working with diplomats and nominated university representatives in a diplomatic, not an educational, venue. Yet despite the relatively few resources available to him, the alternative developed by Hirsch and his carefully constructed Interim Committee on the European University[45] was an ambitious attempt at finding a solution to the European University issue through classic processes of policy modification. Along with his assistant Mercereau, and the committee, Hirsch had tried to build a broad coalition, by recombining existing ideas into a 'new' package.[46] Hence the report made proposals for Europeanising higher education in general. Examples of consensus building included giving a European dimension to the national research and training institutes, as the French wanted, and for making universities more European, through exchanges, as the European rectors' organisation wanted. Hirsch also succeeded in getting agreement that when the European University was established it would be in Florence, as the Italians wanted. So why did the process of advocating an EC policy design, turn to Hirsch's disadvantage?

If we follow Baumgartner and Jones, Hirsch was in the classic trap of the policy maker who needs decision-makers' approval. In putting forward the Interim Committee report, its members drew decision-makers' attention to the fact that the key issue was Community power, not the substantive issue of the universities. Hirsch himself had possibly underestimated the real danger – which did not, in fact, come from the German rectors' organisation, as Hirsch, like Hallstein, had supposed,[47] but from de Gaulle and from member state governments. Once there was widespread unease about using the treaties – together or separately – as the legal base of the European University, as the Commission presidents had advocated, no national government wanted the Commission or even a Community institution as the ultimate decision-maker on the subject.

However there are signs that on this issue, Hirsch never really understood member states' reticence. A telling exchange with de Gaulle, which Hirsch quotes in his memoirs, has him telling off the French president for not respecting Community rules on disclosure of nuclear information, to which de Gaulle responds: 'I am the judge of France's interests.' De Gaulle ensured that Hirsch was not reappointed to his post. The best that Hirsch could manage was to become a shadow minister for de Gaulle's chief challenger, one François Mitterrand, and to promote the cause of the European University in a personal capacity.

Hirsch's experience illustrates that operating in a venue highly exposed to macro-political change exacerbates the chances of linkages between sectoral issues in ways which a policy entrepreneur is unlikely to be able to control. In this case the fact that his interlocutors in the Council of Ministers were ministers of foreign affairs added to the vulnerability of the European University issue.[48] They were going to be far more attentive to the arguments being advanced by de Gaulle that the Community was over-reaching its powers – a tack he pursued in alliance with Germany's Chancellor Adenauer, and through his press conferences – than the possible case for the European University.

In such circumstances, could any policy entrepreneur have succeeded? When late in life Hirsch wrote his autobiography, he was phlegmatic. He entitled it *'Ainsi va la vie'* (That's the way life is).[49]

Taking advantage of a favourable political situation Guichard, the next identifiable individual to change the EC policy agenda, was effective in the short term in securing that change. Like Hallstein, he was favoured by events. The expansionist Hague Summit offered agenda-setting opportunities to anyone with ideas. Guichard wished to advocate an idea that his predecessor as French minister of education had already launched in another forum – the Council of Europe. He was thus recombining an idea consistently upheld by the French, that of inter-governmental cooperation on higher education or education, with the Bonn Summit idea of using an EC forum to do so. Given a growing dissatisfaction with the Council of Europe, he could count on allies among a number of other ministers of education. His fellow ministers did not feel threatened by the new policy idea, which explicitly presented the EC's educational role as helping nation states solve common problems.

Guichard, as an experienced politician, and with a ministry staff at his disposal, had effectively identified his opportunity. The Hague Summit of 1969 was the occasion for a new generation of leaders to demonstrate that 'Europe' was once more 'on the move'. EC leaders seized the opportunity to set out an ambitious Community agenda of enlargement and extended Community powers. De Gaulle's continuous efforts to restrict the powers of the Community had almost destroyed it. Post-war reconciliation was no longer the dominant point of reference. At issue now was the Community's very survival.

A procedural factor that secured a place on the agenda for Guichard's proposal was that his action had the effect of opening a window of opportunity for others.[50] Their combined efforts led to decisions – concrete outcomes and the completion of a policy cycle – with the

1971 decision by Ministers of Education to cooperate as EC ministers.[51] As we have seen, the Italians had been looking for the chance to revive the European University project since the 1961 Bonn Summit, when the Hirsch proposals were formally buried and the Italians were invited to take sole charge of the project. Following the Guichard initiative, the Italians started to look for common ground with the French, at a series of meetings that were followed by inter-governmental conferences on the European University. The Belgians, in alliance with the Commission, then seized the opportunity to bring the issue of an EC ministers of education meeting – promised at the Bonn Summit – to the Community's formal agenda. The new dynamic was also an opportunity perceived by Spinelli to get a basic organisation in place in the Commission. The final piece in the agenda jigsaw was the personal deal between the Italian and French ministers of education to support each other's proposals, come what may.

Procedural issues also explain why Guichard's success in getting the idea of inter-governmental cooperation on the policy agenda was not matched at the implementation stage. First, the process for dealing with the project had the same shortcomings as the increasingly criticised Council of Europe, with the working group of the Committee of Permanent Representatives (COREPER) tackling the issue by intergovernmental bargaining. Second, the participants changed: Guichard was moved to another ministry in 1972 so he did not maintain his personal involvement in the project. It was thus not surprising to find that after 18 months, the combination of circumstances had left working party members in a situation in which they were unable to agree on anything substantive.

Exercising strategic judgement Spinelli's intervention is largely explained as an instance in which preceding events and planned events shaped a policy initiative. The favourable context in which Guichard had operated partially explains Spinelli's effectiveness in helping to establish a policy domain, as he did by ensuring that the EC Ministers of Education met in 1971, and that the Commission created a structure – albeit small – with a responsibility for educational policy.[52]

The Hague Summit had generated a full education agenda. Other than the Guichard proposal for cooperation on education in general, some elements of the Interim Committee's recommendation that universities be made more European also survived. The Belgians wanted trans-border universities. The Italians wanted to resurrect a commitment to a European University. Some university associations wanted to build on the new political wave; others, like the rectors, wanted to ensure they had a place in a policy process. But it was the agreement of the ministers of education to implement the 1961 Bonn Summit recommendation and to meet as EC ministers that provided the procedural push for the Commission to structure some kind of bureaucratic support.

Had Spinelli not had a supportive political climate – that of pressure to implement the Hague Summit proposals before Community enlargement took place – it seems inconceivable that he would have acted. He clearly was not driven by the idea of education as such, although, like so many of his time, he was deeply committed to the Community as a cultural project. His cabinet staff could not recall the issue education as such ever being raised. One factor, confirmed by the Commission official, Mercereau, is that Spinelli himself was not interested in the detail of education policy-making.[53] Mercereau, having been identified by Spinelli, was encouraged to make propositions and to implement the detail, as he did in setting up the expert report on Community policy, chaired by Professor Janne.[54]

Spinelli was, after all, a political figure of the Italian left who wanted visibility on a bigger stage than education. His attention was focussed on research and industry, and the possibility of the environment as an EC policy area. Where education was concerned, Spinelli deployed his efforts in creating alliances within the Commission: with the Commissioner for administration, whose support was needed for an organisational change; and with Emile Noël, with whom Spinelli shared a Resistance past and who was known to be interested in an education dimension to Community activity.

Judging from the files which Noël kept on enlargement, that fact that was around the corner, scheduled for 1973, and that it would include the UK, provided a spur for the Commission to act quickly to install changes the British could not undo. Hence an opportunity arose for a politically-minded individual with highly developed strategic skills to move in quickly. In addition, Spinelli's guile in his dealings within the Commission to ensure that he, rather than a rival, Albert Borschette, should oversee education, are typical of the entrepreneur linking the opportunity and the action.

Although Spinelli was regarded, by British officials at least, as disorganised, he successfully carried out something that none of the previously identified individuals had done in creating conditions for future entrepreneurship in higher education and education more generally. He responded with an effective strategy to an opportunity to act in the policy area of education – an issue given political significance by all member states following the university upheavals of 1968. It was Spinelli who linked intellectual problem-solving to the issue of policy capacity: creating an institutional venue for effective policy-making, building on the interest of EC Ministers of Education to meet, as agreed at the Bonn Summit of 1961. But the price of deciding priorities was that, in contrast, a Community vision of higher education – or a Community policy for education more generally – was scarcely advanced. The Commissioner's agenda was crowded. He gave the issue episodic attention. Hence there was no blueprint prepared for the post-enlargement Community, as Dahrendorf was to remark critically, only the Janne report.

Cumulative effectiveness The outcome of events in 1971, which established an EC education policy domain, relate, in my view, to all four individuals discussed here. Although no one individual completely achieved the objectives they had set themselves, the group had a cumulative effectiveness. In responding to the idea that the Community and universities should have some mutually beneficial relationship, Hallstein, Hirsch, Guichard and Spinelli had – serially – got higher education onto the EC decision agenda, modified the policy with a policy design, started a new agenda for EC level cooperation, and established the machinery for policy-making. Of the four, Spinelli has a special place for making the far from inevitable judgement that the priority action should be to create a dedicated policy venue for education policy making – and one, as befitted an ambitious individual, under his aegis.

Policy making within a recognised domain (i) 1973–76

Why life experience led policy entrepreneurs to intervene

Ralf Dahrendorf In the period following the establishment of education as a recognised domain, Dahrendorf has been identified as a crucial figure in carrying on Spinelli's work.[55] This would seem a plausible suggestion – were it not for the evidence. In 1973, Ralf Dahrendorf was the first Commissioner to have education in his title. However the narrative presented here indicates that, although Dahrendorf's intervention was decisive in negotiating directives on mutual recognition for doctors and others, he had no entrepreneurial ambitions to build on the opportunity for the Community to develop a policy of educational cooperation. As he told one interviewer: 'I felt my chief job was suppressing paper.' Dahrendorf made a different choice. In his view foundations should be left to do innovative work.[56]

Dahendorf's personal scepticism, directed in 1973 towards an institutionalised EC role in higher education or education more generally, may be explained above all by two factors. First, he was, brought up under a constitution that decentralised education policy-making and management. Second, he was a centrist politician, opposed to Spinelli's left wing and federalist politics. A member of Spinelli's federalist cabinet recalls, 'Dahrendorf was the laid-back liberal' who would not have got the EC into new policy areas in the way Spinelli had succeeded in doing.[57] Dahrendorf was equally opposed to what he described as the 'pure theory of the first Europeans', a reference to Hallstein's earlier orientation.[58] As a leading academic with a background in philosophy and sociology, lauded in Germany, the US and the UK – and as a politician – Dahrendorf was one of those respected 'thinkers who could combine professions of belief, practical experience and a political-strategic programme, on the basis of an academic model of reflection'.[59] Ultimately, the issue was a matter of conviction: education had no place in the Community, except as a supporting policy, for example for treaty-linked issues of freedom of movement.

Hywel Ceri Jones Hywel Ceri Jones, architect of an EC education and training policy and co-inventor of the Erasmus programme, had a different life experience from all the individuals discussed above. He was not a grandee – or as the French say, *'un grand commis de l'Etat'* – like Hallstein and Hirsch. Nor did he have the political stature of Spinelli or Dahrendorf. But his life experience did, in combination with his ambition and his energy, make him determined to take a lead on EC education, personally and professionally.

Jones was a convinced European. The UK joining the EEC in 1973 had been a positive and defining moment for him, a moment he viewed as heralding new cultural and economic benefits to the British Isles. Hence his declaration: 'The entry decision was a watershed in British life. I wanted to be part of the new era.'[60] Furthermore, Jones was a politician at heart, albeit an official by profession. He had come to the Commission as a politically committed left-winger who viewed the Community as an instrument with which to advance such values as equality. He had made a name for himself as a radical student politician, president of his Welsh student union. Jones was also highly articulate and a great socialiser. One story which does the rounds is that he always tried to organise EC meetings outside Brussels to coincide with the international rugby calendar.[61]

Jones' own higher education took place in a formative period, when beliefs about conditions for social change were widely discussed. He preceded the 1960s expansion that transformed universities across Europe from highly elite institutions to those taking – in the words of the Robbins report, published in Britain – all those who were qualified for and who desired higher education.[62] But Jones had a prolonged university life which brought him into contact with many who the first in their families to go to university,[63] heralding a generation that was to revolt against the straitjacket of post-war attitudes. Jones was also part of the first generation in Britain to be freed of the obligation of military service. This was a new type of youth.

In contrast with those who had earlier advanced the policy agenda on EC higher education, Jones also had 'hands-on' experience of the education world. After university, including an unfinished dissertation on the Communist-induced split of the 1920s French left, Jones took a postgraduate teaching diploma. He then had ten years' experience as a development officer and administrator in the innovative University of Sussex, just founded in the 1960s. The experience established Jones as an advocate of both teacher and academic initiative, as well as an instinctive opponent of 'harmonisation'. For Jones, 'harmonisation'[64] meant centralised control – anathema to the British education system of his day. An aversion to centralised control profoundly marked Jones' career. Although – after the events discussed here – he would have liked the Treaty of Maastricht to give the Community power to make directives to reinforce cooperation in 1991, he convincingly demonstrated during his professional life that he saw the Community as a resource, not a regulator.[65]

Why policy entrepreneurs were effective (or not)

Political opportunism in responding to and using structure We can see that working to Dahrendorf in 1973, Jones was operating in a context highly favourable to the development in 'new' policy areas. The Paris Summit of 1972, celebrating the EC's successful negotiations to expand the Community to nine member states, specifically welcomed policy development in areas concerned with non-material values'. Furthermore they did not have to fight for what their predecessors had achieved. Spinelli, assisted by Mercereau, had facilitated the acceptance of higher education and education as an EC policy domain. The issue was no longer 'why' there might be EC activity in education, but 'what' activity was envisaged.

Dahrendorf's departure from the Commission in 1974, gave Jones the policy monopoly conditions that are most productive for the development of a policy idea.[66] If he did not totally control the venues in which the policy image was being developed and stabilised – that is, his division in the Commission and in the Education Committee, created in 1974[67] – he was nevertheless in a 'safe haven' that could provide numerous opportunities for a policy entrepreneur to try out new ideas.[68] These venues provided resources.

The first resource Jones could draw on was that he was operating full-time within a specialist bureaucracy. This distinguished him from Hirsch or Spinelli. Jones also had the opportunity and the motivation to take advantage of a policy community's thinking – an opportunity he exploited, developing contacts with interest groups and the self-styled 'Europe of education' – researchers and university activists and educators, many of them associated with the European Cultural Foundation (ECF) – as a way of encouraging the promotion of ideas. Those ideas could then be presented to the Commission and to Ministers, meeting in June 1974. The document presented to ministers was in effect an outline plan, reflecting *'l'air du temps'*, as radical educators viewed it, in terms of educational decentralisation, partnerships between universities, teacher co-operation – and increased opportunities for students and pupils.

The fact that Jones was effective in stabilising the EC education issue in developing an outline for educational co-operation in the Community[69] is best explained by his initial judgement that he could work in a complementary way with Dahrendorf.[70] As an ambitious young official, Jones craved a scheme for imaginative Community action where Dahrendorf did not. However, Jones strongly supported the principle that the Community should explicitly reject any ambition to harmonise national systems. That stance created an atmosphere of trust between the two men. With Jones ready to accept the principles put forward by Dahrendorf, he enjoyed a significant degree of autonomy. This was enhanced by the fact that neither his director nor his director-general appear to have followed the issue of education closely.

Taking risks and countering hazards It is striking in this account that Jones – like all true entrepreneurs – took calculated risks. We can take three examples. First, in drafting the 1974 Commission document on Education in the Community to be approved by the Council, Jones countered the minimalist aspirations of Dahrendorf with a dynamic vision. Jones and his team put forward in the outline plan a limited number of policy issues for development, thus appearing realistic. At the same time, however, they ensured that, in terms of jurisdiction, some issues would be conducted by inter-governmental co-operation which others, derived from common market law, would follow treaty procedures. This strategy of a mixed – and ambiguous – process developed in breadth and depth after the ministers' meeting of 1974, resulting in the action programme for education, approved in 1976. This consisted of 22 headings for action, ranging from encouraging a better diffusion of information about school systems throughout the EC, to pilot schemes for higher education cooperation.

Jones' second gamble was to get the ECF to provide the technical support that was not available from the Commission in 1973–74 – possible under the rules of the time. This success was linked to Jones' good relations with the 'Europe of education', and the creative energy of Raymond Georis, its Secretary-General of the ECF, which created the European Institute of Education in Paris, with French government support. The educators took the view that 'Europe must strive for innovation not harmonisation.... Europe must encourage experiments, new approaches and take risks'.[71] The institute was a huge resource for the Commission both in policy-making and management terms. By the scholar Ladislav Cerych, and with Alan Smith, later of the Commission, managing the pilot projects, the institute explains why both the joint study programmes and Erasmus were able to get under way so quickly.

The third example of risk-taking was Jones' strategic decision to develop links to employment and social affairs ministers, as well as ministers of education. This followed a breakdown in the Council process with ministers of education, who thought the Commission had exceeded its competence – the Grey Areas affair of 1978. The Jones strategy, which included making his directorate part of DGV social affairs, created some ambiguity about the Community's purpose in relation to education. It also increased the suspicions of ministers of education, who, as a UK national official put it, feared they were being manoeuvred into EC 'common policy' when they thought that they were engaging in inter-governmental cooperation, backed by the resources of the Community budget and the expertise of the Commission.'[72] But Jones' efforts effectively opened a door to higher education- related policy development in the interests of the Community. Work in the 1980s related to university cooperation and to information technology, contributed greatly to the Comett and Erasmus decisions.

Working for a creative consensus A significant element of Jones' effectiveness was that he did not attempt to conquer a new policy area by drawing on his well-documented Welsh charm[73] and past political radicalism, to propose new and provocative ideas to a hard-line Commission structure. Jones sought consensus. In 1974, Jones daringly, given his position as a 'new boy' in the Commission, set out to obtain a policy-making structure in which both the Council and the Commission played a role.[74]

It was important to the outcome that Jones had identified a real problem and a creative solution. If the failed Council of Europe model were not to be resurrected, he had to persuade member states that only an EC role supporting activity in volunteer institutions would get away from the 'talking shop' formulae of inter-governmental institutions. And if the EC were to support such as institutional initiative, resources would be needed, requiring a policy-making structure that respected member states' sensitivities over EC interference in national systems, while building a dynamic into co-operation. The support of the EP would also be required in making EC funding available for such activities as conferences, publications and pilot actions.

Jones' success in getting ministers to agree to the Education Committee formula was the essential first step in his policy building venture. The establishment of the 'dual' institution allowed Jones to create the Action Programme in education, out of which most 1990s EC policy action on education grew. The acceptance of the Action Programme principles made it possible to approach the European Parliament, which at the time was able to take initiatives to finance pilot policy schemes. These linked steps gave education a 'line' within the EC budget, and provided stability for the Action Programme. That in turn demonstrated the pilot policy development that was to become the core of the Erasmus programme.

Seizing the complexity of the situation, understanding the institutional 'keys' and having the kind of personality that inspired confidence, Jones became the first individual in the EC to demonstrate a benign form of Community intervention in the sensitive area of higher education and education. The fact that academics and students today take it for granted that they can more easily move around Europe for studies and research on the basis of partnerships, rather than on the basis of (conflicting) national rules and bilateral arrangements owes much to Jones' ability to match an opportunity with appropriate action.[75]

Policy making within a recognised domain (ii) 1985

How life experience led the policy entrepreneur to intervene

Peter Sutherland Peter Sutherland's decisive action to back the development of the Comett and Erasmus programme decisions, in his brief stint in 1985 as Commissioner for education and social affairs establish him as a policy entrepreneur. The issues were outside his main concerns as Commissioner for Competition. He had no obligations in the matter. Few Commissioners for education have been active. He could easily have discouraged his officials. Instead he liked the programmes, he believed they would work, and he took the risk.

Sutherland's action is best explained by his experience of law and politics as Ireland's attorney-general – a role in which he was also a swift decision-maker. He came to the Commission's education portfolio as a man of action, both professionally and physically. (As a young and sporting figure, Sutherland shared Jones' love of rugby.) He had arrived in Brussels with the view that a Commissioner should be an entrepreneur, and he had formed a view about what was appropriate action in higher education or education for the Community. In his view, the Erasmus idea fitted the bill: 'The proposal did not threaten existing national competences on education policy but rather became an attractive adjunct to them'.[76] Sutherland had the kind of imagination which seized on the Erasmus proposal, as harking back to a golden medieval age when Irish students journeyed to Paris, Salamanca and Rome. But rather more important, in terms of eventual and necessary support from fellow Commissioners and the Council of Ministers, he was convinced he could make the case for Erasmus as complementing the single market strategy being developed by Jacques Delors and Arthur Cockfield.[77]

The two individuals on whom Sutherland counted to deliver the higher education projects – Jones and Michel Richonnier – were both knowledgeable about education, and both had a prior experience which made them believe in the Erasmus project. Richonnier, Sutherland's cabinet adviser, was the classical French administrator, trained to think in terms of the strong role for public authority and with an attachment to strategic planning as an instrument of policy development. He had come to the notice of Sutherland's *chef de cabinet* because of his work at the *Commissariat au Plan*. Richonnier's starting point was thus domestic: he viewed the Community as the common base from which to combat a three-fold crisis affecting nation states, namely, unemployment, and the change in the nature of work and social security funding. The EC could, he argued, provide significant investment in education. But he also reflected the values of a member state that considered the Community its playing field, and one where education was vital. Hence his impassioned plea in the French plan document quoted earlier: 'It is not possible to build

Europe without European-minded people.... There will not be a second generation of Europeans – to take on from the heroic first generation – if the youth of today does not acquire a sense of Europe, the reality and the usefulness of the Community construction.'[78]

Why policy entrepreneurs were effective

A favourable climate for a particular idea The Erasmus proposal was another case of educational advance being most immediately conditioned by the larger Community context. In 1985, several events had heralded a new upsurge of energy in the Community after the recession of the late 1970s. The most immediate had been the Fontainebleau Summit of June 1984, held under the French presidency. Having resolved the British budget question, which had poisoned the previous 15 summits, the French head of state, François Mitterrand, had succeeded in getting fellow leaders to focus on the Community's future. The European Council agreed to establish two *ad hoc* committees. One was the People's Europe committee, chaired by the Italian, Pietro Adonnino. The other was the Dooge committee on political, economic and institutional reforms. This was convened to follow up on such initiatives as the Genscher-Colombo proposals, the Stuttgart solemn declaration and the draft Treaty on EU from the EP. But it had an effect on the framing of Sutherland's ideas because it was complementary to the Commission's White Paper of 1985, and the single market project in general.

Erasmus was also a case in which a change of personnel provided a boost for change. The appointment of the new Commission – with Jacques Delors as president, and Peter Sutherland as commissioner for education – opened a political window. Jones had become the entrepreneur with an idea to sell. As the senior policy official on education since 1973 and the 'inventor' of the 1976 Action Programme, Jones carried authority. His track record in piloting most of the 22 points in the Action Programme through to decision and implementation had made him a Commission figure, well known in EC and government and education circles as the advocate of European action in education and training.[79] Jones made no secret that the advancement of higher education was never his first priority. But this did not make him less effective as an advocate. He could calculate without difficulty that this was the sector most likely to produce a breakthrough to a Community decision. Sutherland's willingness to act was the opportunity Jones had been waiting for.

Fulfilling respective tasks with flair The initial steps taken to develop a programme proposal resulted from three individuals fulfilling their respective tasks with above-average determination and creativity. Sutherland, as Commissioner, was the individual whose task it was to bridge the divide between policy development and political decision-making within the Commission, by presenting the Erasmus draft decision as the solution to problems about which the Community leadership was concerned. Jones, as director of education and vocational training and youth policy, was the individual with the task of producing a viable policy 'solution'. Richonnier, the cabinet member, was the individual in the middle, the Commissioner's adviser and the 'safe pair of hands', the go-between who had to ensure that the policy proposal was framed by Jones' team as an effective solution to a political problem that concerned the Commission's decision-makers, and the negotiator with the legal and financial services to get the best resource deal possible.

The opportunity for Sutherland, who had ambitions to become president of the Commission after Delors,[80] was to show how much he could do and how effective he could be. And Sutherland did indeed demonstrate clear leadership, as indicated by his requesting all relevant files from Jones and Jean Degimbe, the director-general of DGV social affairs, for his own policy review, saying, 'Don't worry how big the files are.'[81] Jones' story of Sutherland coming back after a weekend, 'asking the right questions,' adding that 'he had swiftly spotted what was possible,' shows how Sutherland impressed those around him – a classic example of 'certification'.[82] Furthermore, Sutherland stayed involved, despite the fact that education was a minor portfolio for him. He held preparatory meetings with the social affairs staff, took part in cabinet discussions, helped in the preparation of the Commission decisions and, in the case of Comett, took on discussions with university rectors and negotiations with the European Parliament and the Council of Ministers.[83]

Richonnier, Sutherland's specialist adviser, demonstrated how important it was for a cabinet member to move quickly and accurately. He had calculated that the education dossier that would consume, at most, five percent of Sutherland's time.[84] The challenge was to capture Sutherland's attention. He took the most innovative Commissioner as a role model and bait. Drawing on the reputation of Etienne Davignon, who had been highly successful in restructuring and extending Community research policy, Richonnier told Sutherland, 'You could be the Davignon of education and training.'[85] Sutherland was open to persuasion.

But Sutherland was also a careful judge of whether all the conditions for success were present. As we have seen, he had three criteria which persuaded him to commit to developing Erasmus and Comett. These were (i) the opportunity inherent in a dynamic new Commission that had set the goal of completing the single market, (ii) the compatibility with his role as a Commissioner whose main portfolio was competition, and (iii) his judgement on the chances of receiving a viable policy proposal.

The consequence of Sutherland's favourable decision that draft directives for Comett and Erasmus should be developed was that Jones and Richonnier had to work as a team, and to be clear about the objectives and the content of future programmes. The fact that this was not difficult was an important factor. They each believed that a 'solution' to the challenge posed by the technology revolution could be a programme for technology transfer between the universities and their economic regions – the future Comett programme. They also shared a vision for Erasmus of university co-operation and the opportunity for students to study and live in another culture as – in Kingdon terms – a 'solution' to a 'problem'.

However Jones and Richonnier had to deliver on different tasks. Faced with the policy development task, Jones had his solution ready and was able to get his team to start drafting a proposal. At an initial stage, the vision reflected a concern not so much about the Single Market but of a People's Europe. The programme activities were largely lifted from pilot projects run by Jones' directorate in association with a technical agency over the previous eight years. Jones was at this moment in the position of the policy entrepreneur described by Kingdon:

> You have to have a loaded gun and look for targets of opportunity. There are periods when things happen and if you miss them, you miss them.... [So] you keep your gun loaded and you look for opportunities to come along. 'Have idea, will shoot.'[86]

But the ideas had to be credible too. Had the joint study programmes not been so popular and so effectively managed, had they not had credibility within the policy community and at EC leadership level, they might not have the attracted political attention which made them seem viable to Sutherland and Richonnier.

Facing the unexpected pragmatically It is often suggested that it was the European Court of Justice (ECJ) ruling in the Gravier case that enabled the Erasmus decision to be made, by offering the chance to link higher education to the treaty by means of Article 128 – an Article that had the procedural advantage of operating under simple majority voting. Such a voting procedure removed the advantage that the larger states habitually brought to bear, and heralded the promise of far more generous budgets and the development of education and training policy more generally. The downside was to render Community procedures incomprehensible to the general public, and lay the Commission open to the charge that it was using jurisprudence in a domain in which political agreement was the unwritten rule. But Sutherland's cabinet did not hesitate. As one of them put it: 'We took the Erasmus proposal much more seriously after Gravier'.[87]

It is significant that Sutherland, whose role was to win the political support of the Commission and to gauge how best to get a favourable response from the Council, judged that while Gravier was important, its importance should not be exaggerated. As we have seen, his calculation rested on the quality of the proposal and the case that could be made for the programme:

> Hywel Jones and his team together with my Cabinet had prepared a very good proposal. I believed that the Erasmus proposal could capture public imagination and gain the support of education ministers. It was also extremely cost effective and thus finance ministers too could be persuaded. The proposal did not threaten existing national competencies on education policy but rather became an attractive adjunct to them

For Jones, using a vocational training legal base did not provide any problem. Indeed, it was coherent with his political goal of extending educational opportunities through Community mechanisms. He later recalled:

> I had done more than most since 1981 to try and persuade national governments to think of education and employment together. The world we were in needed to think in terms of education and training. Besides I had always been pragmatic about the kind of legal base we would get for Erasmus. I believed that it was so well-established that something had to turn up.[88]

The entrepreneurial calculation that the legal niceties of looking to a vocational training provision of the Treaty would not diminish political support was borne out in June 1985. The European Council in Milan backed both the Dooge report, which interested Sutherland, and the Adonnino report on *A People's Europe*, which requested the Council and Ministers of Education to promote further inter-university co-operation by establishing a programme for student exchanges. This would be supplemented by the introduction of a European system of academic credits transferable throughout the Community. Other important support came from the university rectors, who were ready to lobby ministers in favour of Erasmus. As we have seen, the rector of the prestigious university of Leuven (KUL) rallied persuaded his Minister of Education to back a plan for a conference of the Erasmus universities to coincide with the Council of Ministers discussion.

Success for a team A crucial factor in bringing the draft decision to a successful outcome was the way the three individuals worked together to complete the proposal. This illustrates an aspect of policy entrepreneurship that must be common, although not familiar in the literature in policy change – still less so in the literature on the EC and education. Once the response to the Gravier judgement was decided, the factors accounting for success were linked to teamwork. Policy development was a responsibility which remained shared between Richonnier and Jones, with Sutherland keeping a watching brief.

The challenge to produce a good quality proposal rested on Richonnier's shoulders as well as Jones'. Richonnier recognised that he, Sutherland and Jones had complementary roles. It was Richonnier's responsibility to see that the proposal was delivered on time and with an appropriate legal base and budget. Richonnier's 'added value', drawing on his well-developed ideas on the need for an EC education policy, was ambitious thinking about the scale of the budget, and a certain clout with his fellow Frenchmen in the cabinet of the Commission President, Jacques Delors. Richonnier's 'strong state' background and his prior involvement with the issue inclined him to argue for budgeting for a hitherto unimagined target of 10% student mobility – a figure running at 1% at the time.

This account shows national solidarities were important. Richonnier' a French contacts in the Cabinet of the Commission President, Jacques Delors, were especially valuable, bringing with them support from Delors himself. But the objective was to bring functional pressure to bear. The linkage to Delors' cabinet made for powerful pressure on the Danish Commissioner, Henning Christophersen, responsible for the budget. He was presented with the case that an unexpectedly large demand for an EC education activity was minute in absolute terms, and would be supported by the European Parliament.

Meanwhile, Jones intensified his networking activities. This was as networks within the university community were becoming stronger with their increasing interest and involvement in developments. After almost ten years' work in the field, boosted by his personality and the trust he inspired in the academic community,[89] Jones had developed effective contacts in many places. He had his supporters in universities, among directors in many national ministries and among participants on Joint Study Programmes. In the political world, he regularly met ministers and others through Council meetings.

Sutherland in doing his part to prepare the political stage within the Commission and within the Council and EP for acceptance of the Comett proposal, was also working on behalf of his successor, Manuel Marin. The tough time he had in getting Comett approved had – he was sure – lessons for the parallel case of Erasmus after he had handed over the portfolio.[90]

Policy entrepreneur effort and policy entrepreneur effectiveness

Identifiable entrepreneurs The analysis here most obviously confirms that identifiable policy entrepreneurs emerge when events provide an opportunity for policy change. There were many entrepreneurs in this account. Even in the least active period of policy-making, during the Council of Europe years of the 1960s, there were individuals – the Dutch minister and his senior official – who brought about the important agenda change in making higher education and education a subject of cooperation rather than the object of diplomacy. There were always entrepreneurs in or close to the Commission, who shared such characteristics as tenacity and ambition, all of whom were more or less wily – indeed often, the more wily, the more successful.

The commitment to an idea An important characteristic of these individuals is that they were driven by an idea they wanted to see enacted. Hence in 1955, before higher education had been defined and recognised as a possible area for Community action, Hallstein acted as an advocate for a Community of the Intelligence on the grounds that the EC needed European-minded political leaders and administrators, and that the economies of the Community's member states needed the better research and development that EC backing for higher education would help stimulate.

Hirsch's generation, both in and around the Community and within the universities, took it as read that the 'community of the intelligence' would be Europe-wide. They were acting to create shared beliefs about the need for a Europe of Higher Education what we might call today a European academic area. The EAEC Interim committee on the

European University (1960) which Hirsch chaired foresaw – long before the 1980s research framework programmes were created – that it was in national as well as European interests to support Europe-wide co-operation. For Spinelli too the idea higher education was 'porteur de l'avenir'. Guichard too believed that if the young were not educated to be Europeans, Europe integration would be the weaker. This was linked with their concept of European identity – which in turn was shaped by both the experience of the war, and the institutionalisation of the Cold War.

Changing EC priorities helped shape the driving idea. Jones, the individual who was to dominate education policy making in the EC for 20 years had a different set of beliefs which marked policy development. He did not follow earlier attempts to institutionalise a 'community of the intelligence'. For him, the two most important goals were to use Community institutions to further equal opportunity in education – and to get education linked to the Community's strategic goals and – eventually – established as policy domain of Community competence. But Jones was enough of a realist to realise that there was a political dynamic for Community action on higher education, which could boost the policy sector as a whole.

In the difficult years of trying to implement the Action Programme, and still determined to advance the policy issue, Jones effectively re-branded education, linking it to training in order to fit with social policy and the Commission's employment and social policy aims. Jones was quick to see that when policy leaders' interests changed, he should adapt his strategy and back the technology-related issue, which emerged as the Comett programme.

The very different political circumstances in which Jacques Delors became president of the Commission and Peter Sutherland the Commissioner for Education, with member states committed to backing the Single Market strategy, did not require new agenda setting or new work on shared beliefs, nor even the development of policy capacity. There was, at last, a possibility that the Commission could obtain decisions on non-Treaty but worthy and popular measures like the Comett and Erasmus programmes. Sutherland and his supporting staff – Richonnier and Jones – seized their chance to do the crucial pre-decision work. Characteristically they had the 'solution' ready long before the Commissioners or the Council had identified the precise policy problem they wished to solve. Hence one could say that the Commission had been promoting mobility and university cooperation for over a decade and that was its big idea.

Opportunity recognition Hallstein would not have been motivated to generate the European University idea in a Community context without the opportunity of Messina. Guichard would not have put forward his ideas for cooperation without the specific context of the 1960s in which leaders were determined to relaunch the Community after their conflictual period with de Gaulle. In contrast, Hirsch did not need a big event. Those who modified policy, or tried to, found their opportunities within the process. Hirsch specified an alternative higher education vision because the previous policy proposals had been blocked. An it was the Euratom Commission's responsibility to find a solution. Jones' chance was that the Commissioner chose to step down. The trio of Sutherland, Richonnier and Jones who developed the Erasmus proposal, owed much to the particular opportunities of the new Commission in 1985, as well as to Jones' previous policy work.

A function fulfilled The novelty of this study is what it tells us about function systematically performed, despite the apparent hazards which brought higher education to the attention of decision-makers. In the first cycle of events between 1955–72, we have Hallstein intervening in agenda setting. We have Hirsch specifying an alternative. Guichard produces a new specification. Spinelli's action is partly agenda setting (a not very effective staking out of a Community policy) but more importantly, in terms of a process that does not feature in the Kingdon model, Spinelli was behaving entrepreneurially in building up policy capacity.

In later cycles, 1973–87, Jones emerges first as handling an agreed issue and therefore needing to fulfil the task of crafting a governing formula consisting of a policy design backed by institutional and financial resources. Second, Jones is forced to rethink a strategic vision, and third, once the issue reached the decision agenda, Jones is a member of a team that both exploited the opportunity and prepared the issue for decision. At the same time, Sutherland was an entrepreneur in terms of his determination to get a decision, and providing policy leadership at the crucial pre-decision stage. Richonnier was entrepreneurial in acquiring unexpectedly large resources.

Linked mechanisms of effectiveness Policy entrepreneurs did more than seize an opportunity. They exploited a variety of mechanisms, depending on the policy process involved.[91] We see them calling into play supportive procedures for agenda setting, and using the mechanisms of advocacy; facing a hostile context in which it was impossible to win; taking advantage of favourable events; exercising strategic judgement, benefiting from the accumulation of effective action. All these characterised the different series of policy events in which policy entrepreneurs intervened in the first cycles. When the issue was mature, and education an established Community domain, the activities of the policy entrepreneurs were different. Their success was explained by, for example, taking risks and countering hazards, working for a new consensus, working as a team and fulfilling respective tasks with flair, and facing the unexpected pragmatically.

Context and identity The historical dimension built into this analysis helps advance an understanding of identity as an important factor in explaining individual action, as well as opportunity as a measure of effectiveness.[92] This approach incorporates, however, a certain risk. An immediate consequence of using biographical data is that it produces such a sharp sense of individuals and generations that only the 'great actor' is discerned. But it is argued here that in identifying the individuals within the process of policy generation and change in EC higher education, a valuable causal link has been established with personal resources – brought to bear on context.

The policy entrepreneurs reflected their generation and their professional experience. Hallstein, Hirsch and Spinelli were among the 'founding fathers' of the Community. They were national and European figures, familiar with government. Each was, or had been, a great servant of the state or minister. Professionally they brought the wide-ranging experience of high office to the issue of what higher education could contribute to the Community. Taking Hallstein and Hirsch both born around 1900 and Spinelli born in 1907 – it would have been surprising if they had not been marked by the two World Wars, WW1 as children, WW2 as adults with established values making their stand in the face of Nazism or Fascism. They shared the view that an integrated Community was the best way to stop European nation states going to war. They also expected the proposed European University, and universities in general, to be training and educating 'Europeans'. Hirsch's view, offered in 1960, that it was more important for the European University to focus on the humanities rather than sciences, shaped a policy choice. But these men also expected the universities to contribute to the foreseeable scientific needs of post-war Europe. Hallstein and his German colleagues spoke of the 'community' or the 'common market' of the 'intelligence'.

The later policy entrepreneurs who formulated the Erasmus programme proposal in 1985 had lived through Community enlargements as well as the Community's ambitious project to pitch itself on the world stage through the Single Market. The generation born in the late

1930s and 1940s – Hywel Ceri Jones, Michel Richonnier and Peter Sutherland – were not the elder statesmen figures that typified the period immediately following WWII. Sutherland had held government office as Attorney-General of the Irish Republic and went on to big business. Yet he too had a vision of what it might be to send Irish students once more to Paris, Salamanca and still further-flung parts of Europe, responding to the challenge of his Commission post with both vigour and imagination. Richonnier and Jones were both officials who held strong, motivated views about the EC. Richonnier came to the Community as a French government planner, trained to think strategically – and to 'think big'. Jones was just as much a strategist, in his rather more free-booting way. His views in linking education so closely with training and the Community's Single Market strategy were challenged by some in the university world. But his imaginative and tenacious approach, sustained over a long period, he did much to ensure that EC action differed significantly from that of the Council of Europe – a forum that had established itself as little more than a talking shop for ministers and their officials. Jones had the authority – and took the risk – to back the development of grassroots higher education networks, the rich and distinguishing feature of European higher education co-operation.

Events and institutions as resources The juxtaposition of biography and events also enables us to see clearly the resources inherent to institutions, procedures and ideas, which each of these entrepreneurial individuals was able to interpret as opportunities.

A reasonable assumption to draw from the literature is that events would be the most obvious source of opportunity, and thus an explanatory factor for the advance of higher education policy. The political or focussing events that led to the Treaties of Rome, Community enlargement in 1973 and the Single European Act in 1986 fit such an analysis. However forthcoming events were also important. Spinelli was driven to innovate so that a reform favouring integration would be in place before the Community enlarged to accept more sceptical members. The opportunity for Hallstein to propose the European University lay, in effect, in the meeting of foreign ministers at Messina to consider proposals for the EEC and the Euratom. The opportunity for Guichard to propose co-operation within a Community framework was seized amidst indications, in the run up to the Hague Summit, that existing member states wanted to widen and deepen the Community. The new Commission of 1985 and Delors' expressed commitment to completing the single market provided one – though not the only – opportunity for Erasmus.

Equally, the failure of Hirsch's plan for Europeanised higher education can be put down to the general political mood that followed de Gaulle's attempts to limit the scope of the Communities.

This account clearly indicates that the policy entrepreneur is a master of process, seizing opportunities that arise from institutional rules and procedures – both formal and informal. In this context, the agenda-setting model is particularly useful, carrying the analysis to the heart of the policy process. Applying this model, it is clear that the proposal for a European University survived to become incorporated in the Treaty of Rome EAEC because of a procedural decision, which Hallstein exploited at Messina, to carry forward issues that had not been discussed but to which there were no objections. The issue survived further negotiations – again with the help of Hallstein – because of a second procedural decision that tricky minor issues could be incorporated in the Treaties of Rome with instructions to the Council of Ministers to sort out the difficulties. A reason for the fragility of higher education initiatives in the 1960s was the lack of institutional resources, including those which could have flowed had the policy domain been recognised.

The impact of the new institutional resources which became available in 1973, with Community recognition of a policy domain, offered new opportunities for entrepreneurship. Jones, pursuing the Treaty line that the Commission needed to be able to take initiatives, lobbied for a unique dual membership committee to advise on educational policy. The point of the dual character was to give the Commission the right to bring to bear its 'go-getting' expertise, to create some competition with the careful diplomacy of Council bodies. This included a sophisticated understanding of bundling together issues that had treaty competence with those that did not. Hooking higher education or education onto treaty issues provided access to the most important institutional resource – the right to seek Community funding.

There were other examples with explanatory force in which using particular rules provided a significant advantage to the player concerned. Jones' initiative to move the directorate for education and vocational training to the DG social affairs fell into this category, explained by his view that the social affairs ministers were far more ready to take decisions than education ministers. Similarly, the judgement of the ECJ in the Gravier case presented the Commission with the opportunity to accede to easier decisional rules and hence more generous funding. At the other end of the policy making spectrum, ministers of education worked hard to establish, and then re-establish in the 1980s, that they were prepared to act under intergovernmental rules only. When, with the Erasmus decision, the Council of Ministers (Education) proved that it was not reflecting the general mood of political approval for Erasmus, the rules that counted were those of the European Council. A request from the European Council needed to be acted on quickly. Hence the unusual sight of the Erasmus Decision being given its first positive approval within the Council of Ministers at a meeting of the General Council of foreign ministers – a major change from Council practice under the Education Committee, where rules were used to restrict action.

In conclusion, we can confirm that the distinguishing mark of the effective policy entrepreneurs in this research episode was the extent to which their identity and actions matched the situation. But we can refine an understanding of their effort and their effectiveness or lack of it. While this study makes the case that their life experiences were important in explaining their beliefs, and consequently their efforts, it would, on the basis of this evidence, be a distortion to claim as their main characteristic, that they were able to change the course of policy because they were manipulative individuals primarily driven by self interest. The effectiveness of the policy entrepreneurs discussed here needs to be explained primarily as the match between the problems articulated at a political level and routine policy processes, generic processes and mechanisms that the policy entrepreneurs brought into play. That is to say, the individuals were tenacious, ambitious and res-pected, able to convince colleagues to follow them – but if institutional circumstances had not put them in the right place, at the right time, they could not have begun to function. Accepting the specificity of the policy making *processes* and mechanisms which are allied with the per-sonal characteristics of key actors could enlighten us about EU policy making processes more generally.

10
Conclusions

In setting out to provide a systematic account of the origins and development of European Community (EC) policy-making on higher education I wanted to challenge the dominant assumption of the literature that such policy-making has evolved through 'Community creep' and, specifically, rulings of the European Court of Justice (ECJ). It is not that I deny the role of the Court, and the opportunities which its rulings provided for institutional policy-makers – issues which have been well covered in European Union (EU)-oriented research and scholarship. But I wanted to explore whether there was not likely to be a plausible explanation which recognised the causal force of the day-to-day process of policy-making, and the role of individuals.

To this end I chose a theoretical framework designed to help understand those aspects of the policy process in which real-live policy makers are arguing about ideas and opportunities, about resources and policy capacity, about institutional rules and the scope for breaking with precedent in their efforts to advance policy. That is to say I have been especially interested in the agenda-setting process, as the functional stage of the policy making process in which ideas are debated and refined and particular – possibly powerful – individuals can play a crucial part in ensuring what issues are taken up by decision makers.[1] This way of explaining falls within a new institutionalist, and more specifically a sociological institutionalist framework to which is linked the 'garbage can' literature of organisational sociology. But along with historical institutionalists I recognise the shaping power of context in conjunction with institutional factors, while adding to the explanation, the intervention of policy processes and actors' beliefs.[2]

As explained earlier, I worked on the broad assumption that policy develops as much by day-to-day processes, as by the 'history-making' which we know about in the form of decisions. More specifically I assumed some causal force for the process which produces policy ideas – i.e. the agenda setting process would be part of explanation of outcomes. Thirdly I worked on the methodological assumption that this higher education experience should be conceptualised in terms which were not just *sui generis* but of interest to a wide political science community.

Now almost at the end of this foray, I make three claims for this account. The first is that this methodology, centred on agenda setting, brings to light a hitherto unknown story of the creation and development of a policy of Community cooperation. It has shown that the idea of Community-sponsored higher education activity zigzagged over the full 30 years of Community history, between different sets of institutions and rules, before the Erasmus decision – i.e. the decision in 1987, under EC law and with EC resources setting up an EC wide programme with Community mobility grants, and with encouragement to experiment with a credit transfer system. To recap, decision-makers had considered at least six other proposals:

- For the Community to establish a university level institution (1958)
- For the Community to manage forms of higher education cooperation which would engage all the universities and public research institutes of Europe, around a European University, and would make some student mobility the norm (1960)
- For all higher education cooperation to be developed outside Community institutions (1961)
- For higher education/education cooperation to be managed within Community institutions (1969)
- For EC ministers of education to cooperate on education – and, as part of the deal, to agree to establish an internationally-backed European University Institute (1971)
- For pilot programmes of joint university working, for common rules on admissions, for grants for mobile students, under an action programme (1976) in which intergovernmental action is strengthened by EC resources

The second claim for this account is that by staying so close to the policy making processes it enables us to appreciate the institutional creativity for Community intervention – an aspect which has been somewhat hidden in accounts which have focussed on issues of sovereignty and competence. The institutional constraints of a situation in which the Community was trying to act in an area of national sovereignty – albeit with member state support – caused some intensive work to take place on the type of policy-making machinery. As we have seen, in the years 1974–76, the Commission and Council were in negotiations both about the policy areas in which the Community might act, and the policy rules. The outcome in the Education Committee, as a policy advisory structure, was at the time unique. In a context in which policy advisory committees were either Commission bodies or Council bodies, depending on whether there was Community competence, the Education Committee was 'mixed' or 'dual'. Though managed by the Council secretariat, the Commission was a full member. This allowed a level of involvement which accounted for much of the dynamism behind the early decisions, and notably the Action Programme on education (1976). But the experience also established trust and the belief among the education community – as opposed to some of the politicians – that the Commission was genuinely not working for harmonisation but rather for strong forms of cooperation in which the education actors had a big role. As such, this format, the outcome of institutional constraints, prefigured the flexible arrangements of the Bologna process. More generally it prefigured 'soft' methods in the 1990s in other policy areas which the objective was cooperation rather than legislation.

The third claim for this account is that it enables us to refine our understanding of causality within a general analytic frame which is both institutionalist and processual.[3] The default model of explanation adopted here suggests policy change is the outcome of a situation in which there is a linkage between an accepted idea, the dynamics of European integration at a particular moment in time, and the skilful leadership of EC politicians and entrepreneurial bureaucrats able to use the institutional resources, and bring into play the mechanisms which are appropriate to the generic process of agenda setting or policy modification (alternative specification). That gives us a way of explaining and it provides us with the generalisations which tells us how and why policy change occurs.

However by focussing on the contribution of individuals within the policy process to advancing a policy cause, we are in a better position to explain an aspect of the dynamics which seems generalisable across the different conjunctions of events, institutions and processes which are linked to efforts to change the agenda or to modify policy proposals.

This account has made it clear that *there are almost always politically skilled individuals to respond in specific contextual and institutional circumstances to the opportunity to advance policy ideas.* But on the basis of this account we can, I suggest go further. This account suggests that it is not enough to assume that an appropriately positioned individual *will* exploit the different dynamics of getting agreement on defining the policy issue, or producing a policy solution and seizing the opportunity for action. What this account shows is *how actors responded to and used structure* was crucial to understanding how EC higher education developed. This is a finding confirmed in other studies in which individual action has been taken as part of the explanation for policy outcomes.[4] But this account goes further than the existing literature in showing how beliefs and the life experience exerted a casual connection. If in general we can conclude that where the policy entrepreneurs are concerned, their identity explained their efforts, and that their opportunities and their skills explained their effectiveness,[5] we can add a generalisation consistent with the feedback notions of policy change of new institutionalists.[6] *Their efforts had to be meaningful for them.*[7]

Thus a topic worthy of further investigation is how well individuals in national governments can play a similar role in relation to EU policy-making. We have seen many signs of national initiatives deployed to Community ends.[8] But this account also raises questions relevant for further work on the Commission and its role as policy entrepreneur. As suggested earlier much of the literature has focussed on the Commission as an entrepreneur linked to its interest in expanding the tasks it may undertake[9] and the notion of 'creeping competence'.[10] Yet much of the evidence here is consistent with an important strand of the European integration literature which suggests that the Commission's influence is not exercised simply through its agenda setting powers, but rather through its ability to behave as a leader in circumstances where there is no institutionalised leadership.[11] A greater attention to policy entrepreneurship in the policy-making process could refine our understanding of change in the EU institutions and show how change is effected from deep within the policy process.

Can we not therefore conclude that the evidence mobilised here has moved us a long way from the macro-explanations of an EC or EU role in higher education which attribute policy change to such generalised phenomena as globalisation?[12] And furthermore that single factor explanations for the evolution of EC higher education policy – be it jurisprudence, or the Single European Act, or globalisation – are unable to provide adequate explanations of outcomes.

By making an attempt to conceptualise policy-making in terms which recognise and structure complexity, we may additionally conclude that individuals who are an integral part of the process, have to be part of a better explanation of how and why policy develops in the EU – and elsewhere. This generalisation is explored in an epilogue on the Bologna process.

Epilogue   The Europe of Knowledge: A Renewed European Ambition

The idea that there should be a European dimension to the national higher education systems of the continent is now a political reality. Half a century on from the initial efforts by leading individuals within the EC to establish a Community university, and a decade and half after the Erasmus Decision of 1987, 41 governments within Europe are committed to modifying national systems to create a common academic space to be known as the European Higher Education Area.

Many observers see an uncertain future in which the only likelihood is major and possibly threatening change. To create the EHEA is seen as moving into uncharted waters.[1] The European higher education area may be set to transform the European states' higher education institutions as fundamentally as the nation state changed the medieval universities. Among their concerns is that it is not clear who shapes the process and it is not clear what the process is: will universities continue to be seen as a public good or will their prime characteristic be their contribution to Europe's competitiveness?[2]

Having seen the limited way Europe has impacted on universities over the last half century – largely a matter of what individual academics and students have wanted to make of it – it would be impossible to deny that universities in Europe today are embarked on a huge undertaking, and one with novel dynamics. Formally what their governments are doing by signing up to the Bologna process is agreeing to implement ten action lines which will mesh together the national practices of Europe's higher education systems. In a first package of six measures, agreed at Bologna in 1999, ministers committed their system to adopting a system of 'easily readable and comparable' degrees; to a degree system essentially based on two cycles differentiated between

192

undergraduate and postgraduate; to establish a system of credits; to promote mobility; to promote cooperation in quality assurance; and to promote a European dimension to higher education, meaning a European element to curriculum development, integrated programmes of study training and research etc.

Ministers added a second package at the Prague summit in 2001: recognising lifelong learning as a guiding principle of all education and training policy in Europe and an element in creating the European Higher Education Area; recognising the part that higher education institutions and students have to play in the achievement of an EHEA, and committing themselves explicitly to an implicit am of the process from the beginning, promoting the attraction of the EHEA.

At the Berlin summit in 2003, ministers agreed that doctoral studies should be considered as the third cycle in the Bologna process, and that synergies between the European Research Area should be strengthened. They also agreed that an awareness of the 'social dimension' (e.g. access) should inform their action in general.[3] Furthermore they were still working to a timetable to complete by 2010 – the year in which EU leaders have targeted for the completion of the Lisbon process, the establishment of a European Research Area and the implementation of a single market in services, which would be a highly divisive issue if higher education is included. For 2005, at the half way point, ministers expected a stocktaking on national progress, related to quality assurance, the two cycle structure and a framework for recognition of qualifications.

There are many signs that getting agreement to new procedures will be complex. In a system in which the bachelors/masters structure has always existed – such as the countries of the UK – it is expected that 50% of students on getting an undergraduate degree will leave university for the labour market, initially at any rate, knowing the degree is respected by employers. In Europe as a whole, where there are different traditions, the expectation is that a mere 17% will not stay on for a higher qualification. In Germany the figure is 10%, in Austria, Italy, Spain and Portugal between 6 and 10%, in France 4%.[4] Leave aside the case of medicine and dentistry, course lengths and credit ratings mark another European division. In the UK there are prestigious masters' degrees which last a calendar or an academic year, and which can be calculated in the newly required credit terms as 60–90 points. Most European systems count two years – and 120 points. Many countries aim for a balance which brings undergraduate plus masters to 300 points – a UK total would be 240. Where is the compatibility between them? As for doctoral studies, Europe remains evenly divided over whether a doctorate is an essentially individual (and usually lengthy) project or whether it can be a (shorter) partly taught programme. Some say the answer is in a retreat to the technical language of 'descriptors' which portray learning outcomes rather than length of course.

It is worth insisting that there are several scenarios. Implementation is always a process of interpretation – at least where there is no binding law. Furthermore there is compelling evidence where EU implementation is concerned that there is no 'one size fits all' even where the EU has direct powers.[5] Since higher education policy is one of those policy domains where the EU has only supporting powers, and states will be responsible for implementation, it would be astonishing if there is not a very wide spectrum of outcomes.

In any event, governments may choose to implement the structural change to which the Bologna process commits them formally – but do no more than pass laws. In which case reform will have a hollow core. On the other hand institutions may engage in the reform in a consistent and comprehensive way and, backed by governments, and the Bologna process may become a set of tools for improving the quality of higher education and this is recognised. In the scenario most compatible with EU aspirations for a Europe of Knowledge, but probably furthest from reality, the Bologna process will be no less than part of the paradigm shift in education and in society, towards life-long learning as the norm, with all that implies in terms of more diverse groups of students, more diverse methods of learning and more student-originated demands.[6]

This final chapter argues that the Bologna process might be better understood – and possibly applied – if it were to be presented as neither necessarily catastrophic nor miraculous, but rather as a policy process with its own opportunities and constraints. Hence these final pages look at how the policy vision of the Bologna process, and the policy capacity, have been shaped by events and by rules. That is to say I take up the explanatory model which underpinned the study at the core of this book.

Developing the Bologna vision

For many observers, the Bologna process began not in Italy, but in France. Claude Allègre, the French minister of education, with some aplomb, 'europeanised' the problem of getting university systems to adapt to the era of the knowledge economy in May 1998, as part of the celebrations for the 800th anniversary of the founding of the Sorbonne. Like other French policy-makers before him, it was essentially a natio- nal problem which had made him think European. French govern- ments have long faced pressing national problems ready to bring thousands in the university world out in the street. Recent reports list these as inadequate funding for universities, a higher education system divided between a mass university sector and a well-resourced selective sector of *grandes écoles*, high drop out in the universities, students ill-prepared for the changing graduate job market, and the need to train researchers.[7]

A typical policy entrepreneur, Allègre made the Sorbonne celebra- tions the opportunity to act collectively, bringing together the minis- ters responsible for higher education in Germany, Italy and the UK to join him in an appeal to other European governments.[8] He openly admitted, to the fury of those who had been left out, that if these three joined France to make such a plea, the others would of course follow.[9]

The four ministers urged other European governments to work for a common university 'architecture' defined as a structure of two-cycle structure of bachelors and masters degrees. They also advocated mech- anisms for making higher education cooperation work familiar to the higher education community since the early days of the Erasmus programme.[10] These included a credit system, such as the European Credit and Transfer Scheme (ECTS). Students and academics should be strongly encouraged to study or research in countries other than their own – a semester in the case of students. The 1997 Lisbon con- vention on basic requirements for higher education recognition would, they thought, make mobility easier. Higher education should be taken to include appropriate lifelong learning. But it was also a mission to humanise Europe. The ministers put their names to the declaration that

> Europe is not only that of the euro, of the banks and the economy. It must be a Europe of knowledge as well. We must strengthen and build upon the intellectual, cultural, social and technical dimen- sions of our continent. These have to a large extent been shaped by our universities, which continue to play a pivotal role for their development.[11]

The not-so-hidden agenda for the original signatories was that the great university systems of Europe should develop the features widely seen as making the American system a world-beater. They needed to counter the European brain drain to the US, especially in science, and to do more to attract bright students to the EU. As Allègre – a world class scientist himself and visiting US professor – told a meeting of university rectors and others a year later, Europe needed to emulate the American system of masters diplomas as a qualification for employment, and develop the widely respected PhD for research.[12]

The proposal made by the 'Sorbonne four' were, in general, well-tried ideas emerging from two sources. The specific ideas on such issues as a credit system, recognition procedures had, in Neave's words, been 'appropriated' from programmes such as Erasmus and Tempus.[13] The European higher education area had been proposed in the Socrates-Erasmus programme of 1995.[14] But the general view that Europe needed to exploit its higher education systems better, if not to improve them, derived from the contemporary thinking within the EU at large about structural shifts to the knowledge economy. The integration of such thinking into EU strategies had started back in 1993 with Delors' 1993 White paper *Growth, Competitiveness and Employment*[15] and was working its way through European Councils at the time of Allègre's intervention. It had been given fresh urgency by the prospects of EU enlargement to take in ten countries with much lower GDPs than existing member states and looking for forms of collaboration.[16]

However it was only because they were national ministers that the French, the German and the Italian ministers, supported by the British, introduced the biggest novelty in European higher education policy for 50 years, and in effect, the glue which would hold the Bologna process together. They argued for the two-cycle structure which, they recognised privately, offered them significant economies. And they also knew, because they were acting collectively, that they then had the political strength to go home and legislate for the bachelors/masters or BaMa as it became known – as the French, German and Italian ministers did.[17] (The British government in contrast believed that Bologna would not have any impact on UK structures but would open the way to Europe-wide competition for students and resources at which the British expected to do well).[18]

Within a year, 29 governments from the EU, the future enlarged EU and neighbouring states, declared their readiness to meet at Bologna to agree on a European strategy. Within five years the Bologna process was even more diverse, stretching to Russia and Turkey and including every state of the continental landmass excluding some of the Balkan states and those on Russia' southern periphery. Even central Asian republics were asking for help to 'do' Bologna. And other areas of the world, including South East Asia and Latin America were looking to establish a similar scheme of regional convergence.[19]

Within Europe, support was understandable. Almost all national governments had undergone two decades of forced changed in higher education.[20] This almost everywhere had taken the form of more regulation, less direct central control. The new controls focussed on the quality and financial management measures typical of the contemporary evaluative state. In general in Western Europe, issues of management, organisation of academic institutions and quality assurance became central, whether or not governments were actually able to achieve change, a far cry from the preoccupations of a generation earlier, when the dominant issue was equality.[21] The countries of eastern Europe had supplementary concerns. They had already engaged in major transformations after the collapse of the Soviet Union. All were looking for new policy horizons, even to the point of further reform.

The opportunity created by Allègre's action to put europeanisation on the agenda with a higher profile than ever accorded to it before, had created the opportunity for others with strong and different views to modify the policy vision before it was considered at Bologna. Employability was a point at issue. A number of ministers considered the Sorbonne declaration weak on the need to make graduates more employable within a global economy – they were later to be backed by the heads of higher education institutions who considered, in a ratio of nine to one, that was part of their duty to graduates.[22]

The two Europe-wide university associations – the Brussels-based Liaison Committee of Rectors and the Geneva-based Standing Conference of European Rectors, the two forerunners of the European University Association – were the first to seize the chance to get a foot in the policy process. They gave Guy Haug, well known in the unofficial 'Europe of Education' networks, the job of 'improving' on the Sorbonne declaration. They wished to ensure that a Bologna declaration would commit explicitly to improving the international competitiveness of the European systems of higher education by developing cooperation in quality assurance, with a view to developing comparable criteria and methodologies.[23]

Haug had the energy, authority and tenacity of the typical policy entrepreneur. In 1999 he was well-established as an expert on European and American higher education making cooperation work. Back in the 1970s he had been involved in a pioneer experiment to create a joint courses between institutions from different national systems and with different status – public, private and semi-private institutions – in ways consistent with academic autonomy. Four were involved.[24] 'I *know* this kind of cooperation can be made to work, if there is trust'[25] he says.

He thus had an interest born of experience in getting quality assurance written into the Bologna declaration as a demonstration of the project's trustworthiness.[26] His line was that what was needed was a flexible frame of reference for qualifications and an enhanced European dimension in quality assurance and accreditation based on coordination and independent evaluation.[27] But his first task turned out to be allaying fears of the Sorbonne declaration and a future Bologna declaration. In an influential paper which made up part of the *Trends* report, on 'what the Sorbonne declaration does say and what it doesn't' he produced a textual analysis, before the ministers' meeting at Bologna, to show that there was no hint of harmonisation of content, curricula or methods, nor of a single model of bachelor, masters, doctoral degrees, nor of a European recognition system for the diversity of qualifications. Plans for 'Europe', let alone those infamous unelected Brussels bureaucrats of popular imagery, to impose structures on national systems, simply did not exist.

Probably Haug's key contribution was reframe the problem of why europeanisation was needed. Drawing on views expressed by ministers in and around the Sorbonne debate, Haug argued that interpretations of the Sorbonne declaration which failed to recognise its concerns about competitiveness 'would be severely short-sighted and dangerously wrong'. Europe's future role in the world market for students, teachers and researchers made politicians rightfully talk in terms of an emergency. Higher education policy needed to recognise the emergence of an ever more European and international labour market. The survey of existing structures (later known as *Trends I*), which he and colleagues carried out for the university associations in readiness for Bologna, confirmed also that national systems were faced with mounting challenges from American and others setting up branch campuses, franchising and e-learning courses delivered in English for profit. It also showed that the diversity and complexity of degree structures within Europe was extreme. Though there was a trend towards shorter studies, there was no significant convergence to the 3–5–8 model.

By the time the 29 governments came to sign the joint declaration, a consensus had emerged. The Bologna objective was make their systems 'more compatible and comparable' – a formula less open to mistranslation than 'harmonisation'. This took a lot of work, says Haug with rich understatement.[28] This was part of an extraordinary period of work and intellectual leadership, over three years, on policy design and monitoring, during which the CRE and the Confederation were in the throes of a difficult merger. Among the other outcomes was a survey of higher education systems in 'Bologna countries' entitled *Trends* – the pioneer volume in an increasingly elaborate and well financed series which is transforming our knowledge of Europe's systems.[29]

Once the Bologna declaration had been signed, competition to clarify the policy vision continued – a finding which squares with the literature on open-ended agenda processes in European policy-making.[30] Ministers have modified the Declaration's proposed action and objectives at every meeting since Bologna, and changed the order of priorities. Their declaration at Prague in 2001 formalised their recognition that universities' staff and students were a necessary part of the EHEA process, that universities were a public good 'and should remain a public responsibility'. At the Berlin ministerial meeting of 2003 there was more of what some UK university presidents derisively call 'Eurospeak'. Ministers 'reaffirmed the importance of the social dimension of the Bologna process' meaning at least equal opportunities in terms of access.[31]

These initiatives have largely come from the representative bodies of the universities and of students, the European University Association and the ESIB, the conference of national unions of students of the higher education community in Europe. As of January 2005, the EUA, open to membership from individual universities and national rectors' conferences, as well as associations and networks of higher education institutions had 759 members in 45 countries across Europe and the whole of Russia and into Azerbaijan. ESIB claims to represent 11 mn students in 43 unions across 33 countries. In 2000–01, when there was little competition from participant governments, they filled a gap with the 'public good' statement. This drew from the 2001 Salamanca convention of the EUA, and the student bodies' Göteberg Declaration.[32]

At first the Commission was out of policy-making range. Despite the received wisdom, it is not an institution in permanently expanding mode. Both the education directorate and the Commissioner's office were divided as to whether there was 'anything in Bologna for them' knowing that member states were suspicious – a real contrast with the policy drive demonstrated by the Commissioner, Viviane Reding, at Berlin four years later. In 1999 the Commission's education arm lacked morale and clear leadership. Its role had been constrained by the Treaty of Maastricht.[33] It had suffered the fall-out from the Commission's resignation in 1999, caused by the Education Commissioner, Edith Cresson.[34]

ESIB took the opportunity to air its hostility to conceptions of higher education derived from world trade regulation, GATS-style or the EU's planned directive to complete the single market in services: 'Education is a human right and human rights can never be trade-able'. It was strongly critical that some ministers were failing to take into account the social implications of the Bologna process.[35] The EUA, traditionally an advocate for the cultural diversity of Europe within a common cultural and civic European identity, has consistently supported the case for wide accessibility to higher education and the need for higher education to enhance social cohesion.[36]

The EUA had a double aim. It was especially keen – in parallel with a move by the Commission – to work to maintain and strengthen the organic links between teaching and research. As the EUA had been urging since 2001, and repeated at their convention in Graz in 2003, universities believed in a 'Europe of knowledge based on strong research and research-based education in universities across the conti-nent'. But the rector-politicians behind the EUA's creation were also determined that the universities corporately should have been able to influence the process. 'It's your job to get us into the policy-making', Lesley Wilson remembers being told on her appointment.[37] The EUA was thus ready from the start to be a contributor, not just to policy thinking, but to providing practical help. It was especially concerned, as a grass roots *animateur*, to strengthen the role of institutions – another theme of its convention at Graz in 2003. To this end, with help from the EC Socrates programme, it launched pilot projects on the ECTS and the diploma supplement and models for running joint masters' courses.[38]

While a distinctive contribution from the EUA has been to keep min-isters and a wider public informed on the implications of Bologna for universities, it has consistently presented the Bologna process as closely linked to Community action, current and previous, in this policy area. This was not surprising. The EUA, and its predecessor the CRE, had been used to working across the Community with the Commission – from the days of the education unit in the 1970s, through to the Education DG, set up after the Treaty of Maastricht. A characteristic outcome of EUA/Commission collaboration has been the Erasmus Mundus programme. Lesley Wilson, chief executive of the EUA, claims the programme idea evolved from a meeting in which the commissioner, Reding, asked the EUA 'what can you do for us?'. The EUA had an answer up its sleeve to make European systems more attractive – what eventually emerged as Erasmus Mundus, a programme which provides generous scholarships for students from outside Europe to spend a period in at least two universities in different member states, over a full university year.[39]

The Commission's influence on policy has become clearer since 2001 when it became a participant in the Bologna process. Though even here some of its action – and non-action – has been unexpected. Making the obvious links to the EU's strategic goal to create a more effective knowledge economy as formulated by the Lisbon goals – it has been active in promoting the idea of a European Research Area, and more EU funding for research some of it administered by a research council controlled by scientists. It would also like to structure Europe's research capabilities to guarantee 30–50 European centres of excellence.[40] This was on-going business. Paradoxically the working links between the research and education arms of the Commission have not been clear in practice.[41]

Creating organisational capacity

The issue of organisational back-up for the Bologna process had become of concern by 2001. After 1999, ministers were up against the dilemma experienced in previous years when intergovernmentalism had been tried. The intermittent attention of national administrations, and the lack of resources for a common cause, features which characterise political cooperation, were evident drawbacks for a project which showed every sign of having been able to expand within the wider Europe, attracted by the ideas and methods of the Bologna process.

The ministers' first step at their Prague meeting was to set up an organisation which they controlled, the Bologna Follow-Up Group, (generally known as BFUG). It would represent signatories, special participants and the European Commission and would be chaired by the EU presidency, with a representative of the host country for the subsequent ministerial meeting being made deputy chair. Its main objective was to keep all members in touch and deliver professional help on implementation. This has taken the form of international seminar on such thorny issues as what makes a masters' course and/or how to create cooperation between accreditation agencies A preparatory element, similarly chaired by the EU presidency, was initially composed of representatives of the countries hosting the previous ministerial meetings, two EU member states and two non-EU member states, and the Commission. At Berlin, ministers went a step further in the recognition of the need for leadership, in agreeing that the BFUG should have a board and a secretariat, furnished for two years by the country hosting the following ministerial meeting.

From 2001, the Commission's expertise was fully recognised. It had, after all, been developing higher education as a policy domain for European cooperation for decades, in partnership with the universities and national governments. It had devised the programmes, a model credit system, and a conception of quality assurance – all instruments of coordination, operating by incentives not harmonisation. It had been a promoter of the 1997 Lisbon convention on recognition of qualifications. It had done much to fund the networking on curriculum and exchange which gave the European dimension its reality within higher education institutions. It also had the expertise in international relations which the ministers wanted, to make the EHEA more attractive world-wide.

By 2001 Commission officials could see the wider opportunities to create synergies with new Community action on the broader Lisbon agenda and, potentially, with the internal market legislation, which builds on regulatory consistency.[42] Predictably the Commission involvement showed almost immediately some of the benefits it could offer. The development of the Erasmus Mundus, approved by the Council and the European Parliament in 2003 was one of the more spectacular. In 2004 the first 80 EU institutions were chosen.[43] The Commission also moved swiftly on the issue of learning outcomes, as a tool to support flexible course lengths rather than a common 'architecture'. Its 'Tuning' project with volunteer universities was designed to demonstrate the possibilities of codifying competences and learning outcomes in selected disciplines and at different levels of attainment at bachelors' and masters' levels. The objective has been to reference these to values within the European Credit Transfer Scheme with the hope of transforming the currently small mobile labour force into something far bigger.[44]

The overlaps for the Commission with the Lisbon process have become more obvious as time has gone on, though national responses to the Lisbon process itself have been half-hearted.[45] For example, it ensured the Tuning project included a vocational training qualification of the type covered by freedom of establishment legislation.[46] Following the Berlin conference the Commission became an even more central actor.[47] The ministers' demand for stocktaking reports of national action on Bologna by the halfway mark – 2005 in Bergen –

also required a response to the request for a feasible European framework scheme on quality assurance, designed to make national frameworks 'convertible' into a different European higher education system 'currency'. They also wanted the framework of qualifications which would make the two cycle system make sense. The Commission was already prepared with its proposals on supporting the working parties of the European Network for Quality Assurance (ENQA) in their work on the standard, procedures and guidelines, and also on institutional evaluation, competence based learning and the work of certain professional accrediting agencies. It has also produced indicators for education and training which could be used system-wide.[48]

This evidence on policy-making in higher education through the Bologna process leads me to conclude that what we are seeing is a new kind of partnership, with state actors and with non-state actors, suggesting a new conception of European policy-making in higher education based on cooperation not legislation. This conforms to the view repeatedly expressed by Helen Wallace, a great and pioneering scholar of the European phenomenon. There are key points which she makes from her extensive knowledge over the whole field of European politics and policies which fit the Bologna process like a glove. The first is that there is no single and predominant mode of policy making but interestingly different modes across sectors. The second is that to achieve a shared EU policy regime requires only that compatible approaches are evident – congruence but not convergence. The third is that the EU is only part of a wider pattern of policy-making beyond the nation state. The fourth is that the politics of the EU are normal politics. Most of the policy makers who devise and operate EU rules are people who are national policy-makers most of the time. For them the European dimension offers an extended policy area in which opportunities and in constraints arise from the multi-level and multi-layered processes and may indeed inspire differences in behaviour. So in order to understand the EU we need to understand the national institutional settings too.[49]

I personally believe that the Bologna process, taking place as it does in the shadow of the EU has much life in it for the coming years, provided those who make up its diffuse institutional leadership do not lose their nerve and revert to an intergovernmental process without the dynamic of shared targets and shared forms of development. But it is precisely because of the engagement of national actors who are determined to get change within national systems that the process has a legitimacy which keeps it in being. Thus far many of these national actors have found the dense networks and the expertise in and around the EU a support for achieving national change their way.

We can confidently predict that some of the participants will do the minimum, and that, at the other extreme, there will be astute and tenacious individuals and organisations who find in the EU/European domain a way of advancing their ideas. This variety is the nature of intergovernmental processes. And for the majority, the Europe of Knowledge is an idea whose time has come.

Appendix

Table 1   Higher Education in the Treaties

TREATY OF ROME EAEC, 1957
Article 9 (2)
An institution of university status shall be established: the way in which it will function shall be determined by the Council acting by QM on a proposal from the Commission

Article 216
The Commission proposals on the way in which the institution of university status referred to in Article 9 is to function shall be submitted to the Council within one year of the entry into force of the Treaty

TREATY OF ROME EEC, 1957
Selected specific and implied powers:

Article 57
In order to make it easier for persons to take up and pursue activities as self-employed persons, the Council shall issue directives for the mutual recognition of diplomas, certificates and other evidence of formal qualifications. In the case of medical and allied and pharmaceutical professions, the progressive abolition of restrictions shall be dependent upon co-ordination of the condition for their exercise in the various Member States

Article 235
If action by the Community should prove necessary to attain, in the course of the operation of the common market, one of the objectives of the Community and the Treaty has not provided the necessary powers, the Council shall, acting unanimously on a proposal from the Commission and after consulting the European Parliament, take the appropriate measures

TREATY OF MAASTRICHT, 1991
[additional objectives of the EU]
Article 3
(p) a contribution to education and training of quality and to the flowering of the cultures of the Member States

Article 126
1 The Community shall contribute to the development of quality education by encouraging co-operation between Member States and, if necessary, by supporting and supplementing their action, while fully respecting the responsibility of the Member States for the content of their teaching and the organisation of education systems and their cultural and linguistic diversity.

Table 1   Higher Education in the Treaties – *continued*

2 Community action shall be aimed at:
o developing the European dimension in education, particularly through the teaching and dissemination of the languages of the Member States
o encouraging mobility of students and teachers, inter alia by encouraging the academic recognition of diplomas and periods of study
o promoting co-operation between educational establishments
o developing exchanges of information and experience on issues common to the education systems of the Member States
o encouraging the development of youth exchanges and of exchanges of socio-educational instructors
o encouraging the development of distance education
3 The Community and the Member States shall foster co-operation with third countries and the competent international org in the field of education, in particular the Council of Europe
4 In order to contribute to the achievement of the objectives referred to in this Article, the Council:
o acting in accordance with the procedure referred to in Article 189b, after consulting the Economic and Social Committee and the Community of the Regions, shall adopt incentive measures, excluding the harmonisation of the laws and regulations of the Member States
o acting by a qualified majority on a proposal from the Commission, shall adopt recommendations

TREATY OF AMSTERDAM, 1997
Additional objectives
'to promote the development of the highest possible level of knowledge for their peoples through a wide access to education and through its continuous updating'

Renumbers Articles. TEU Articles 126 an 127 become TEU Articles 149 and 150

DRAFT CONSTITUTIONAL TREATY, 2004

Part I
Title 1 Definition and objectives of the Union
Article 1-2 The Union's [educated-related] objectives
1.The Union's aim is to promote peace, its values and the well-being of its citizens
2. The Union shall offer its citizens an area of freedom, security and justice without internal frontiers, and a single market where competition is free and undistorted
3. The Union shall work for the sustainable development of Europe, based on balanced economic growth, a social market economy, highly competitive and aiming at full employment and social progress, and with a high level of protection and improvement of the quality of the environment. It shall promote scientific and technological advance.

Table 1 Higher Education in the Treaties – *continued*

It shall combat social exclusion and discrimination, and shall promote social justices and protection, equality between men and women, solidarity between generations and protection of children's rights.

It shall promote economic, social and territorial cohesion, and solidarity among Member States. The Union shall respect its rich cultural and linguistic diversity, and shall ensure that Europe's cultural heritage is safeguarded and enhanced....

Article 1-4 Fundamental freedoms and non-discrimination
Free movement of persons, goods, services and capital, and freedom of establishment shall be guaranteed within and by the Union...

Title III Union competencies
Areas of supporting. coordinating or complementary action
Article 1-16
1. The Union may take supporting, coordinating or complementary action.
2. The area for supporting, coordinating or complementary action shall be, at European level,
– industry
– protection and improvement of human health
– education, vocational training, youth and sport
– culture
– civil protection
3. Legally binding acts adopted by the Union on the basis of the provisions specific to these areas...may not entail harmonisation of Member States' laws or regulations

Part III
The policies and functioning of the Union
Article 111- 182
1 The Union shall contribute to the development of quality education by encouraging co-operation between Member States and, if necessary, by supporting and complementing their action. It shall fully respect the responsibility of the Member States for the content of their teaching and the organisation of education systems and their cultural and linguistic diversity...[sport]
2 Union action shall be aimed at:
o developing the European dimension in education, particularly through the teaching and dissemination of the languages of the Member States
o encouraging mobility of students and teachers, inter alia by encouraging the academic recognition of diplomas and periods of study
o promoting co-operation between educational establishments
o developing exchanges of information and experience on issues common to the education systems of the Member States
o encouraging the development of youth exchanges and of exchanges of socio-educational instructors and encouraging the participation of young people in democratic life in Europe
o encouraging the development of distance education

Table 1   Higher Education in the Treaties – *continued*

3 The Community and the Member States shall foster co-operation with third countries and the competent international org in the field of education, in particular the Council of Europe

4 In order to contribute to the achievement of the objectives referred to in this Article, the Council:

o   acting in accordance with the procedure referred to in Article 189b, after consulting the Economic and Social Committee and the Community of the Regions, shall adopt incentive measures, excluding the harmonisation of the laws and regulations of the Member States

o   acting by a qualified majority on a proposal from the Commission, shall adopt recommendations

4. In order to contribute to the achievement of the objectives referred to in this Article

(a)   European laws on framework laws shall establish incentive actions, excluding any harmonisation of the laws and regulations of member states, They shall be adopted after consultation with the Committee of the Regions and the Economic and Social Committee

(b)   (b)   the Council of ministers, on a proposal from the Commission, shall adopt recommendations

Table 2 Vocational Training in the Treaties

Treaty of Rome EEC, 1957

Title II Employment and Equality of Treatment

Article 7
1. A worker who is a national of a Member State may not, in the territory of another Member State be treated any differently from national workers by reason of his nationality. In respect of conditions of employment and work, in particular as regards remuneration, dismissal and should he become unemployed, restatement or re-employment
2. He shall enjoy the same social and tax advantages as national workers
3. He shall also, by virtue of the same right and under the same conditions as national workers, have access to training in vocational schools and retraining centres
4. Any clause of a collective or individual agreement or of any other collective regulation concerning eligibility for employment, employment, remuneration or other conditions of work or dismissal shall be null and void in so far as it lays down or authorises discriminatory conditions in respect of workers who are nationals of the other Member States

Article 48 (1)
Freedom of movement for workers shall be secured within the Community by end of the transitional period at the latest

Article 118
Without prejudice to other provisions of this Treaty and in conformity with its general objectives, the Commission shall have the task of promoting close co-operation between Member States in the social field, particularly in relation to matters relating to:
- employment
- labor law and working conditions
- basic and advanced vocational training
- social security
- prevention of occupational accidents and diseases
- occupational hygiene
- the right of association and collective bargaining between employers and workers

To this end the Commission shall act in close contact with Member States by making studies, delivering opinions and arranging consultations both on problems arising at national level and those of concern to international organisations.
Before delivering the opinions provided for in this Article the Commission shall consult the Economic and Social Committee

Article 128
(rendered null and void by the Treaty of Maastricht)
The Council shall, acting on a proposal from the Commission and after consulting the Economic and Social Committee, lay down general principles for

Table 2   Vocational Training in the Treaties – *continued*

implementing a common vocational training policy capable of contributing to the harmonious development both of the national economies and of the common market
- vote: by simple majority

TREATY OF MAASTRICHT, 1991
Article 127
1 The Community shall implement a vocational training policy which shall support and supplement the action of the Member States, while fully respecting the responsibility of the Member States for the content and organisation of vocational training.
2 Community action shall aim to:
o   facilitate adaptation to industrial changes, in particular through vocational training and retraining
o   improve initial and continuing vocational training in order to facilitate vocational integration and re-integration into the labor market
o   facilitate access to vocational training and encourage mobility of instructors and trainees and particularly young people
o   stimulate co-operation on training between educational or training establishments or firms
o   develop exchanges of information and experience on issues common to the training systems of Member States
3 The Community and the Member States shall foster co-operation with third countries and the competent international organisations in the sphere of vocational training
4 The Council, acting in accordance with the procedure referred to in Article 189c, and after consulting the Economic and Social Committee, shall adopt measures to contribute to the achievement of the objectives referred to in this Article, excluding any harmonisation of the laws and regulations of the Member States

DRAFT CONSTITUTIONAL TREATY, 2004
Part III
The policies and functioning of the Union
Article III-183

Subsection 1–3 as in the Treaty of Maastricht Article 127
Subsection 4 as in the Draft Constitutional Treaty Article III-182

Table 3 Selected Policy Entrepreneurs and Policy Process in EC Higher Education Policy, 1955–87

Agenda setting	Walter Hallstein	1955–1957	Head of German foreign ministry	Proposed European University Proposal Treaty article
Alternative specification	Etienne Hirsch	1959–1960	President Euratom Commission	Delivered Interim Committee report for Europeanising higher education
Agenda setting	Olivier Guichard	1969	French Minister of Education	Proposed European Centre for Development of Education
Domain creation	Altiero Spinelli	1971	EC Commissioner for Research and Industry	Created Education group and Inter-servis Education Group Commissioned report on an EC policy for education (Janne)
Alternative specification/ agenda setting	Ralf Dahrendorf	1973–1974	EC Commissioner for Research, Science and Education	Proposed a much more *limited* vision of education in EC
Policy design and domain modification	Hywel Ceri Jones	1973–1976	Head of Division Education and Youth	Delivered Commission Communication on policy vision and education advisory machinery (Education Committee) Delivered draft Action Programme resolution I976 in negotiation with Education Committee Partially implemented Action programme
Advocacy for Erasmus idea Preparing the decision	Hywel Ceri Jones	1985–987	Director Education Training and Youth	Proposed action on Erasmus Developed Erasmus proposal Acted as advocate for Erasmus decision in policy community

Table 3   Selected Policy Entrepreneurs and Policy Process in EC Higher Education Policy, 1955–87 – *continued*

Making the choice to present a decision	Peter Sutherland	1985	EC Commissioner for Education, Social Affairs and Competition	Proposed and delivered Erasmus programme decision Oversight of development of Erasmus proposal Acted a sponsor and advocate in Commission and other EC institutions and with university rectors
Preparing the decision. Design for resources and legal base	Michel Richonnier	1985	Member Sutherland Cabinet	Negotiated Erasmus decision budget Advocate for Erasmus decision with Delors cabinet and French government

Table 4   The Bologna Process Commitments to Institute a European Higher Education Area by 2010

Introduced in the Bologna declaration 1999
  1. Adoption of a system of easily readable and comparable degrees
  2. Adoption of a system essentially based on two cycles
  3. Establishment of a system of credits
  4. Promotion of mobility
  5. Promotion of European co-operation in quality assurance
  6. Promotion of the European dimension in higher education

Introduced in the Prague Communiqué 2001
  7. Lifelong learning
  8. Higher education institutions and students
  9. Promoting the attractiveness of the European Higher Education Area

Introduced in the Berlin Communiqué 2003
  10. Doctoral studies and the synergy between the EHEA and ERA (Educational Research Area)
      The social dimension of higher education might be seen as an overarching or transversal action line

Notes

Chapter 1   Ideas Do Not Arrive Out of the Blue

1 Naming policy: the terms EEC, Euratom and the Community are used for any years before 1993 when the Treaty of European Union came into force.

2 The UK government *White Paper*, 'The future of higher education,' (2003) proposes to change the system so that the title of 'University' can be awarded to institutions on the basis of their taught degrees, without requiring evidence of research (pp. 14–15).

3 Diversification is a theme taken up widely in the higher education literature – see Scott, 1998, Kogan 1997, Hackl, 2001, Blumenthal, Goodwin et al (1996), Green, Wolf and Leney (1999), Kälvermark and van der Wende (1998), Neave and van Vught (1991).

4 COM (2003) 58.

5 Bologna declaration official website http://www.bologna-bergen2005.no

6 See Commission website for Lisbon process http://europa.eu.int/growthandjobs/index_en.htm

7 See COM (2004) 2 final/3 'Proposal for a directive of the European parliament and of the Council on services in the internal market' and the Commission website Directorate General Internal Market and services (http://europa.eu.int); For a critical view: 'Facing the challenge, the Lisbon strategy for growth and employment', Report from the High Level Group chaired by Wim Kok (November 2004) http://europa.eu.int/growthandjobs/group/index_en.htm.

8 Davies, H. (2004) UACES-online (www.uaces.org) has summarised these issues. See also Universities UK Presidency speech annual conference 2004 'Develop global competitiveness, urges Universities UK President' (Ivor Crewe, 15 September 2004) http://www.universitiesuk.ac.uk/mediareleases/show.asp?MR=396

9 Scott 1998: 1 on internationalisation. Callan and Teichler in the same collection treat Europeanisation as a variant on internationalisation.

10 Beukel 2001: 124.

11 Mény et al 1995: 8–9. There is a vast literature of Europeanisation and its different meanings. See Ladrech 1994: 69; Héritier 2002; Knill 2001; Featherstone and Radaelli 2003: 340–41.

12 Gellert 1993; Kogan 1999.

13 COM (2003) 58 'The role of universities in the Europe of Knowledge' Between 1999–2025 in the EU 15 population of 350 million, a fall of 9.4 million is forecast for the 16–20 age group and an increase of 37.2 million in the over 60s.

14 COM (2003) 58; A. Sapir et al (2003) 'An agenda for a growing Europe, making the EU economic system deliver', Report of an independent high

level group established on the initiative of the President of the Commission. 'Measures to improve higher education/research relations in order to strengthen the strategic basis of the European Research Area (ERA), Report of an independent high level expert group set up by the Commission (DG Research).

15 COM (2003) 58.
16 COM (2003) 58: Tertiary expenditure accounts for 1.1% of GDP in the EU, 2.3% in the US. R and D expenditure (boosted by defence expenditure) accounts for 1.0% in the EU, 2.7% in the US. Sources are quoted to suggest that higher education and research are a service producing 3% added value in the EU, 5% in the US.
17 *Magna Charta Universitatum* website www.magna-charta.org.
18 See an extensive literature on ideas as an explanation in policy making including Kingdon 1984; Goldstein and Keohane 1993.
19 See Peterson and Bomberg 1999: 5; Peterson 2001: 294; Cram 1997.
20 Nugent (5ᵗʰ ed) 2003 Chapter 4.
21 Education and vocational training were affected by the re-numbering. The relevant Treaty articles of Maastricht, Articles 126 and 127 became Articles 149 and 150 under the Treaty of Amsterdam (see Table 1, Chapter 2).
22 See for example Dinan, 1999: 1–101 for a masterly survey of history, facts and figures.
23 Neave 1984: 6.
24 de Witte 1989.
25 McMahon 1995; Field 1998; Moschonas 1998; Shaw 1999; Beukel 2001, van Craeyenest (1989).
26 Shaw 1999: 556.
27 Sprokkereef, A. 1993: p. 340
28 Interview 23 June 1999 with Richard Mayne, speechwriter to Hallstein 1958–63 and personal assistant to Jean Monnet 1963–66. More recently Blitz (2003: 198) uses Monnet's own memoirs to demolish the view.
29 See Chapters 2 and 9.
30 Higher education is not an issue for major studies e.g. Moravscik (1998).
31 In addition to de Witte, McMahon, Shaw, see Frazier (1995); Hervey (1998); Lenearts (1989, 1994); Lonbay (1989).
32 Blitz 2003: 197: 'a policy that was not anticipated in the original EEC programme but which developed as a result of the Single Market plan and the gradual acknowledgement that educational issues were related to common economic concerns'.
33 Beukel 2001: 124 for a recent assessment.
34 Shaw 1999: 557. Carole Frazier, *L'Education et la Communauté Européenne* (1995) treats education as a domain in which the single market interacts with individual rights.
35 EU Draft Constitutional Treaty Article 1-16 and Articles III-182, III-183.
36 See bibliography.
37 See bibliography.
38 Palayret, J.-M. 1996.
39 Cerych as actor features in Chapter 6.

40 *Journal of the Association of European Universities* No. 115 – Supplement 40 years of history. Ruegg's definitive history of the universities in the postwar period is awaited.
41 Hall and Taylor 1996 review these.
42 Hall 1986: 19.
43 Thelen and Steinmo 1992.
44 See Pierson 1996 and the subsequent discussion.
45 DiMaggio and Powell 1991; Hall and Taylor 1996. See also Craig Parsons 2003.
46 Max Weber 1864–1920, German political economist and sociologist considered as the founder of modern study of sociology and public administration. His major works are in the sociology of religion, and government. His is famous for his definition of the state as having a monopoly of legitimate violence.
47 See Michael Barzelay (2003: 255) for his advocacy of the worth and feasibility of a robust process understanding of policy-making.
48 March and Olsen 1989. This logic of appropriateness is to be contrasted with the 'rational' logic of consequences.
49 This reading of Kingdon owes much to Barzelay (2001), (2003).
50 Baumgartner and Jones term the moment of change as 'punctuated equilibrium'.
51 Schumpeter, J. [1934] 1961: 93 quoted in Swedberg 2000: 16.
52 Baumgartner and Jones 1993: 3.
53 Roberts and King 1996.
54 Kingdon [1984] 1995: 180–181.
55 Weiler 1991; Burley and Mattli 1993.
56 Peters 1994; Pollack 1994.
57 Sandholtz and Zysman 1989.
58 Ross 1995.
59 Marks 1993.
60 Sandholtz 1992; Peterson and Sharp 1998.
61 See Pollack (2000) for a review of this literature.
62 Cram 1994: 212.
63 Schink, European University Institute, 1993.
64 Nihoul 1999, Policy formation in the European Union, the case of educational policy.
65 Dudley and Richardson 1999.
66 Dyson and Featherstone 1999: ix.
67 Ragin 1987: 31 the aim of a case study as being to establish a meaningful dialogue between ideas and evidence (1997: 52). In this instance the field of general discussion is EC policy-making, with evidence drawn from EC higher education policy making. Hence gaining insight into policy change in the EC requires us to analyse EC higher eduation policy change in terms that can be related to EC policy change.
68 See for insights on historiography H. White (1984) for a review of concepts of historical understanding and Gardiner (1974) for selected texts on the debate 'what is history?'.
69 Interviews were conduced with some 60 individuals – see appendix.
70 Under the EU (DG Research) EUSSIRF scheme, see Acknowledgements.

Chapter 2   Origins: The Proposal for a European Community University, 1955–57

1   Serra 1989 contains the archive-based account of historians and their confrontation with key actors. Among the historians, Dumoulin, Guillen, Harryvan, Küsters, Trausch. Among the actors, Emile Nöel, Calmès. See Spaak 1971; Hallstein 1972 for participant accounts. Mayne 1970, who knew many of the participants provides a high-level journalistic account.
2   Spaak 1971: 227.
3   Young, H. 1998: 78.
4   Jansen 1996: 97–121; Loth et al 1998: 2.
5   Palayret 1996: 43.
6   Serra 1989: 177 intervention by C. Calmès.
7   Müller-Armack 1971: 173 my translation.
8   Karl Deutsch's introduction to Karl Jasper's *Idea of a University* (1960: 15) quoted in Husemann 1978: 158.
9   Bird 1978: 147.
10 Husemann p. 162 quoting Robert Birley.
11 Bird 1978: 156.
12 Palayret pp. 18–23.
13 Küsters 1998: 66.
14 ECHA EH-26 Hirsch archives: Inauguration of the European University Institute, 1976, intervention of Max Kohnstamm, first president of the EUI: Allocations prononcées à l'occasion de l'inauguration de l'Institut universitaire européenne.
15 Müller-Armack p. 173.
16 Ophüls worked for Adenauer while Müller-Armack worked for the Chancellor's rival, Ludwig Erhard, the powerful economics minister and later Chancellor.
17 Müller-Armack p. 173.
18 Nugent 1999: 39.
19 Spaak p. 228.
20 Mayne 1970.
21 Serra p. 122.
22 Quoted in Stirk 1996.
23 Palayret p. 51.
24 Spaak 1971: 239.
25 Uri 1991: 123.
26 Nihoul 1999: 73 refers to ECSC Treaty Article 56.
27 Palayret p. 45.
28 Spaak p. 256 and Pineau 1991: 183.
29 Interview with Félix-Paul Mercereau, 19 June 1999.
30 Palayret p. 46.
31 Palayret gives Hallstein the credit (Palayret p. 46) Müller-Armack says it was thanks to Ophüls (Müller-Armack p. 176).
32 Hallstein, W. 1972: 199, Calmès in Serra 1989 p. 177.
33 Kingdon, J. 1984: 3.
34 Cohen M., March J., Olsen, J. 1972: 1.
35 McAdam, Tarrow and Tilly 2001: 121.
36 Even his own ministry of foreign affairs and the West German rectors were caught out. Palayret 1996: 46.

Chapter 3   Conflicting Visions of Europeanised Higher Education, 1958–61

1 Palayret 1996.
2 The term is Félix-Paul Mercereau's – interview 19 June 1999 – noting that the French were the only nuclear power of the time.
3 Rüegg 1999: 31.
4 Rüegg pp. 31–33.
5 Palayret 1996: 20; Cerych 1999: 10–11.
6 Palayret 1996: 37.
7 See Coombs 1964 on education and culture as 'the fourth dimension of foreign policy'.
8 Georis 1999: 28.
9 Palayret p. 26; Deering 1992: 116–9.
10 Palayret p. 28.
11 See Deering 1992: 292.
12 Palayret p. 26.
13 Palayret p. 35.
14 Palayret p. 21.
15 The following draws heavily on the accounts of Palayret 1996 pp. 50–53 and Hallstein 1972 p. 197 and Vedovato 1968.
16 Palayret 1996: 53.
17 Palayret 1966: 60.
18 Mercereau, 19 June 1999.
19 Hirsch 1988: 163.
20 ECHA file correspondence Denis de Rougement to Christian Calmès.
21 Hallstein p. 200.
22 Hirsch p. 166.
23 Palayret p. 64.
24 Palayret 1996: 57–59.
25 Mercereau, 19 June 1999; Palayret p. 69.
26 Hirsch 1988: 163.
27 Palayret pp. 61–4.
28 Vedovato 1968: 10.
29 Hirsch, pp. 164–166.
30 Mercereau, 19 June 1999.
31 Hirsch 1988: 164.
32 ECHA Jules Guérin dossier 89, Visit by the presidents of the three Communities to the United States, chapter IV: 14.
33 Hirsch 1988: 163–4.
34 Palayret 1996: 69.
35 Müller-Armack p. 178.
36 Palayret 1996: 73.
37 Report from Interim Committee on the European University to the EEC and EAEC Councils, 27 April 1960.
38 Palayret on the Interim Committee pp. 69–92.
39 Palayret 1996: 96.
40 Palayret 1996: 109.

41 Kingdon 1995: 199.
42 Hirsch himself (p. 166) talks of the five ministers not daring to oppose.
43 Baumgartner and Jones 1993: *passim.*

Chapter 4   Experimenting with Intergovernmentalism, 1961–69

1   Dinan 1999: 43.
2   Palayret 1996: 125.
3   See also accounts in Vedovato 1968.
4   Palayret pp. 132–133.
5   Haigh 1970: 12.
6   Palayret pp. 123–133.
7   Palayret pp. 118–120.
8   Hirsch p. 164.
9   See Coombs 1964.
10 See Haigh pp. 19–24.
11 Quoted in Haigh.
12 Interview with R. Georis, 22 November 2000.
13 Georis papers: Memorandum 'Considération sur le transfert des activités' dated '20 août 1959' and marked 'Confidentiel, Exemplaire no 4'.
14 Haigh 1970: 28.
15 Haigh p. 28.
16 Haigh p. 24.
17 Haigh 1970: 133; Palayret.
18 ECHA EH-26 Table ronde sur la co-opération universitaire, p. 7 intervention of M Antoine, Brussels, Jan 11, 1972.
19 Dinan 1999: 60.
20 In separate incidents Hallstein and Hirsch accused the French president of not respecting EC treaties – leading de Gaulle to ensure their EC careers were ended prematurely. The clash with Hallstein in 1965 was over the Commission proposal to change the base of its income from national contributions to own resources. The French president refused to allow his government to participate in EC decision-making for six months – an incident known as the Empty Chair Crisis. The crisis was partly resolved in 1966 by the 'Luxembourg Compromise', which recognised the veto when crucial national interests were at stake. Hirsch had told de Gaulle that France was not respecting the Euratom Treaty – to which de Gaulle replied 'France is the only judge of France's interests'. – Hirsch pp. 168–172.
21 Bousquet 1998: 12. Bousquet is a rare source in citing these European Parliament resolution and showing the evolution of educational policy-making decisions from 1961.
22 *EC Bulletin* 12–69.
23 Guichard in Jarvis.
24 Hall, P. 1986.
25 Guichard in Jarvis.

26 The word harmonisation inspires controversy, as we will see. The context of Guichard's remarks makes harmonisation appear to be for practices to converge, rather than the equalising practice introduced by EC law in the form of a directive.
27 Guichard in Jarvis.
28 See Palayret 1996: 156–163.
29 Kohnstamm talked of his 'respect and emotion' in paying tribute to Cattani for his work on the European University, Florence 1976.
30 Final communiqué of the Hague Summit conference EC Bulletin 12–69.
31 Jarvis pp. 2–3 and Appendix 1.
32 Neave 1984: 6.
33 Baumgartner and Jones 1993: 32–5.
34 Kingdon 1995: 98.

Chapter 5 Creating a Policy Domain for Education, 1970–72

1 Guichard (1971) Le Monde July 9 1971, translated and published in Jarvis (1972) Appendix 3.
2 The word harmonisation inspires controversy, as we have already seen in Chapter 4. The context of Guichard's remarks, as Faure's before him, makes it appear to be negotiated agreement that practices converge, rather than a practice introduced by EC law in the form of a directive.
3 Guichard in Jarvis.
4 Neave 1984: 6.
5 Neave p. 7.
6 Jarvis pp. 12–14?
7 ECHA EN-159, 1972 'Préparation Sommet de Paris'.
8 Palayret recounts this story, p. 163; ECHA EN-159, 1972.
9 Jarvis Appendix 4; Palayret pp. 164, 188; ECHA Hirsch archive EH-26.
10 Neave p. 6, a meeting cited as 'the first of its kind since 1957'.
11 Resolution of the Ministers for Education meeting within the Council of 16 November on co-operation in the field of education (in Council of the European Communities, 1988: 9); Jarvis pp. 14–17.
12 Rüegg 1999: 33.
13 Council Decision of 2 April 1963 laying down general principles for implementing a common vocational training policy (63/266/EC) in Council 1988: 197.
14 Rüegg 1999: 32.
15 Dinan 1999: 61–7.
16 Rüegg p. 33.
17 ECHA Hirsch archive EH-26.
18 Hirsch archive.
19 ECHA EN-391 1970. Fiche de transmission à M. Ruggiero chef de cabinet de M le President et photocopie de la note du 19/10/70 de M. Rabier.
20 ECHA EN-1064 aide-mémoire (March 15 1971) from Spinelli's cabinet.
21 ECHA EN-391 Secretary General's note dated 1 February 1971 to Borschette and other Commissioners.

22 ECHA EN-391 correspondence E. Noël to H. Lesguillons, dated 1 March 1971.
23 ECHA EN-391 ref Aide-mémoire for M. Spinelli dated March 15, 1971.
24 ECHA EN-391 SEC (71) Note à l'attention to MM les Membres de la Commission, le 22 février 1971.
25 ECHA EN-391 Secretary General's note dated 1 February 1971 to Borschette and other Commissioners.
26 Corbett, R. 1996: 186; Correspondence with Christopher Layton, a member of Spinelli's cabinet, August 1999.
27 Corbett, R. p. 186; Spinelli 1972 Servan-Schreiber 1967: *Le défi américain* (The American Challenge).
28 ECHA EN-1064 Co-ordination dans le domaine de l'éducation, note de G. Speranza – cabinet Spinelli – 16/06.
29 There are many witnesses to Noël's brilliance as an administrator and to his insights and intelligence. 'He was a fixer in the best sense. Those of us who have laboured in the salt mines of Siberia [i.e. diplomacy] do not underestimate the importance of fixing', said the British diplomat, Sir David (now Lord) Hannay, who referred to Noël as an 'inspiration' when he was part of the UK representation in 1973. (Conference Tribute to Emile Noël, London, 24 October 1997, European Commission, Storeys Gate London SW1). Noël was described as sitting 'quietly in the drafting committee saying nothing until they had exhausted themselves talking and then said: "I have been taking note of your discussions. Would you like me to summarise them?"'
30 Noël's lifelong interest in education has not been researched before. My access to his files in the ECHA collection makes it clear that there is room for more substantial work than is possible in this book.
31 Hannay, October 1997.
32 ECHA – Noël's personal files bear this out, for example his dealings with Lichnérowicz and Lesguillons.
33 SEC (72) 4250 'Bilan et perspectives'.
34 ECHA EN-391 Secretary General's note dated 1 February 1971 to Borschette and other Commissioners, Lichnérowisz 1970.
35 ECHA EN-391 SEC (71) Note à l'attention to MM les Membres de la Commission, le 22 février 1971.
36 Spinelli.
37 Mercereau, correspondence, Aug 2000.
38 Mercereau Aug 2000.
39 See Chapter 2.
40 Mercereau, 19 June 1999.
41 Mercereau, 19 June 1999.
42 ECHA EN-1064 Rapport à Monsieur le Commissaire Spinelli sur la coordination des activités de la Commission dans les domaines de l'Education et de la Jeunesse, Bruxelles, le 4 juin 1971 (rapport Mercereau).
43 ECHA EN-1064 'rapport Mercereau'.
44 A grade staff – the policy-making and policy management grade Nugent 2003: 169.
45 SEC (72) 4250 'Bilan et perspectives'.
46 e.g. DGIII which had some responsibilities for Education and Training alongside its concern for pure research.

47   ECHA EN-917, SEC (71) 2644/2.
48   SEC 9(1971) 2644/2 Annexe gives details of a budget of 7mn units of account and recipients of information related to study of the Community.
49   Jean-René Rabier later created Eurostat.
50   ECHA EN-1064 Note from Speranza to Secretary-general, dated 16 June 1971. Spinelli's chef de cabinet Speranza, was in touch with Noël to discuss Mercereau's report, as well as Spinelli's view on the subject and the personnel changes involved.
51   ECHA EN 917: SEC (72) 2644/2 texte révisé du document SEC (71) 2644 du 9.7.1971 travail en matière d'enseignement et d'éducation (Communication de M. Spinelli en accord avec M. Coppé) Brussels le 19 juillet 1971.
52   According to Hannay, Noël's weekly chef de cabinets meetings 'were not an indulgence – he was extremely hard headed about it. He believed – he knew – the best chance to influence policy was at the formative stage and preferred to put in his influence at this stage rather than face to face contact with Commissioners. He was always extremely courteous. You knew when he began 'Cher ami' lights were flashing at red.' (Hannay conference Tribute to Noël, London Oct 1997).
53   ECHA EN-917 Note complémentaire to SEC (71) 2644.
54   OJ 73/2 point 20: SEC (71) 2644/2 l9 juillet (texte révisé du document SEC (71) 2644 de 9.7.1991).
55   See Jones' view Chapter 6.
56   SEC (72) 4250 'Bilan et perspectives'.
57   ECHA EN-110, 1971: 'Réunion de travail spéciale consacrée a l'examen de la situation générale de la politique européenne' incl. M. Spinelli: Quelques idées concernant les politiques communes industrielles, de la recherche scientifique et technologique, de l'environnement, régionale, qui devraient être inscrites dans les propositions de la commission pour la préparation du sommet'. See Spinelli 1972 *The European Adventure* for the public form to these views.
58   ECHA EN-110, 1971.
59   ECHA EN-11 Note A. Borschette 'Contribution pour réunion de travail spéciale'.
60   ECHA EN-1972 'Items concerning EN speech to Civil Service College on eve of UK entry and talks with Lord Jellicoe and Sir William Armstrong'.
61   ECHA EN 1205 'Lettre à K-H. Narjes 31 mai 1972' P/337/72.
62   Free translation.
63   Dinan 1999: 90.
64   Interview with Hywel Ceri Jones, 19 March 2002.
65   Mercereau, 19 June 1999.
66   Interview with J-L. Quermonne 31 October 2001.
67   Interview with S. Maclure 13 February 1998.
68   L. Cerych in the Liber Amicorum R. Georis.
69   Jones, 9–11 November 1998.
70   Bousquet 1998: 13. Bousquet notes that the issues on which experts agreed and the nuances between them remain the same today.
71   The English version of the Janne report in the *EC Bulletin* is a superficial translation – which might account for the report's later difficulties when policy-makers were faced with such words as regulation and harmonisation.

72 The British vice chancellors were reported to be very enthusiastic about the issue – which is what eventually became the Erasmus model.
73 *EC Bulletin Supplement* 10/73: 57.
74 See Noël's letter to Karl Narjes ECHA EN-1205.
75 Communiqué *EC Bulletin* 10/72.
76 Interview with Sir Christopher Audland 24 October 1997.
77 Neave p. 6.
78 Mercereau, 19 June 1999.
79 Neave 1984: 6, Beukel 2001: 157–8.
80 Kingdon 1995; Hedstrom and Swedberg 1998; McAdam, Tarrow and Tilly (2001).
81 Coombs 1964.
82 See March and Olsen.
83 Baumgartner and Jones 1993: 37, March and Olsen 1989.

Chapter 6   Stabilising the Policy Domain, 1973–76

1   De Witte 1989: 9.
2   *EC Bulletin Supplement* 10/73: For a Community policy on education (Janne).
3   SEC (72) 4250.
4   *EC Bulletin Supplement* 10/73: 57 (Janne report).
5   *EC Bulletin Supplement issue.*
6   Crozier, M. 1970 Le Seuil Paris: translated as The Blocked Society Viking Press, 1973.
7   *EC Bulletin Supplement* 10/73, p. 6.
8   Interview Mercereau, 19 June 1999.
9   Pratt 1974: 54.
10 Interview with Stuart Maclure, 13 February 1998.
11 Maclure, 13 February 1998.
12 *EC Bulletin Supplement* 10/73 p. 26.
13 *EC Bulletin Supplement* 10/73 p. 57.
14 *EC Bulletin Supplement* 10/73 p. 13.
15 *EC Bulletin Supplement* 10/73 p. 26.
16 *EC Bulletin Supplement* 10/73 p. 22.
17 *EC Bulletin Supplement* 10/73 p. 12.
18 *EC Bulletin Supplement* 10/73 p. 13.
19 *EC Bulletin Supplement* 10/73 p. 13.
20 *EC Bulletin Supplement* 10/73 p. 24.
21 *EC Bulletin Supplement* 10/73 p. 23.
22 *EC Bulletin Supplement* 10/73 p. 21.
23 Interview with Ralf Dahrendorf, 6 March 1998.
24 The President of the Commission, a former minister in France.
25 Sir Christopher Soames, British politician, former minister and son-in-law of Sir Winston Churchill. Soames was the senior British Commissioner.
26 Interview with Ralf Dahrendorf, 6 March 1998.
27 SEC (73) 2000: 5.
28 Dahrendorf, interview.

29 SEC (73) 2000: 9.
30 SEC (73) 2000: 9.
31 The mutual recognition of three-year university qualifications was agreed in 1988: Zilioli 1989.
32 Rüegg p. 32.
33 Interview with Hywel Ceri Jones, 9 November 1998.
34 Dahrendorf in interview with Cesare Onestini, 3 February 1995 in 'Federalism and Lander autonomy: the higher education policy network in the Federal Republic of Germany 1948 to 1998' Chapter 7 European cooperation programmes. Unpublished D. Phil thesis Oxford University 2001.
35 Beck 1971, Mallinson 1980.
36 *EC Bulletin Supplement* 10/73: 5.
37 Neave p. 7.
38 Correspondence with Christopher Layton, August 1999.
39 Nugent 1999: 110–117.
40 Daiches 1964. Daiches' book was a manifesto for the new universities of the 1960s.
41 Interviews with Rod Kedward, and Sian Reynolds, Sussex academics, contemporaries of Jones, 20 June 2000. However this is a difficult proposition to support on the basis of this chapter's evidence.
42 Jones, 30 June 1998.
43 Correspondence with George Thomson, 5 December 1997.
44 Vice chancellor of Sussex University at the time.
45 A Welshman and good friend of Jones. Later an EU Ambassador.
46 Thomson, correspondence.
47 Jones, 5 July 1997.
48 Jones, 5 July 1997.
49 Jones, 5 July 1997.
50 Correspondence with Jones, 18 January 2002.
51 Council 1988: 17 Council resolution of 6 June 1974 on the mutual recognition of diplomas. certificates and other evidence of formal qualifications.
52 *EC Bulletin* 3–1974 point 2242.
53 Jones, 9 November, 1998. Correspondence with Raymond Georis, March 2002. Those who knew Janne well tell the same story.
54 'Education in the European Community' speech by Hywel Ceri Jones North of England Education Conference, Liverpool, 5–7 January 1983.
55 Jones, 9 November 1998.
56 COM (74) 253 reprinted in *EC Bulletin Supplement* 4/74 'Commission communication on Education in the European Community'.
57 Those listed were the Hague Summit 1969, Council guidelines on vocational training July 1971, the EC Ministers of Education resolution of November 1971, the Paris Summit declaration Oct 1972, the Janne report Feb 1973.
58 *EC Bulletin Supplement* 3/74 para 31.
59 *EC Bulletin Supplement* 3/74: 15.
60 Interview with Jones, 9 November 1998. See also Fogg and Jones (1985: 294).
61 COM (74) 253 final/2 and *EC Bulletin Supplement* 3/74, Draft decision.

62   *EC Bulletin Supplement* 3/74: 6.
63   See Chapter 4.
64   Fogg and Jones, 1985: 293.
65   Dahrendorf, interview; interview with John Banks, 13 June 1997.
66   Fogg and Jones p. 294.
67   Commission of the ECs, *Eighth General Report* point 323. Resolution of
      the Ministers for Education meeting within the Council of 6 June 1974
      on co-operation in the field of education OJ C 98 20/08/1974; Council
      1998: 15.
68   Interview with UKREP official, 2 July 2001.
69   Fogg and Jones p. 294.
70   Fogg and Jones p. 294.
71   Fogg and Jones, p. 293.
72   Jones, 9 November 1998.
73   *EC Bulletin* 10–75 pt. 2260.
74   OJ C 239 20.10.1975.
75   *EC Bulletin* 12–75 pt. 1101.
76   OJ C 38, 19.02.1976 resolution of the Council and of the ministers for
      Education meeting within the Council of 9 Feb 1976 comprising an
      action programme in the field of education.
77   See Neave p. 86 for other examples.
78   Neave p. 96.
79   Interview with Domenico Lenarduzzi, 23 March 1998.
80   Interview with Guy Haug 26 May 1998.
81   Fragnière 1976: 187.
82   This strand is especially associated with Denis de Rougement – see
      Chapter 2.
83   See Chapter 4.
84   Fragnière 1976: 193. Final report of the education section of Plan Europe
      2000.
85   On Georis' retirement from the ECF in 1995, his friends contributed a
      Liber Amicorum a historic document of this epoch of European policy
      activity in education (Georis papers).
86   Interview with R Georis, 22 November 2000. In a contribution to Gemelli
      (1998: 433) Georis attributed this particular formulation – 'my Bible' – to
      his 'good friend' Shepherd Forman, the Director of the International
      Affairs Program of the Ford Foundation New York speaking in 1979. The
      circles were small. Forman attributed it to a six point speech made the
      previous year by Ralf Dahrendorf, then a Ford Foundation trustee.
87   Fragnière 1976: 193.
88   Georis, 22 November 2000.
89   Paper from Georis collection dated November 1979 Institut d'Education
      de la Fondation Européenne de la Culture (ECF): *Le Bureau de Bruxelles et
      son avenir*.
90   Part of the ECF Institute moved back to Brussels in 1987, when Alan
      Smith, in charge of all the development work on Erasmus at the
      Institute, moved so that what had become the technical agency would be
      close to the Commission.
91   Georis document as above.

92   In 1979, Jacques Delors, then Professor at the University of Paris IX-Dauphine was to become a member of the Institute's Council.
93   Jones, 5 July 1997.
94   See Chapter 3.
95   The ECF established a network of institutes in different policy sectors, including the European Institute for Environmental Policy, the Centre for European Policy Studies (CEPS) in Brussels, the European Centre for Political Studies in London directed by Roger Morgan.
96   McMahon, de Witte, Neave.
97   Pépin, L. (in press) 'L'éducation et la formation dans la construction de l'Union Européenne, trente ans d'histoire'.
98   Peters 2001: 79.
99   Wallace, H. 1983: 64.
100 Baumgartner and Jones 1993: 20.

Chapter 7   Implementing the Action Programme in Education, 1976–84

1   Neave 1984 on education as 'a taboo issue' (p. 6) Europe as 'controversial' (p. 3) the quest to find a basis for cooperation 'difficult' (p. 11) etc. Cf Fogg and Jones 1985, p. 293.
2   *EC Bulletin* 12/75 points 1101 and 1102.
3   Jones, 9 November 1998.
4   Jones, 9 November 1998.
5   De Witte 1989.
6   Neave p. 79 – using Masclet 1975 – suggests 20,000 students out of the total of 4.5 million in the EC10 were mobile.
7   Jones, 9 November 1998.
8   *EC Bulletin* 3/76 point 2276.
9   See Tabatoni.
10 *EC Bulletin* 11/76 point 1201.
11 *EC Bulletin* 6/76 point 2261.
12 *EC Bulletin* 11/77 point 2269, 2270, 2404.
13 *EC Bulletin* 11/76 point 1204.
14 Christopher Price – a political journalist and Labour MP (1966–70 and 1974–83) with a special interest in education, whose career included being Parliamentary Private Secretary to the Secretary of State for Education (twice) and chair of the Parliamentary Select Committee on education, before becoming Director of Leeds Polytechnic (later Leeds Metropolitan University) 1986–92.
15 Interview with Price, 29 May 1997.
16 Jones, 9 November 1998.
17 Council 1988: 35; Council Directive of 15 July 1977 on the education of migrant workers children (77/486/EEC).
18 The event did not stay in the mind of the politicians most closely concerned.
19 Banks, 1982: 11.
20 *EC Bulletin* 6–78 pt. 1.4.3.
21 Banks p. 13.

22   SEC (78) 3650.
23   Jones, November 1998.
24   'Admission to institutions of higher education of students from other member states' drafts and correspondence: private papers of Smith.
25   COM (78) 468 'Admission to institutions of higher education of students from other member states'.
26   See Chapter 8.
27   Interview with John Banks, 13 June 1997.
28   *EC Bulletin* 7/78 pt. 2.1.126.
29   Interview with British ministry official, 15 June 1996; Banks, 13 June 1997.
30   *EC Bulletin* 12/78 point 2.1.60; OJ C 6 of 8.1.1979.
31   SEC (78) 3650.
32   SEC (78) 5057 'Note for Members of the Commission, Report of the inter-departmental working party on 'Grey Areas', 6 January 1979.
33   *EC Bulletin* 10/72.
34   ECHA EN-1872 COM (78) 'PV485 2e partie 9 séance du 16 septembre 1978, Comblain-la-Tour'.
35   ECHA EN-1872 (78) 'Conférence de presse du President Jenkins, le 18 sept 1978: réunion informelle de la Commission à Comblain-la-Tour'.
36   SEC (78) 5057: 3 'Grey areas'.
37   ECHA EN-1982, 1978, 'Note a l'attention for Monsieur E. Noel stricte-ment personnel', Bruxelles, le 30 novembre 1978, signed Henri Etienne.
38   See Chapter 6.
39   ECHA EN-1982, 1978, Note, Etienne.
40   SEC 5057: 8 'Grey areas'.
41   SEC (78) 5057: 9 'Grey areas'.
42   SEC (78) 5057 'Grey areas'.
43   SEC (78) 5057/2 Annexe to report to Grey Areas January 6, 1979 and Jones private papers.
44   Treaty references here include EEC: 117 and 118 vocational training, EEC: 128 on a common vocational training policy, EEC: 123–127 the European Social Fund.
45   Social action programme OJ C 13 of 12.02.1974, the Council resolution of 6 June 1974 on co-operation in the field of education OJ C 98 of 20.08.1974 and the Commission's Communication submitted to the Council on 14 March 1974 COM (74) 253 final/2.
46   The Euratom treaty articles on nuclear research and the European University; the EEC articles on free movement (EEC: 48 and 49) and recognition of qualifications (EEC: 57); Council resolutions in favour of a social action programme OJ C 13 of 12.02.1974 and co-operation in the field of education OJ C 98 of 20.08.1974; and the Commission's Com-munication, submitted to the Council on 14 March 1974 COM (74) 253 final/2.
47   Jones memo 1978: 10 – a reference to the resolution of the ministers of education in June 1974.
48   SEC 5057.
49   Jones, 9 November 1998.
50   Jones, 7 July 1997.

51 Former official in private correspondence 13 March 2003.
52 *EC Bulletin* 11/79 point 2.1.113; OJ C 309 of 10.12.1979.
53 See chapter 6.
54 Was it a presidency? – see 1976.
55 EC Bulletin 11/75 point 2245.
56 P. Gaiotti di Biase whose report was adopted on 11 March 1982 – an important element, along with a EP report in 1984 on higher education (rapporteur N. Péry) in enabling educational cooperation to move up a gear according to Pépin.
57 *EC Bulletin* 3/79 point 2.1.31.
58 Council 1988: 47.
59 Commission document XII/1130/77; Smith 1980: 94.
60 SEC (80) 1773; OJ C583 03.12.1980.
61 Interview with Jones, 9 November 1998.
62 Interview with Jones, 9 November 1998.
63 Interview with Jones, 9 November 1998.
64 OJ L199 of 30.07.1975.
65 Directorate Education Training and Youth. 'The development of education and vocational training policy 1963–1988, an overview of main developments at Community level, situation on 30 June 1988, prepared with the help of the Eurydice European Unit.' Internal un-headed document.
66 OJ C 13 of 12.02.1974.
67 OJ L 39 of 13.02.75.
68 OJ L 185 of 21.07.1979.
69 OJ C of 31.1.1980. This was followed in 1983 by Commission approval for pilot projects in this domain financed by the European Social Fund, and a report on the implementation (COM (84) 132 final).
70 Jones, 9 November 1998.
71 Interview with Ivor Richard, 25 November 1997.
72 Cerych 1980: 7.
73 Banks 1982: 12.
74 Banks 1982: 12.
75 Richard, 25 November 1997.
76 Dinan 1999: 94.
77 The Belgian Etienne Davignon was an innovative figure in the Community creation of research policies – see next chapter.
78 Richard, 25 November 1997.
79 Correspondence with Nick Stuart, member of the Jenkins cabinet, April 2000.
80 Interview with Jacqueline Lastenouse, 25 March 1998. Lastenouse ran the university information activities of DGX and helped iniate the 'Jean Monnet' professorial chairs.
81 Interview with Nick Stuart, member of the Jenkins Cabinet, 28 March 1988.
82 Jones 1983 speech to the North of England conference full ref.
83 Preston 1998: 6.
84 DG XII document.
85 Lenarduzzi, 23 March 1998.

86   Smith 1980: 77.
87   DG XII document. See Tabatoni's account.
88   Tabatoni 1995.
89   Institut d'éducation, Fondation européenne de la culture (1979) 'Con-
      férence sur les programmes communs d'étude dans l'enseignement
      supérieur au sein de la CE Edimbourg 3–5 avril 1979 rapport final' [joint
      study programmes].
90   Smith, 23 March 1998.
91   See also Masclet 1975; Capelle 1977.
92   *Studies in Education* No. 7, 1979.
93   Georis, 2 November 2000.
94   'Leuven conference'.
95   Tindemans 1986 in 'Leuven conference'.
96   Dinan 1999: 101 – proposals that were essential precursors of the EC's
      revival in 1984.
97   Thatcher 1993: 314.
98   Council 1998: 97.
99   See Favier and Martin-Rolland 1991 for a French perspective.
100   Council 1988: 89–91, Conclusions of the Council and of the Ministers
      for Education meeting within the Council of 2 June 1983 concerning the
      promotion of mobility.
101   Council 1987: 89–91, Conclusions of the Council and of the Ministers
      for Education meeting within the Council of 2 June 1983 concerning the
      promotion of mobility.
102   COM (85) 134 final: 30.
103   See the argument advanced in Fogg and Jones 1985: 299.
104   COM (85) 134.
105   COM (85) 134 final: 1.
106   *EC Bulletin* 06/84 point 1.1.6 Fontainebleau summit communiqué.

Chapter 8   Attaining a Goal: The Erasmus Decision, 1985–87

1   Interview with Richard, 25 November 1997.
2   Interviews with officials June 1998.
3   A view taken in the literature (de Witte 1989, Shaw 1999).
4   Interview with Jones, 22 November 2000.
5   Interview with Jones, 22 November 2000.
6   Correspondence with Peter Sutherland, April 2002.
7   This was the future Comett programme.
8   See Council 1988: 81.
9   Interview with André Kirchberger, 29 June 1998.
10   Interview with André Kirchberger, 29 June 1998 and H. C. Jones,
      22 November 2000.
11   Comett stood for Co-operation between Universities and Enterprises
      regarding Training in the field of Technology. A. Kirchberger 29 June
      1998.
12   See Chapter 6. The Commission's concern was initially expressed in 1974
      in *Education in the Community*.

13   Smith 1985: 269.
14   Correspondence with Richonnier, 26 June 1998.
15   Richonnier 1985 *Les Métamorphoses de l'Europe de 1989 à 2001* Paris Flammarion.
16   Richonnier, 26 June 1998.
17   See Chapter 5.
18   Richonnier, 26 June 1998.
19   Sutherland, April 2002.
20   Drake 2000: 29–30.
21   EC Bulletin Supplement 1/85 'The thrust of Community policy'.
22   *EC Bulletin* 1/85 point, Haug and Tauch 2001.
23   Kirchberger, 29 June 1998.
24   Lenarduzzi, 23 March 1998.
25   Jones, 22 November 2000.
26   Sutherland, April 2000.
27   i.e. the officials in the Directorate for Education, Vocational Training and Youth Policy most closely concerned.
28   Richonnier, June 1998.
29   Jones, 22 November 2000; Kirchberger, 29 June 1998.
30   Smith, 28 March 1998.
31   Jones, 22 November 2000; Kirchberger, 29 June 1998.
32   Commissariat au Plan 1983.
33   Case 294/83 Gravier (1985) ECR 593.
34   De Witte (1989), Lenearts (1989), McMahon (1995), Lonbay (1989), Shaw (1999).
35   OJ L 257 of 19.10.1968 (Council 1998 p.).
36   Decision 63/266/EEC OJ L 26.04.1963.
37   Interview with Alan Forrest, 5 July 1996.
38   Case 294/83 Gravier (1985) ECR 593.
39   Case 9/74 (1974) ECR 773.
40   de Witte 1989: 1.
41   Case 152/82(1983) ECR 2323.
42   McMahon 1995: 70.
43   Interview with Cabinet member.
44   Treaty EEC Article 235.
45   Jones, 22 November 2000.
46   Sarah Evans had been part of the legal service team working for the Audland working party. Jones persuaded her to get a placing with the education and training directorate.
47   Evans, 28 March 1998.
48   Decision 63/226/EEC. See Council 1988: 197.
49   EC Bulletin 06/84 point 1.1.8.
50   Lenarduzzi, 23 March 1998.
51   Lenarduzzi, 23 March 1998.
52   *EC Bulletin* 9/84 pt 1.1.1; (COM (84) 446 final).
53   See Chapter 6.
54   *EC Bulletin* 9/83: 2.1.48 and OJ C 264, 4.10.1983.
55   *EC Bulletin* 2/84: 2.1.163 and 2.1.164.
56   *EC Bulletin* 6/85 pt 2.1.64.

57   *EC Bulletin* 6/85 pt 2.1.70.2.1.71.
58   *EC Bulletin* 6/84 2.1.65, 2.1.68., 2.1.71.
59   COM (85) 210 or 310 Completing the Internal Market.
60   COM (85) 310 p. 26 Completing the Internal Market.
61   Dinan 1999: 94.
62   Interview with François Lamoureux, 2 July 1998.
63   See Chapter 7.
64   Jourdain 1995: 82.
65   Dinan 1999: 115.
66   *EC Bulletin* Supplement 7/85 pt 5.8.
67   *EC Bulletin* Supplement 7/85 pt 5.8.
68   OJ C 234, 13.09.1985; Sutherland, April 2002.
69   Sutherland, April 2002.
70   Sutherland, April 2002.
71   Alan Smith private papers.
72   COM (85) 756 final 'Proposal for a Council decision adopting the European Community Action programme for the mobility of university students (ERASMUS)'.
73   COM (85) 756 final.
74   COM (85) 756 final.
75   COM (85) 756.
76   *EC Bulletin* 1/86 point 2.1.63 COM (85) 756 final.
77   OJL 199, 06.08.1977; Jones, 9 November 1998. Jones defined co-operation measures as 'soft' Fogg and Jones. See Wellens and Borschadt, 1989.
78   The Action Programme resolution OJ C 38, 19.02.1976; Council 1988: 21.
79   OJ C 38, 19.2.1976 *Tenth General Report* pt 402 see 104.
80   COM (85) 756 final.
81   Sutherland, April 2002.
82   Co-decision between the Council and the European parliament was not introduced until the Treaty of Maastricht, 1991, and first was put into operation in 1995 – the co-decision on the Socrates programme.
83   Nugent 2003: 36.
84   Nugent 2003: 134–151.
85   See Council 1988: 155; OJ L 222, 08.08.1986.
86   Forrest, 5 July 1996.
87   The new Commissioner had a booklet printed for the occasion of the achievements of the ten years in which the frontispiece was himself and an EC 'founding father'.
88   Interview with Robert Jackson, 25 November 1997. Minister of higher education 1987–90 and notably more pro-Europe than his (Conservative) party.
89   Slang – a sharp operator – an elision of 'Mafia' and 'Taffy' slang for a Welshman.
90   Jackson, 25 November 1997.
91   Interview with UK civil servant, 15 June 1996.
92   *EC Bulletin* 4/86 point 2.4.47.
93   OJ C 148, 16.6.1986 MEPs used the term 'the gradual alignment of courses'. If this was happening it was due to academics' choice. *EC Bulletin* 6–86 point 2.1.74.

94   *EC Bulletin* 5/86 point 2.1.72.
95   Forrest, 5 July 1996.
96   *EC Bulletin* 6/86 point 2.1.106.
97   Interview with former UK deputy ambassador, 27 Nov 1997.
98   Forrest, 5 July 1996; Jones, 5 July 1997; Kirchberger, 29 June 1998; UK civil servant, 15 June 1996.
99   The UK had already taken action to stop EC students accessing the generous grants made by local education authorities.
100   Shaw 1992; Field 1998.
101   Jones, 9 November 1998; Kirchberger, 29 June 1998; Evans, 23 March 1998.
102   Jackson, 25 November 1997.
103   Jackson, 25 November 1997.
104   Katholieke Universiteit Leuven.
105   Jones, 5 July 1997.
106   Interview with Roger Dillemans, 13 September 2000.
107   Conférence des Recteurs, Erasmus Conference 25–27 Nov 1986 Katholieke Universiteit Leuven 1986.
108   Dillemans, 13 September 2000.
109   Dillemans, 13 September 2000.
110   Conférence des Recteurs (1986) Telegram to Ministers of Education.
111   Conférence des Récteurs (1986) Telegram to Ministers of Education.
112   Council 1987: 34th Review of the Council's work and *EC Bulletin* 6/1986 point 2.1.106.
113   *EC Bulletin* 6/86 point 2.1.106.
114   OJ L 222, 08.08.1986 Council 1988: 155.
115   Lenearts 1989; *Agence Europe* 28 November 1986 no 4439 new series p. 9.
116   Their reasoning was much like the Germans' in 1955.
117   The Belgians had launched an unsuccessful challenge to the Gravier ruling.
118   Interview with member of cabinet of French Minister of Education, 5 February 1996.
119   Interview with British official 15 June 1996, Forrest, 5 July 1996.
120   Baker, 21 November 1997; Jackson, 25 November 1997.
121   Baker, 21 November 1997 and serving official 6 November 1999.
122   See *Agence Europe* 1–2 Dec 1986 4441 new series.
123   *Agence Europe* 1–2 Dec 1986.
124   Lenarduzzi, 23 March 1998.
125   Evans, 23 March 1998.
126   Thatcher, pp. 557–559.
127   Thatcher, pp. 557–559.
128   Dillemans, 13 September 2000.
129   Dillemans, 13 September 2000.
130   Attali 1993: 217.
131   Masterson went on to be President of the European University Institute in Florence, 1993–2001.
132   Garret Fitzgerald 1991: 601–602.
133   Fitzgerald, 1991: 610–602.
134   Attali, p. 218.
135   *Agence Europe* 17 Dec 1986, 4454 new series.
136   *Agence Europe* 10 Dec 1986, 4448 new series.

137   *Agence Europe* 12 Dec 1986, 4450 new series.
138   Thatcher, p. 558.
139   Jones, 5 July 1997; Lenarduzzi, 23 March 1998; Smith, 23 March 1998.
140   Monory cabinet member, April 1997.
141   Vergès, 1989: 137.
142   Jones, 9 November 1998.
143   British education ministry official, 12 June 1998.
144   See below.
145   *Agence Europe* 15 May 1987, 4550 new series and EC Bull 5–86.
146   Jones, 5 July 1997; D. Lenarduzzi, 23 March 1998; A. Smith, 23 March 1998.
147   *EC Bulletin 5–87* Special feature 'Council reaches agreement on Erasmus'. The programme came into operation on 1 July 1987.
148   March 1994: 160.
149   In this instance a new policy cycle began when the Commission initiated legal action – as it had threatened in May 1987 – which led to a short term triumph. It was able to introduce new programmes with large budgets – not necessarily as assumed by Pollack (1994) because of political will – but because the Commission won a legal victory. The Commission had challenged the ruling of the ECJ arguing that Article 128 was a sufficient basis for the decision. The Court found in favour of the Council because universities were not just training institutions, they also conducted research which could not be covered by Article 128. However the Single European Act included research as an area of Community competence and thus it could have provided the necessary underpinning. But the deal, in which a Council legal adviser was highly active, consisted of suppressing the research references in the Erasmus decision. The net contributor governments did not look on this with a favourable eye since Article 128, operating with a simple majority, effectively guaranteed that they would be outvoted on budgets by the other governments – a situation which lasted until 1993 when the Treaty of Maastricht came into force – see Lenearts, 1989; Field 1998, also author's interview with Council legal officer 25 March, 1998.

However when the intergovernmental conferences of 1990–91 opened up the prospect of a new bargain, education was a policy area on which member states seized. One camp wanted to use any new treaty to restrict Community action to the acquis of 1989–90; a second camp wanted to use a treaty to extend Community competence, basing an explicit education article on Article 128. The outcome of the member state bargain was the – more or less restrictive but explicit – Treaty of Maastricht Articles 126 and 127, See Lenearts 1994, Barnard 1995, McMahon 1996, Shaw 1999.

Chapter 9   Policy Entrepreneurship in EU Higher Education: Process, Actions, Identities

1   This study is focussed on policy entrepreneurship in and around the Commission. Another analysis could have included the French official, *Gaston Berger*, who in 1959 advocated a European dimension for all research and

training institutes; the Dutch official *Dr Reininck*, who in the early 1960s persuaded his minister, *Joseph Cals*, to take the initiative to advance a strategy for higher education cooperation to advance the sector, rather than higher education for diplomatic (that is, Cold War) ends; and the Secretary-General of the European Cultural Foundation, *Raymond Georis*, who, in the 1970s and 1980s, provided an answer on policy capacity at the moment it was needed to advance Jones' policy design for higher education cooperation, thereby providing the base of experience from which Erasmus eventually emerged. Similarly, the long-serving French Commission official *Félix-Paul Mercereau*, who was part of the Treaty of Rome negotiations for the atomic energy community and who served under Hirsch and Spinelli until the 1973 enlargement, drafted the first plan for an educational bureaucracy and helped to secure the deal on the European University Institute. He was the 'memory' of higher education in the period up to 1972, although his main interest was in atomic energy, and he certainly had to take blows from the French government for his strong Community line. Pierre Messmer, French prime minister at the time of Mercereau's retirement, personally saluted the efforts of officials such as Mercereau in an arena that inevitably pitted them against purely national interests. *Jacques Delors*, the Commission president and another Frenchman, had a lifelong interest in education and incorporated an education element in his single market strategy. He also intervened decisively, after the events discussed here, and in the preparation of the Maastricht Treaty in 1991 to ensure that education was a subsidiarity issue. Delors himself, whose interest in education was well known. Before he arrived in the Commission, Delors enjoyed his role as a pedagogue. He was passionate about the function of education in enabling people to learn about themselves and the world around them. In 1971, the French Parliament passed legislation on life-long learning, paid for by a payroll tax, which Delors had inspired and developed – an action that first brought Delors to public attention. Before he became a minister in the Mitterrand government, Delors had a period as professor at the Paris Université-Dauphine, in a research unit examining the changing nature of work and training – a period when Jones worked with him on an EC training conference.

2 Roberts and King 1996.
3 Schneider, Teske and Mintrom 1995.
4 Dudley and Richardson 1999: 223–48.
5 Dyson and Featherstone.
6 Kingdon 1995: 180–82.
7 Kingdon 1995: 181.
8 Dyson and Featherstone 1999: x. See also Goldstein and Keohane on 'road maps'.
9 Resolution of the Ministers of Education meeting within the Council of 16 November 1971, on co-operation in the field of education.
10 Decision to create the European University Institute in Florence, 1972: *EC Bulletin* 3/75 points 1401–3.
11 Resolution of the Council and Ministers of Education meeting within the Council on 9 February 1976, comprising an action programme in the field of education OJ C 38, 19 February 1976.

12 Council Decision of 15 June 1987 adopting the European Community action scheme for the mobility of university students (Erasmus) (87/327/EEC) OJ L 166, 25 June 1987.

13 See Chapter 2.

14 But Jones' ambition to secure the right to make directives for education in domains that were essentially cooperative failed. Under the 1991 Treaty of Maastricht, the Community had to operate in education under subsidiarity rules, confining it to making a contribution, and thereby acknowledging that primary policy competence continued to lie with member states.

15 March's conception of the 'logic of appropriateness' This is based on the observation that effective decision-makers, wherever they are, imagine explicitly or implicitly three questions. First, the question of recognition: what kind of situation is this? Second, the question of identity: what kind of person am I or what kind of organisation is this? And third, the question of rules: what does a person such as me, or an organisation such as this, do in a situation such as this?

16 See Mashaw and Harfst, 1990 on policy change in US road safety, Weir 1992 on policy change in US employment policy. There is again some overlap with Dyson and Featherstone who use 'inherited beliefs and historical memories' as explanatory factors (Dyson and Featherstone 1999: x).

17 Barzelay 2003 Research methodology report to the Inter-American Development Bank, IIM, LSE.

18 Kingdon [1984] 1995: 181–2.

19 Dahrendorf 1973, Loth et al 1998: 2.

20 Hallstein 1972: 199.

21 See Loth, Wallace and Wessels (eds) 1998 on Walter Hallstein, the forgotten European? Mayne, who worked for Hallstein, confirms the more generous interpretation (Interview with Mayne, 23 June 1998).

22 Jansen 1998: 168.

23 Mayne, 23 June 1999.

24 Loth et al 1998.

25 Interview with Mayne, 23 June 1999.

26 Hallstein 1972: 199.

27 Palayret 1996: 43.

28 Hirsch 1988: 103.

29 Preface to Hirsch 1988 *Ainsi va la vie.*

30 ECHA EN–1204 correspondence to E. Hirsch, Bruxelles, le 20 décembre 1961.

31 Hirsch, 1988: 163.

32 Hirsch, 1988: 101.

33 Hirsch, 1988: 166.

34 Le Monde, le 9 juillet 1971.

35 Corbett, R., 1996: 179 [no relation].

36 Spinelli, 1972 *The European adventure.*

37 Spinelli, 1972: 1.

38 Spinelli, 1972: vii.

39 Spinelli, 1972: 150–51.

40 Müller-Armack 1971: 173.

41 Spaak, 1971: 228.
42 Interview with Félix-Paul Mercereau, 19 June 1999.
43 Kingdon p. 153.
44 Kingdon pp. 181–2.
45 See Chapter 2.
46 See Kingdon 1995 on the 'policy soup'.
47 Hirsch 1988: 166.
48 See Houben 1964. The Member State representatives, the ministers and officials were not education experts but diplomats. It was an exceptional event when Ministers of Public Instruction were invited to the Council as they were in the session on the Interim Report.
49 Hirsch 1988.
50 Kingdon while recognising policy entrepreneurs are found in many locations (179) ignores this siluation.
51 See Council 1988: 11 Resolution of Ministers of Education meeting within the Council of 16 November 1971on cooperation in the field of education.
52 See Chapter 4.
53 Correspondence with Félix-Paul Mercereau, August 1999.
54 Mercereau 19 June 1999 – but this seems confirmed by the ECHA archives.
55 Beukel 2001: 158.
56 See Chapter 5.
57 Correspondence with Christopher Layton, 11 August 1999.
58 Dahrendorf, 1973 reviewing Hallstein's book *Der unvollendete Bundesstaat*.
59 Wessels 1998: 240–241.
60 See Chapter 5.
61 Interview with P. Masterson, Florence, 23 March 2000.
62 *Higher Education*, report of the committee appointed by the Prime Minister, 1963, Cmnd2154, HMSO The Robbins report].
63 Neil Kinnock, a contemporary fellow Welshman and friend of Jones – and leader of the Labour Party in the early 1990s, famously described himself as 'the first Kinnock in a thousand years to go to university'.
64 Educationists of the day – and still in the years 2000 – often interpret harmonisation as meaning voluntary convergence – 'different instruments playing in tune'.
65 See Chapters 3, 4 and 5.
66 Baumgartner and Jones 1993: 3.
67 Baumgartner and Jones p. 25.
68 Baumgartner and Jones p. 3.
69 COM (74) 253 Education in the Community.
70 Jones is publicly on record for his admiration of Dahrendorf's stand against harmonisation. See Neave 1984: 8.
71 Fragnière 1976: 173.
72 Banks 1982: 13.
73 see Chapter 7. British minister, Robert Jackson, described him in 1987 as a 'twinkling Welshman'.
74 Baumgartner and Jones 1993.
75 March 1994
76 Correspondence with Sutherland, 4 April 2002.

77 Arthur Cockfield Commissioner for the internal market tax law and customs 1985–88, a British tax specialist and industrialist appointed to government and then the EC by Margaret Thatcher.

78 See Chapter 8.

79 See Chapter 7, interview with Ivor Richard, Commissioner 1981–84 'If you want to talk about education don't talk to me, talk to Hywel Jones'. Others included Emile Noel, the Secretary General for the Commission (interview with Christopher Audland, 24 October 1997) and Jacques Delors, President of the Commission (Interview with Jean-Marc Ouazen, 28 March 1998).

80 See European Voice 24–30 June 2004: 16.

81 See Chapter 8.

82 McAdam, Tarrow and Tilly p. 121, certification as the validation of actors, their performances and their claims by external actors.

83 Correspondence with Sutherland, 4 April 2002.

84 Correspondence with Richonnier 26 June 1998 and with Sutherland, April 2002.

85 Correspondence with Richonnier 26 June 1998.

86 Kingdon [1984] 1995: 183.

87 See Chapter 8.

88 See Chapter 8.

89 Interview with Dillemans, 13 September 2000.

90 Because Sutherland held the education portfolio for one year only, he did not complete the Erasmus task. The crucial brokering role within the different political venues was left largely in the hands of his successor, Manuel Marin from Spain.

91 McAdam, Tarrow and Tilly (2001); Barzelay (2003).

92 March 1994 p. 58 Weick 2001 p. 3.

Chapter 10   Conclusions

1 Kingdon 1995.

2 Skocpol 1992, Thelen and Steinmo 1992, Mahoney and Rueschemeyer 2003.

3 Barzelay 2003: 254–5.

4 Dyson and Featherstone 1999: 33.

5 The personal and organisational characteristics of the policy entrepreneur, and the quality of their judgement as to the kind of proposals they could advance which command the assent of member states and still nudge the EU in a more integrative direction.

6 Reflexivity is defined as direct feedback from knowledge to action See, Pierson 1993.

7 See March 1994; Dyson and Featherstone 1999 refer to needing to take into account these individuals' beliefs which functioned as 'road maps'.

8 See the examples of Seydoux and Berger 1959–69. See Chapter 3.

9 Majone 1996 *Regulating Europe*.

10 Pollack 1994.

11 Pollack 2000.

12 For more macro explanations see Field 1998; Moschonas 1998: 97; Scott 1998.

Epilogue

1 Reichert S. and Tauch, C. 2004: 275.
2 Hackl 2001: 13(3) 99–114.
3 See Appendix, Table 4.
4 Trends III (2003).
5 Héritier 2002.
6 See Reichert and Tauch 2003: 275–88; Adam, S. (2003).
7 OECD Education at a Glance (2004) on France; Attali 1998.
8 The ministers were Luigi Berlinguer of Italy, Jürgen Rüttgers of Germany and Tessa Blackstone for the UK.
9 Hackl 2001: 105.
10 See Socrates information on EU Commission website www.europa.eu.int.
11 Sorbonne declaration 1998 – http://www.bologna-bergen2005.no.
12 Allègre's speech to rectors 40th anniversary of the Standing conference of European Rectors (CRE), Bordeaux 20 and 21 May 1999.
13 Neave 2003: 186.
14 Hackl 2001: 107 – it was defined as an open European area for cooperation in education.
15 COM (1993) 700.
16 Sapir et al (2003) notes that the new member states bring with them a much lower standard of living, a legacy of old industrial investment, environmental damage and poor public administration. Grabbe 2004: 70 notes that enlargement will probably encourage the EU to develop new areas of integration.
17 In France where the new structure was known as the LMD – licence, maître, doctorat.
18 Interviews with officials May 1998.
19 Interview official 15 June 2003.
20 Eurydice report (2000: 21). Two decades of reform in higher education.
21 See discussions in Bleiklie and Kogan, 2000: 13.
22 Reichert and Tauch 2003.
23 Bologna declaration http://www.bologna-bergen2005.no.
24 This was the joint degree course between the business schools of Reims, Middlesex Polytechnic, Reutlingen in Germany and ICADE in Madrid.
25 Interview with Guy Haug, 17 January 2005.
26 Haug 2003: p?
27 Knudsen, I.; Haug, G.; Kirstein, J. (1999) Trends in learning structures.
28 Haug, 17 January 2005.
29 Trends, 1999.
30 Peters, G., 1994 Ch. 1 [Richardson and Mazey-policy style] or Peters 2000: 80–2.
31 Berlin communiqué (2003) http://www.bologna-bergen2005.no.
32 Hackl 2001: 114.
33 Lenearts 1994.
34 Interview with official, 18 June 2000.
35 ESIB declaration; Lourtie 2001: 8 on the Gothenburg (Göteberg) declaration. Many ministers supported ESIB according to Wächter 2004: 267; 2004: 266.

36 Zgaga para. 25 p. 22.
37 Interview with Lesley Wilson, 23 January 2005.
38 Zgaga p. 24.
39 Interview with L. Wilson, 23 January 2005.
40 Ref COM (2003) 58 final, 'The role of universities in the Europe of Knowledge'.
41 Davies, H. (2004) p?
42 Davies p. 1.
43 http://www.europa.eu.int/pol/educ/index_en.htm.
44 An average of [3] % of European nationals work outside their home country – Eurostat.
45 COM (2003) 58 and Kok report 2004.
46 See Davies.
47 Europe Unit 2004 Commission publishes new indicators for Lisbon.
48 European Commission DG EAC From Berlin to Bergen, the EU contribution draft 2 October 2003.
49 Wallace, H., 2000: 7–9 and 45.

Primary Sources

Interviews and/or correspondence

Audland, Christopher, Deputy Secretary-General EEC Commission 1973–81; 24 Oct 97.

Baker, Kenneth, Secretary of State for Education and Science 1986–89; 21 November 1997.

Banks, John, Under-Secretary, head of International Relations Branch, Dept Education and Science UK in 1976–77; 13 June 97.

Booth, Clive, Private secretary to Secretary of State for Education and Science in 1976–77 (Shirley Williams); 1 Nov 1997.

Blackstone, Tessa, Minister of State Dept for Education 1997–2001; August 1997.

Bostock, David, UK permanent mission to EC 1973–75, 1985–89, 1995–98; 28 February 2001.

Boswell, Tim, Parliamentary Under Secretary of State, Dept for Education, 1992–95; 10 April 2000.

Bousquet, Antoine, Inspecteur Général Ministère de l'Education Nationale; 26 October 1998.

Briggs, Asa, vice chancellor Sussex University 1967–76 and member of Council of European Institute of Education 1975–90; correspondence June 1999.

Clémenceau, Patrice, DGXXI Administrateur principal; 5 July 1996.

Dahrendorf, Ralf, Commissioner Research Science and Education 1973–74; 6 March 1998.

Dillemans, Roger, Rector Catholic University of Leuven (KLU) in 1986–87; 13 September 2000.

De Longeau, Jean-Yves, Chef du Départment des affaires internationales de l'enseignement supérieur, Ministère de l'Education Nationale; 22 February 1997.

Evans, Sarah, legal officer Directorate Education, Vocational Training and Youth 1981–93; 23 March 1998.

Forrest, Alan, Council of Ministers: Head of Division General Secretariat, Education Culture Youth, 5 July 1983–96; 25 March 1998.

France, Sian, lecturer, Sussex University 1970s, 20 June 2000.

Franjou, Patrick, conseiller Conférence des Présidents d'Université; September 97.

Georis, Raymond, Secretary-General European Cultural Foundation 1974–1995; 22 November 2000.

Halimi, Suzy, conseillère aux relations internationales de l'enseignement supérieur et de la recherche; 22 Feb 1997.

Hannay, David, member UK Delegation, Chef de cabinet and UK ambassador between 1960's–90's; 24 October 1997.

Hodkinson, Elizabeth, Director European Division, Department for Education; 15 July 1998.

Jackson, Robert, Parliamentary Under Secretary of State, Department for Education and Science, 1987–90; 25 November 1997.

Jallade, Jean-Pierre, Director European Institute for Education and Social Policy, Paris; 2 January 1998.

Jarvis, Fred, General Secretary National Union of Teachers 1975–89; 14 July 1997.

Jones, Hywel Ceri, 5 July 1997; 9–11 November 1998; 22 November 2000 and correspondence.

Jouve, Michel, Directeur, Agence Socrates France; 25 May 1998.

Kedward, Rod, lecturer Sussex University 1970s, 20 June 2000.

Kern, Barbara, seconded German official to DGXXII Dir A; 12 December 1996.

Kirchberger, André, DGXXII; 29 June 1998.

Kirchberger, Kristine, secretary to Education Group 1972, DG XXII; 9 November 1998.

Knudsen, Inge, Director Confederation of European Union Rectors' Conferences; 29 June 1998; 9–11 Nov 1998.

Lamoureux, François, Deputy Director of Jacques Delors' Cabinet; 2 July 1998.

Lastenouse, Jacqueline, Head of Unit Action Jean Monnet and University information, DGX Information, Communication, Culture and Audovisual; 25 March 1998.

Layton, Christopher, member of Spinelli cabinet; correspondence August 1999.

Lenarduzzi, Domenico DGXXII Director Socrates; 23 March 1998.

Maclure, Stuart, Editor Times Educational Supplement 1970's; 13 February 1998.

Masterson, Patrick, Master University College Dublin in 1986; 23 March 2000.

Mayne, Richard, official within the Commission, speechwriter for W. Hallstein, 1958–63, PA to Monnet 1963–66; 23 June 1999.

Mercereau, Félix-Paul, Euratom and EEC Commissions 1960s, 1970s, chef de cabinet of E. Hirsch; 19 June 1999 and correspondence August 1999.

Mitchell, Irving DGXXII Head of Erasmus Unit; 3 July 1998.

Nabavi, Ginette, DGXX administrator, Dir A responsible ECTS; 23 March 1998.

Ouazan, Jean-Marc, Member of Cabinet Cresson 1998 and long-time collaborator of Jacques Delors; 24 March 1998.

Palayret, Jean-Marie, Director of the European Community Historical Archives.

Pépin, Luce, Head of the European Unit, Eurydice; Sept 2000.

Pokorny, Adam, DGXXII seconded UK official; 2 July 1998.

Price, Christopher, Chair of UK Erasmus committee 1980's; 12 March 1998.

Quermonne, Jean Louis, Président Université de Grenoble 1970's; 31 October 2001.

Reilly, John, Director of UK Socrates-Erasmus 1990's; December 1996.

Richard, Ivor, Commissioner Social Affairs 1981–84; 25 November 1997.

Richonnier, Michel, Member of Cabinet of Commissioner Peter Sutherland 1985; correspondence, 26 June 1998.

Rosselle, Dominique, Directeur exécutif PôleUniveritaire Européen de Lille; 1997.

Ruberti, Antonio, Commissioner Research and Education 1993–94; April 1997.

Smith, Alan, European Institute of Educational and Social Policy Director of the technical Assistance Office; 13 December 1996; 23 March 1998.

Smith, Sir Trevor, Chairman of UK Socrates-Erasmus Council; May 1997.

Stuart, Nick, Member of Cabinet of Commission President Roy Jenkins; 1979–81; correspondence April 2000.

Sutherland, Peter, Commissioner for Social Affairs and Education Training and Youth 1985; correspondence April 2002.

Teichler, Ulrich, scholar Erasmus expert; May 1997.
Thomson, George, UK Commissioner 1973–77; correspondence 12 November 1997.
Van Craeyenest, Félix, Legal service Council of Ministers; 25 March 1998.
Van der Hijden, Peter, DGXXII; 24 March 1998.
Verli-Wallace, Angelika, DGXXII Deputy Head of Erasmus Unit; 29 June 1998.
Wächter, Bernd, Head of Dept Erasmus Technical Assistance Office Socrates and Youth; 11 Dec 1996.
Williamson, David, Secretary-General of EEC Commission 1987–97; 2 March 1999.
Officials whose anonymity is respected. Dates of interviews in endnotes

Documents

(i) Personal papers

Dillemans, Roger
Georis, Raymond
Jones, Hywel Ceri
Richonnier, Michel
Smith, Alan

(ii) Historical Archives of the European Communities (ECHA)

Collection European Atomic Energy Commission
CECA, 1960 'Rapport du Comité intérimaire aux Conseils de la CEE et de la CECA', Florence: Comité intérimaire pour l'université européenne.
Fonds Emanuelle Gazzo
EG-232 1987 Emploi, éducation et politique sociale au sein d'Europe communautaire.
Fonds Etienne Hirsch
EH-26 Négotiations relatives à la création de l'Institut universitaire de Florence.
Fonds Jules Guéron
JG-89 1959 'Notes prises au cours du voyage des Présidents aux Etats-Unis par F-P Mercereau, juin 1959, Ch IV "Weekend at Princeton"'.

Fonds Emile Nöel
EN-83 1973 'Groupe suites du sommet 1973'.
EN-103 1987 'Comité de liaison des Conférences des Présidents/recteurs d'universités de la CE: liaison avec le comité, travaux'.
EN-110 1971 'Val Duchesse 13/10' 'Réunion de travail speciale consacrée a l'examen de la situation générale de la politique européenne...le 13 oct 1971 a Val Duchesse'.
EN-159 1972 'Réunions' 'Preparation Paris Summit 1972 notes de synthese relations exterieures and union economique et monetaire'.
EN-160 1972 'Réunion 13/04 (précédée d'un échange de vues de la Commission à Val Duchesse le 12/04...Préparation de la prochaine réunion des Ministres des Affaires Etrangères...'.
EN-391 1971 'Associations pour l'étude des problèmes de l'Europe'.
EN-819 1972 'Conférence au Civil Service College sur 'The present state of the Community'.

EN-917 1971 'Politique de l'éducation'.
EN-1064 1971 'A. Coppé et son cabinet'.
EN-1097 1973 'R. Dahrendorf et son cabinet, relations extérieures, recherche, science, éducation 1972–73'.
EN-1204 1961 'Hirsch (E) 1961–85'.
EN-1205 1972 'Narjes (KH) – commissaire – 1969–82'.
EN-1575.1 1979 'Conseil de l'Europe: réunion du comité des délégués des ministres du Conseil de 'Europe en présence d'EN à Strasbourg'.
EN-1754 1983 'Stuttgart 17–19/06 1983'.
EN-1808 1985 'Milan 28–29/06'.
EN-1852 1984 'Fontainebleau 25–26/06 1984'.
EN-1872 1978 'Comblain-la-Tour 16–17/09'.
EN-2037 1988 'Politique de l'éducation : perspectives à moyen terme 1988–1992'.
EN-2054 1988 'Conseil universitaire pour l'action Jean Monnet'.
EN-2079 1987 'Politique de l'éducation'.

(iii) Commission archives

SEC (71) 2644/2 'texte revisé du document SEC (71) 2644 du 9.7.1971 travail en matière d'enseignement et d'éducation (Communication de M. Spinelli en accord avec M. Coppé) Brussels le 19 juillet 1971'.
SEC (72) 4250 'Bilan et perspectives de l'activité du Groupe Enseignement et Education'.
SEC (72) 4250 'Communication de Monsieur Spinelli OJ 2306/12/1972'.
SEC (73) 2000 'Working program in the field of research, science and education (personal statement by Mr Dahrendorf)'.
SEC (78) 5057 'Grey areas'.
SEC (91) 1753 'First progress report on action undertaken by the Member States and by the European Community with a view to strengthening the European dimension in education'.
SEC (91) 1991 'Report on the activities of the Commission of the ECs in the field of education, training and youth during 1990'.

(iv) Commission official publications

COM (74) 253 'Education in the European Community'.
COM (78) 400 'Education action programme at Community level: equal opportunities in education and training for girls'.
COM (78) 468 'Admissions to institutions of higher education of students from other Member States'.
COM (78) 469 'Education action programme at Community level: a European Community scholarships scheme for students'.
COM (84) 466 'A People's Europe: implementing the conclusons of the Fontainebleau European Council'.
COM (84) 722 'Commission communication on the new information technologies and the school systems in the European Community'.
COM (85) 167 'Communication setting out the broad lines if Community action for the period 1985–88 in the field of vocational education and the new information technologies'.

COM (85) 355 'Commission proposal on a general system for the recognition of higher education diplomas'.

COM (85) 431 'Proposal for a decision adopting an action progranne of the Community in Education and Training for technology (COMETT)'.

COM (85) 134 'Education and Vocational training within the European Community, activities of the Commission of the European Communities in 1983 and 1984, a contribution to the standing conference of European Ministers of Education, to be held in Brussels on 6–10 May 1985', Brussels: Commission of the European Communities.

COM (85) 310 'The completion of the internal market'.

COM (85) 756 'Proposal for a Council decision adopting the European Community Action programme for the mobility of university students (ERASMUS)'.

COM (88) 192 'Erasmus programme annual report, 1987'.

COM (88) 203 'The teaching of foreign languages'.

COM (88) 280 'Education in the European Community, medium-term perspectives, 1989–92'.

COM (88) 841 'Proposal for a Council Decision establishing the Lingua programme to promote training in foreign languages in the European Community'.

COM (89) 275 'Proposal for a Council decision on the right of residence of students, on the right of residence for employees and self-employed persons who have ceased their occupational activity and on the right of residence'.

COM (89) 372 'proposal for a Council Directive on a second general system for the recognition of professional education and training which complements Directive 89/48'.

COM (89) 568 'Community charter of basic social rights for workers'.

COM (89) 236 'Education and training in the European Community, Guidelines for the Medium Term 1989–92'.

COM (90) 600 'Opinion on Treaty on European Union/IGC'.

COM (90) 334 'The rationalisation and co-ordination of vocational training programmes'.

COM (91) 349 'Memorandum on higher education in the European Community'.

COM (92) 407 'Proposal for a Council Decision adopting the second phase of the trans-European co-operation scheme for higher education'.

COM (92) 457 'European higher education-industry co-operation: advanced training for competitive advantage'.

COM (92) 2000 'From the Single Act to Maastricht and beyond: the means to match our ambitions, the commission's programme for 1992, structural and financial measures 1993–1997'.

COM (93) 183 'Guidelines for Community action in the field of education and training'.

COM (93) 209 'Proposal for a Council Directive on the right of residence for students'.

COM (93)700 'Growth, competitiveness and employment: the challenges and the way forward into the 21st century'.

COM (93) 151 'EC Education and Training Programmes 1986–92, report from the Commission to the Council, the European Parliament and the Economic and Social Committee'.

COM (93) 457 'Green Paper on the European Dimension of Education'.

COM (93) 'Green Paper on the future of Community initiatives under the structural funds'.

COM (94) 264 'Proposal for a European Parliament and Council Decision establishing 1996 as the European Year of Lifelong earning'.

COM (94) 596 'Commission communication on recognition of qualifications for academic and professional purposes'.

COM (94) 708 'Proposal for a decision of the European Parliament and the Council establishing the Community action programme, Socrates'.

COM (95) 590 'Teaching and learning, towards the learning society, Commission white paper'.

COM (96) 462 'The obstacles to trans-national mobility'.

COM (96) 471 1996 'Learning in the information society: action plan for a European education initiative 1996–98'.

COM (96) 462 'Education-training-research, the obstacles to transnational mobility, Green Paper', Luxembourg: OOPEC.

COM (97) 563 'Towards a Europe of Knowledge, Communication from the Commission'.

COM (2002) 401 final 'Proposal for a European Parliament and Council Decision establishing a programme for the enhancement of quality in higher education and the promotion of inter-cultural understanding through cooperation ith third countries (Erasmus World) (2004–2008)'.

Commission 1986 'proposal for COMETT decision'.

Commission 1989 'The Community charter of fundamental social rights of workers'.

Commission 1989 'Education and training in the European Community: guidelines for the medium term, 1989–1992'.

Commission 1990 'Activites de la Commission dans les domaines de l'education, de la formation et de la politique de la jeunesse en 1989'.

Commission 1990 'Structures of the Education and Initial Training Systems in the Member States of the European Community'.

Commission 1991 'Memorandum on open distance learning in the EC'.

Commission 1991 'Synopsis of the activities of the Task Force for HR ETY of the Commission of the ECs during 1989–1990'.

Commission 1992 'Communication to the Council and the EP concerning European HE-industry co-operation: advanced training for competitive advantage'.

Commission 1992 'Memorandum on vocational training in the EC in the 1990's'.

Commission 1994 'Key data on education in the European Union, 94'.

Commission 1994 'proposal for a co-decision on the Leonardo programme'.

Commission 1995 'Communication social action programme and programme 1995–1997'.

Commission 1995 'Results of the pilot action of the European school partnerships 1992–1994'.

Commission 1996 'Education and training: tackling unemployment'.

Commission 1996 'For a Europe of civic and social rights: report by the comite des sages'.

Commission 1996 'Report on the evaluation of Tempus'.

Commission 1997 'Accomplishing Europe through education and training, report of a study group'.

Commission 1997 'Learning in the information society: action plan for a European education initiative 1996–1998'.

Commission 1997 'Towards the Fifth Framework programme: scientific and technological objectives'.

Commission 1997 'Veil report, High level group on freedom of movement'.

Commission 1993 'Responses to the Memorandum on higher education in the European community'.

Commission 1995 'Preparation of the accession for the associated countries of Central and Eastern Europe into the internal market of the Union'.

Commission 1996 'Socrates: manual of good practice on Erasmus under the Socrates programme: where to find information, which persons to involve, which steps to take'.

Commission 1997 'Arion scheme of study visits for education specialists: report of activities'.

Commission 1997 'The Erasmus Experience'.

Commission 1997 'Guide to programmes'.

EC Bulletin periodical, monthly

EC Bulletin Supplement 10/73 'For a Community policy in education (the Janne report)'.

EC Bulletin Supplement 4/74 'Commission communication on education in the European Community'.

EC Bulletin Supplement 3/76 'Action programme in favour of migrant workers and their families'.

EC Bulletin Supplement 12/76 'From education to working life'.

EC Bulletin Supplement 7/85 'A People's Europe, reports from the *ad hoc* committee'.

EC Bulletin Supplement 2/91 'Inter-governmental conferences: contributions by the Commission'.

Education Training and Youth Studies no 5 1994 'Co-operation in education in the European Union, 1976–1994'.

Le Magazine periodical from the Task Force, later DGXXII, published from 1994.

Social Europe 'The role of education and training in the completion of the Single Market' 3/88.

Social Europe 1988 'The social dimension of the internal market: interim report'.

Studies in education 1978 'Nouveaux models de l'enseignement superieur et egalite des chances'.

Studies in education 7 1979 'Joint programmes of study an instrument of European coop in HE'.

Studies no 2 1993 'The outlook for higher education in the European Community, responses to the Memorandum'.

Eurydice 1988 *European community co-operation, the first decade.*

Eurydice and CEDEFOP 1995 *Structures of the education and initial training systems in the EU.*

(iv) Council of Ministers

Council of the ECs 1987 'European Educational Policy Statements, third edition', Luxembourg: OOPEC.

Council of the ECs 1989 'Council decision of 28 July 1989 establishing an action programme to promote foreign language competence in the European Community'.

Council of the ECs 1990 'European Educational Policy Statements, supplement (Dec 1989) to the third edition'.

Council of the ECs 1992 'European Educational Policy Statements, supplement no 2 to the third edition (1990–1992)'.

Council of the EU 1998 *'Statements on education, training and young people, 3rd Edition'*.

(v) European Parliament

European Parliament 1981 'Report drawn up by Mrs P. Gaiotti de Biase on a Community programme in the field of education'.

European Parliament 1983 'Report drawn up by Mrs N. Pery on higher education and the development of co-operation between higher education establishments'.

European Parliament 1985 'Report drawn up by Mr E. McMillan-Scott on the proposal from the Commission to the Council for a decision adopting an action programme in education and training for technology (Comett)'.

European Parliament 1986 'Report drawn up by Mr A. Coimbra Martins, on student mobility and the proposal from the Commission to the Council for a decision adopting Erasmus'.

European Parliament 1988 'Report drawn up by Mrs J. Larive on Community education policy: medium term perspectives (1989–1992)'.

European Parliament 1989 'Report drawn up by Mr A. Coimbra Martins on the Commission proposal to the Council for a decision modifying the Community action programme on student mobility Erasmus'.

European Parliament 1990 'Report drawn up by Mrs A. Hermans on the European dimension at university level, and notably the mobility of students and academics'.

European Parliament 1992 'Report drawn up by Mrs A. Hermans on education and training policy in the run up to 1993'.

European Parliament 1993 'Report drawn up by Mr M. Elliott in response to the Commission memorandum on higher education'.

European Parliament 1993 'Report drawn up by Mrs P. Rawlings on the development of EC/US cultural co-operation'.

ECJ 1974 'Case 9/74 Casagrande [1974] ECR 773'.
ECJ 1983 'Case 152/82 Forcheri [1983] ECR 2323'.
ECJ 1985 'Case 293/83 Gravier v City of Liège [1985] ECR 593'.
ECJ 1986 'Case 24/86 Blaizot [1988] ECR 379'.
ECJ 1986 'Case 263/86 Humbel [1988] ECR 5365'.
ECJ 1987 'Case 45/86 EC Commission v EC Council [1987] ECR 1493'.
ECJ 1989 'Case 56/88 UK v Council (PETRA) [1989] ECR 1615'.
ECJ 1989 'Case 242/87 Commission v Council (ERASMUS) [1989] ECR 1425'.
ECJ 1991 'UK, France and Germany v Council (COMETT II)'.

Bibliography

Adam, S. (2003). 'Qualification structures in European higher education' study prepared for the Danish Bologna seminar, Copenhagen, 27–28 March 2003 – see www.bologna-bergen2005.no.

Allègre, C. (1999). Speech to rectors, 40th anniversary of the Standing Conference of European Rectors (CRE), Bordeaux 20 and 21 May 1999.

Attali, J. (1998). Pour un modéle européen d'enseignement supérieur, rapport de la commission présidée par Jacques Attali Paris, ministére de l'éducation national, de la recherche et de la technologie.

Attali, J. (1993). Verbatim 1 1981–1986. Paris: Fayard.

Bache, I. (2004). 'Europeanisation and Higher Education: Towards a Core Curriculum in European Studies?' Paper presented to the ESRC/UACES Study Group and Seminar Series on the Europeanisation of British Politics and Policy-Making, Sheffield, 23 April, 2004. (www.shef.ac.uk/ebpp).

Banks, J. (1982). 'European cooperation in education.' *European Journal of Education* 17(1): 9–16.

Barnard, C. (1995). The Treaty on European Union, education and vocational training D. Phillips. *Oxford Studies in Comparative Education* 5(2): 13–28.

Barzelay, M. (2001). *The new public management: improving research and policy dialogue*. Berkeley, Los Angeles: University of California Press.

Barzelay, M. (2003). 'Introduction: the process dynamics of public management policy-making.' *International Public Management Journal* 6(3): 251–81.

Baumgartner, F. and B. Jones (1993). *Agendas and instability in American politics*. Chicago: University of Chicago Press.

Berlin communiqué (2003). Realising the European Higher Education Area, communiqué of the Conference of Ministers responsible for higher education in Berlin 19 September 2003 www.bologna-bergen2005.no.

Beukel, E. (1993). Education. *Making policy in Europe, the Europeification of national policy-making*. S. Andersen and K. Eliassen. London: Sage.

Beukel, E. (2000/2001). Educational policy: institutionalisation and multi-level governance. S. Anderson and K. Eliassen *Making policy in Europe* 2nd ed London: Sage, pp. 124–39.

Bird, G. (1978). The universities. *The British in Germany, educational reconstruction after 1945*. A. Hearnden. London: Hamish Hamilton.

Bleiklie, I., and M. Kogan (2000) Comparisons and theories. *Transforming Higher Education, a comparative study*. M. Kogan, M. Bauer, I. Bleiklie, and M. Henkel. London: Jessica Kingsley.

Blitz, B. (2003). 'From Monnet to Delors: educational cooperation in the EU.' *Contemporary European History* 12(2): 197–212.

Blumenthal, P., C. Goodwin, A. Smith and U. Teichler, (eds) (1996). *Academic mobility in a changing world, regional and global trends*. London: Jessica Kingsley.

Bousquet, A. (1998). *Education et formation dans l'Union Européenne*. Paris: La Documentation française.

Burley, A. and W. Mattli (1993). 'Europe before the court: a political theory of legal integration.' *International Organisation* **47**: 841–76.

Callan, H. (1998). Internationalisation in Europe. *The globalisation of higher education*. P. Scott. Buckingham: Society for Research in Higher Education and Open University Press.

Capelle, J. (1977). La mobilité des étudiants diplomés, des chercheurs et des enseignants. Strasbourg: Council of Europe.

Cerych, L. (1980). 'Retreat from ambitious goals?' *European Journal of Education* **15**(1).

Cerych, L. (1999). *The CRE, NGOs and European integration CRE-40th anniversary CER-action, review of the Association of European Universities*, no. 115/1999 Supplement.

Cerych, L. and P. Sabatier (1986). *Great expectations and mixed performance: the implementation of higher education reforms in Europe*. Stoke on Trent: Trentham Books.

Cohen, M., J. March and J. Olsen (1972). 'A garbage model of organisational choice.' *Administrative Science Quarterly* **17**(1): 1–25.

Commission (2003) 58 *The role of universities in the Europe of Knowledge*.

Commission (2004) 2 *Proposal for a directive of the European Parliament and the Council on services in the internal market*.

Commission (2004) Facing the challenge – The Lisbon strategy for growth and employment, report from the High Level Group chaired by Wim Kok, November 2004.

Coombs, P. (1964). *The fourth dimension of foreign policy: education and cultural affairs*. New York: Harper and Row.

Corbett, R. (1996). *Spinelli and the Federal Dream. Eminent Europeans, personalities who shaped contemporary Europe*. Bond, M., J. Smith and W. Wallace. London: The Greycoat Press, pp. 179–92.

Corbett, A. (2002). 'Ideas, institutions and policy entrepreneurship in European Community Higher Education Policy 1955–95', unpublished PhD dissertation, University of London.

Cram (1994). 'The European Commission as a multi-organisation.' *Journal of European Public Policy* **21**(2).

Cram, L. (1997). *Policy making in the EU, conceptual lenses and integration processes*. London, Routledge.

Crewe, I. (2004). 'Universities, Europe and the globalisation of higher education' speech 13 July 2004, London: Centre for European Reform.

Crozier, M. (1973). *The blocked society*. London: Viking Press [Translation of *La société bloquée*] Paris: Fayard.

Dahrendorf, R. (1973). *Plädoyer für die Europäische Union [An appeal for European Union]*. Munich.

Daiches, D. (ed.) (1964). *The idea of a new university: an experiment at Sussex*. London: Deutsch.

Davies, H. (2004). 'Higher education in the internal market.' *UACES European studies On-line essays*.

De Witte, B. (1989). 'Introduction' *The Community law of education*. B. de Witte Baden-Baden Nomos.

Deering, M.-J. (1992). *Denis de Rougemont, l'européen, combats acharnés*. Geneva: Fondation Jean Monnet pour l'Europe.

DiMaggio, P. and W. Powell (eds) (1991). *The new institutionalism in organisa-tional analysis.* Chicago: University of Chicago Press.

Dinan, D. (1999). *Ever closer union? an introduction to the European Community.* Basingstoke, Hants: Macmillan.

Drake, H. (2000). *Jacques Delors, perspectives on a European leader.* London: Routledge.

Dudley, G. and J. Richardson (1999). 'Competing advocacy coalitions and the process of "frame reflection": a longtitudinal analysis of EU steel policy.' *Journal of European Public Policy* 6(2): 225–48.

Dyson, K. and K. Featherstone (1999). *The road to Maastricht, negotiating economic and monetary union.* Oxford: Oxford University Press.

Eurydice (2000). *Two decades of reform in higher education, 1980 onwards.* Brussels: Eurydice.

Favier, P. and M. Martin-Rolland (1991). *La décennie Mitterrand.* Paris: Le Seuil.

Featherstone, K. and C. Radaelli, C. (eds) (2003). *The politics of Europeanisation.* Oxford: Oxford University Press.

Field, J. (1998). *European Dimensions, Education, Training and the European Union.* London: Jessica Kingsley.

Fitzgerald, G. (1991). *All in a life: an autobiography.* London: Macmillan.

Fogg, K. and H. Jones (1985). 'Educating the European Community – ten years on.' *European Journal of Education* 20(2–3): 293–300.

Frazier, C. (1995). *L'éducation et la communauté européenne.* Paris: CNRS editions.

Fragnière, G. (ed.) (1976). *Education without Frontiers, a study of the future of edu-cation from the European Cultural Foundation's 'Plan Europe 2000' with a foreword by John Vaizey.* London: Duckworth.

Gardiner, P. (ed.) (1974). *The philosophy of history.* Oxford: Oxford University Press.

Gellert, C. (ed.) (1993). *Higher education in Europe.* London: Jessica Kingsley.

Georis, R. (1998). Post-scriptum: Foundations' culture in Europe. *The Ford Foundation and Europe (1950s–1970s), cross-fertilisation of learning in socialscience and management.* G. Gemelli. Brussels: European Inter-University Press: 431–442.

Goldstein, J. and R. Keohane (1993). Ideas and foreign policy: an analytic frame-work. *Ideas and foreign policy: beliefs, institutions and political change.* J. Goldstein and R. Keohane. New York: Cornell University Press.

Grabbe, H. (2004). What the new member states bring the EU London N. Nugent *European union enlargement.* Basingstoke: Palgrave Macmillan.

Grant, C. (1994). *Delors, inside the house that Jack built.* London: Nicholas Brealey.

Green, A., A. Wolf, and T. Leney (1999). *Convergence and divergence in European education and training systems.* London: University of London Institute of Education.

Hackl (2001). 'The intrusion and expansion of Community policies in higher education' *Higher Education Management* 13(3) 99–114.

Haigh, A. (1970). *A Ministry of Education for Europe.* London: Geo Harrap.

Hall, P. (1986). *Governing the economy: the politics of state intervention in Britain and France.* Cambridge: Polity Press.

Hall, P. and R. Taylor (1996). 'Political science and the three new institution-alisms.' *Political Studies* 44(4): 936–957.

Hallstein, W. (1972). Europe in the Making, [trans of Der unvolleridere Bundesstaat 1969] London: Charles Roetter.

Haug, G. (2003). 'Quality assurance/accreditation in the emerging European higher education area: a possible scenario for the future.' *European Journal of Education* 38(3): 229–240.

Haug, G. and C. Tauch (2001). Trends in learning structures in higher education II [Trends II] follow-up report prepared for the Salamanca and Prague conferences of March/May 2001. Helsinki, National Borad of Education.

Hedstrom, P. and R. Swedbery (eds) (1998). *Social mechanisms: an analytical approach to social theory*. Cambridge: Cambridge University Press.

Héritier, A. (ed.) (2002). 'New modes of governance in Europe: policy-making without legislating' in A. Héritier, *Common goods: reinventing European and international governance*. Lanham, MD: Rowman and Littlefield Publishers.

Hervey, T. (1998). *European social law and policy*. London: Longman.

Hirsch, E. (1988). *Ainsi va la vie*. Lausanne, Fondation Jean Monnet pour l'Europe.

Houben, P. H. J. M. (1964). *Les conseils de ministres de communautés européennes*. Leyde: AW Sythoff.

Husemann, H. (1978). Anglo-German relations in higher education. *The British in Germany, Educational reconstruction after 1945*. A. Hearnden. London: Hamish Hamilton.

Jansen, T. (1998). Walter Hallstein after the presidency. *Walter Hallstein: the forgotten European*. W. Loth, W. Wallace and W. Wessels Basingstoke: Macmillan.

Jarvis, F. (1972). The educational implications of membership of the EEC. London: National Union of Teachers.

Kälvermark, T. and M. van der Wende (1998). *National policies for internationalisation in higher education in Europe*. Stockholm: Högskoleverket [National agency for higher education].

Kingdon, J. [1984] (1995). *Agendas, alternatives and public policies*. Boston: Little, Brown.

Knill, C. (2001). *The Europeanisation of national administrations: patterns of institutional change and persistence*. New York: Cambridge University Press

Knudsen, I., G. Haug, and J. Kirsten. (1999). *Trends in learning structures* [Trends I]. Geneva, Conférence des Recteurs Européens.

Kogan, M. (1997). 'Diversification in higher education: differences and commonalities.' *Minerva* 35: 47–62.

Kogan, M. (1999). 'The culture of academe.' *Minerva* 37(1): 63–74.

Küsters, H. (1998). Hallstein and negotiations on the Rome Treaties. *Walter Hallstein, the forgotten European*. W. Loth, Wallace W. and Wessels W. Basingstoke: Macmillan.

Lenearts, K. (1989). Erasmus: legal base and implementation. *European Community law of education*. B. d. Witte. Baden-Baden.

Lenearts, K. (1994). 'Education in Community law after Maastricht.' *Common Market Law Review* 31: 7–41.

Lichnérowicz, A. (1970). *Rapport general introductif: Les aspects modernes du concept de coopération internationale*. La coopération entre les universites européennes, Grenoble, l'Association Europe-Universitaire et l'Université des Sciences Sociales de Grenoble.

Lonbay, J. (1989). 'Education and law in the Community context.' *European Law Review* 14: 363–87.

Loth, W., W. Wallace and W. Wessels (eds) (1998). *Walter Hallstein, the forgotten European?* Basingstoke, Hants: Macmillan.

Lourtie, P. (2001). Furthering the Bologna process, report to the Ministers of Education of the signatory countries. Prague, Follow-up group of the Bologna process.

Mahoney, J. and D. Rueschemeyer (eds) (2003). *Comparative historical analysis in the social sciences*. Cambridge: Cambridge University Press.

Majone, G. (1996). *Regulating Europe*. London: Routledge.

Mallinson, V. (1980). *The Western European idea in education*. Oxford: Pergamon Press.

March, J. (1994). *A primer on decision-making*. New York: Free Press.

March, J. and J. Olsen (1989). *Rediscovering institutions*. New York: Free Press.

Marks, G. (1993). Structural policy in the European Community. *Euro-politics: institutions and policymaking in the 'new' European Community*. A. Sbragia. Washington: Brookings Institution.

Masclet, J.-C. (1975). *The intra-European mobility of undergraduate students*. Paris: Institute of Education of the European Cultural Foundation.

Mashaw, J. and D. Harfst (1990). *The struggle for auto safety*. Cambridge, MA: Harvard University Press.

Mayne, R. (1970). *The recovery of Europe, from devastation to unity*. London: Weidenfeld and Nicolson.

McAdam, D., Tarrow, and S. Tilly, C. (2001). *Dynamics of contention*. Cambridge: Cambridge University Press.

McMahon, J. (1995). *Education and culture in European Community law*. London: Athlone Press.

Mény, Y., P. Muller, et J. L. Quermonne (eds) (1995). *Politiques publiques en Europe*. Paris: L'Harmattan.

Moravscik, A. (1998). *The choice for Europe: social purpose and state power from Messina to Maastricht*. Ithaca, NY: Cornell University Press.

Morgan, R. (1972). *West European politics since 1945: the shaping of the European Community*. London: Batsford.

Morgan, R. and C. Bray. (eds) (1986). *Partners and rivals in Western Europe: Britain, France and Germany*. Aldershot: Gower.

Morgan, R. (2000). 'A European society of states – but only states of mind?' *International Affairs* 76(3): 559–574.

Moschonas, S. (1998). *Education and training in the European Union*. Aldershot: Ashgate.

Müller-Armack, A. (1971). *Auf dem Weg nach Europe*. Tubingen and Stuttgart: Rainer Wunderlich and C. E. Poeschel.

Neave, G. (1984). *Education and the EEC*, Trentham Books.

Neave (2003). 'Anything goes: or how the accommodation of Europe's universities to European integration integrates an inspiring number of contradictions'. *Tertiary Education and Management* 8: 181–197.

Neave, G. and F. van Vught (1991). *Prometheus bound: the changing relationship between government and higher education in Europe*. Buckingham: Pergamon Press.

Nihoul, G. (1999). Policy formation in the European Union: ideas and institutions in the making of education policy. *Faculty of Social Science, Sub-faculty of Politics (unpublished D. Phil dissertation)*. Oxford: Oxford University Press.

Nugent, N. (1999). *The government and politics of the European Union.* Basingstoke: Macmillan.

Nugent, N. (2003). *The government and politics of the European Union.* (5th ed.) Basingstoke: Macmillan.

OECD (2004). *Education at a Glance.* Paris: Fayard.

Palayret, J.-M. assisted by R. Schreuers (1996). *A university for Europe, prehistory of the European University Institute in Florence (1948–1976).* Rome: Presidency of the Council of Ministers, Dept of Information and Publishing.

Parsons, C. (2003). *A certain idea of Europe.* Ithaca: Cornell University Press.

Pépin, L. for the Commission (in press). L'éducation et la formation dans la construction de l'Union Européenne, trente ans d'histoire. Brussels, Commission.

Peters, G. (1994). 'Agenda setting in the European Community.' *Journal of European Public Policy* 1(1): 9–26.

Peters, G. (2000). Agenda setting in the European Union. J. R ichardson. European Union, power and policy-making. 2nd ed.

Peterson, J. (2001). 'The choice for EU theorists: establishing a common framework for analysis.' *European Journal of Political Research* 39: 289–318.

Peterson, J. and E. Bomberg (1999). *Decision-making in the European Union.* London and New York: Macmillan and St Martin's Press.

Peterson, J. and M. Sharp (1998). *Technology policy in the European Union.* Basingstoke: Macmillan.

Pierson, P. (1993). 'When effect becomes cause: policy feedback and political change.' *World Politics* 45: 595–628.

Pierson, P. (1996). 'The path to integration, a historical institutionalist analysis.' *Comparative Political Studies* 29(2 April 1996): 123–163.

Pineau, C. (1991). *Un grand pari: l'aventure du Traité de Rome.* Paris: Fayard.

Pollack, M. (1994). 'Creeping competence, the expanding agenda of the European Community.' *Journal of Public Policy* 14(2): 95–145.

Pollack, M. (2000). The Commission as an agent. N. Nugent. *At the heart of the Union, studies of the European Commission,* 2nd ed. Basingstoke, NY: Macmillan/ St Martin's Press.

Pratt, J. (1974). 'Education in the EEC.' *Higher Education Review* 2: 51–58.

Preston, J. (1998). *Competing through human capital: EU trairung and education policy. European industrial policy: concepts and instruments.* T. Lawton, Macmillan.

Ragin, C. (1987). *The comparative method, moving beyond qualitative and quantitative strategies.* Berkeley, LA: University of California Press.

Reichert, S. and C. Tauch (2003). *Trends 2003. Progress towards the European Higher Education Area. Bologna four years after: steps towards sustainable reform in Europe.* Brussels: European Universities Association.

Reichert, S. and C. Tauch (2004). Trends IV.*European universities implementing Bologna.* Brussels: European Universities Association.

Richonnier, M. *Les métamorphoses de l'Etat.* Paris, Fayard.

Roberts, N. and R. King (1996). *Transforming public policy, dynamics of policy entrepreneurship and innovation.* San Francisco: Jossey-Bass.

Ross, G. (1995). *Jacques Delors and European integration.* NY: Oxford University Press.

Rüegg, W. (1999). La CRE, autonomie et cadre européen. *CRE-action,* Review of the European Universities Association. Supplement to 115: 31–33.

Sandholtz, W. (1992). 'ESPRIT and the politics of international collective action.' *Journal of Common Market Studies* 30(1): 1–21.

Sandholtz, W. and Zysman, J. (1989). '1992 Recasting the European bargain.' *World Politics* 42(1): 96–128.

Sapir, A., P. Aghion, M. Hellwig, J. Pisani-Ferry, D. Rosati, J. Vinals and H. Wallace (2003). 'An agenda for a growing Europe, making the EU economic system deliver.' Report of an independent high level study group established on the initiative of the President of the Commission. Brussels.

Schink, G. (1993). *Kompetenzerweiterung umHandslungs-system des Europischen Gemeinschaft: Eigendynamik und 'Policy Entrepreneurs'.* Baden-Baden: Nomos Verlagsgesellschaft.

Schneider, P., P. Teske and Mintrom, M. (1995). *Public entrepreneurs, agends for change in American government.* Princeton: Princeton University Press.

Scott, P. (1998). *Massification, internalisation and globalisation.* The globalisation of higher education. P. Scott. Buckingham, Society for Research in Higher Education and Open University Press.

Serra, E. e (1989). Il Rilancio dell' Europa e i trattati di Roma, actes du colloque de Rome, 25–28 mars 1987, Bruylant/Bruxellw; Giuffre/Milan; LGDJ/Paris; Nomos Verlag/Baden-Baden.

Servan-Schreiber, J.-J. (1967). *Le défi américain.* Paris: Denoël.

Shaw, J. (1999). From the margin to the centre: education and training law and policy from Casagrande to the 'Knowledge society'. *The evolution of EU law.* P. Craig and G. de Burca. Oxford: Oxford University Press.

Skocpol, T. (1992). *Protecting soldiers and mothers: the political origins of social policy in the United States.* Cambridge, MA: Belknap.

Smith, A. (1980). 'From "Europhoria" to "Pragmatism": towards a new start for HE cooperation in Europe.' *European Journal of Education* 15(1).

Smith, A. (1985). 'Higher education cooperation 1975–1985: creating a basis for growth in an adverse economic climate.' *European Journal of Education* 20(2–3).

Spaak, P.-H. (1971). *The continuing battle: memoirs of a European, 1936–1966.* London: Weidenfeld and Nicolson.

Spinelli, A. (1972). *The European Adventure, task for the enlarged community.* London: Charles Knight and Co Ltd.

Sprokkereef, A. (1993). *Developments in European Community education policy. The European Community and the challenge of the Riture. J. Lodge.* London: Pinter: 340–7.

Stirk, P. (1996). *A history of European integration since 1914.* London, Pinter.

Swedberg, R. (ed.) (2000). *Entrepreneurship.* Oxford: Oxford University Press.

Tabatoni, P. (1995). 'The European Institute of Education and the building of Europe'. *European Journal of Education* 30(4): 479–91.

Teichler, U. (1998). The role of the European Union in the internationalisation of higher education. *The globalisation of higher education.* P. Scott. Buckingham.

Teichler, U. and F. Maiworm (1997). The Erasmus Experience, major findings of the Erasmus evaluation research project. Luxembourg, Office of Official Publications of the European Communities. 1987–1995

Thatcher, M. (1993). *The Downing Street years.* London: Harper Collins.

Thelen, K. and S. Steinmo (1992). Historical institutionalism in comparative politics. *Structuring politics: historical institutionalism in comparative analysis.* S. Steinmo, Thelen, K. and Longstreth, F. (eds). Cambridge: Cambridge University Press.

Uri, P. (1991). *Penser pour l'action, un fondateur de l'Europe.* Paris: Odile Jacob.

van Craeyenest, F. (1989). La nature jundique des résolutions sur la coopération en matiéére d'éducation. *The Community law of education.* B. de Witte. Baden-Baden, Nomos Verlagsgesselschaft.

Vedovato, G. (1968). *L'Universita Europea a Firenze.* Firenze, Biblioteca Della 'Rivista di Studi Politici Internazionali.

Vergès, J. (1989). La voie intergouvernementale: 'le livre bleu'français. *The Community law of education.* B. de Witte. Baden-Baden: Nomos.

Wächter, B. (2004). 'The Bologna process: developments and prospects.' *European Journal of Education* 39(3): 265–273.

Wallace, H. (1983). Negotiations, conflict and compromise: the elusive pursuit of common policies. *Policy-making in the European Community* 2nd ed. Chichester and New York, Wiley.

Wallace, H. (2000). The institutional setting. H. Wallace and W. Wallace *Policy-making in the European Union* Oxford: Oxford University Press.

Wallace, H. (2000). The policy process. H. Wallace and W. Wallace *Policy-making in the European Union* Oxford: Oxford University Press.

Weick, K. (2001). *Making sense of the organisation.* Oxford: Blackwell.

Weiler, J. (1991). 'The transformation of Europe.' *Yale Law Journal* 100: 2403–83.

Weir, M. (1992). Ideas and the politics of bounded innovation. *Structuring politics: historical institutionalism in comparative analysis.* S. Steinmo, K. Thelen and F. Longstreth. Cambridge: Cambridge University Press: 188–216.

Wessels, W. (1998). Walter Hallstein's contribution to integration theory. *Walter Hallstein, the forgotten European?* Loth, W., W. Wallace, et al (eds) (1998). *Walter Hallstein, the forgotten European?* Basingstoke: Hants, Macmillan.

White, H. (1984). 'The question of narrative in contemporary historical theory.' *History and Theory* 23.

Young, H. (1998). *This Blessed Plot, Britain and Europe, from Churchill to Blair.* London and Basingstoke: Macmillan.

Zgaga, P. (2003). *The Bologna process between Prague and Berlin, report to the Ministers of Education of the signatory countries.* Berlin: Follow-up group of the Bologna process.

Zilioli, C. (1989). The recognition of diplomas and its impact on educational policies. *The Community law of education.* B. de Witte. Baden-Baden, Nomos.

Index